When Business Harms Human Rights

When Business Harms Human Rights

Affected Communities that are Dying to Be Heard

Editors
Jena Martin
Karen E. Bravo
Tara Van Ho

ANTHEM PRESS

Anthem Press
An imprint of Wimbledon Publishing Company
www.anthempress.com

This edition first published in UK and USA 2020
by ANTHEM PRESS
75–76 Blackfriars Road, London SE1 8HA, UK
or PO Box 9779, London SW19 7ZG, UK
and
244 Madison Ave #116, New York, NY 10016, USA

British Library Cataloguing-in-Publication Data
A catalogue record for this book is available from the British Library.

ISBN-13: 978-1-78527-226-4 (Hbk)
ISBN-10: 1-78527-226-8 (Hbk)

This title is also available as an e-book.

CONTENTS

PREFACE

by Jena Martin

For me, this book is personal.

At first glance, I grew up in a typical household. My mother was (and still is) a registered nurse (RN). My father was trained as an accountant. When we were younger, my brother and I went to school and then let ourselves into our apartment to wait for one of my parents to come home and make dinner ('latchkey kids' is the term they used back then). I went on to graduate high school, then college, then law school, before taking a job, first at a law firm, then at a government agency, before eventually ending up in my dream job – teaching as a law professor in the United States.

And yet, in many ways, my life was not typical at all. When I was eight, my mother moved my brother and myself to Canada. After my mom and dad separated, I ended up living most of my teenage years with my dad and my stepmom, helping to take care of my younger siblings. We moved a lot. My dad and my stepmom became serial entrepreneurs, chasing various business opportunities (both in the United States and Canada), trying to provide for our ever-growing family. This provided for a less than stable life, but it was the only life I knew so I didn't mind. In the meantime, my mother was trying to make it as a part-time single mom, taking care of my older brother – trying to put him in the best schools, trying to provide him with a solid foundation.

Although I didn't know it then, the growing intersection between businesses and the larger society around us was fundamentally shaping the world in which I lived. My mother, who has been practicing as an RN since 1959, has become first disillusioned and now downright cynical about the role that pharmaceutical companies and insurance companies have had on our right to health. Much of the reason why my father turned to running his own business is because of the outright discrimination he faced at the hands of accounting firms that didn't feel comfortable having a black face examine the books of their white shoe companies. As a teenager, my first full-time job that didn't involve working for one of my family's businesses was at McDonald's in Canada, where I worked my way up to becoming a shift manager while I was in college. In many ways, I'm very grateful for that opportunity; the company gave me a scholarship that helped pay for one semester of college. But I also saw the inner workings of a publicly traded corporation up close, with all of its frustrations and foibles.

Watching my family struggle trying to eke out a life of stability amidst the chaos of uncertainty has fundamentally shaped who I am. Working for a mammoth-sized publicly traded corporation for four years has fundamentally shaped who I am. Working for the US Securities and Exchange Commission as an investigative attorney who examined the fraud that abounds in both public and private corporations – all of these things have brought me to where I am today: a person who cares deeply about social justice. An attorney who tries to help small businesses grow. A professor who spends time examining the intersection of business and human rights.

So, why am I telling you all of this?

Because too often in the academic world we tend to look at phenomena and policy through divorced, seemingly objective lenses. Empirical writing has become increasingly fashionable in legal scholarship, providing facts and figures to substantiate our perspective. Let me be clear – it is absolutely crucial that we do all of this – empiricism and policy help us to understand what we are struggling with in a way that mere speculation and conjecture cannot.

As long as we don't forget the why.

And, for me, 'the why' at the heart of what I do has been and will always be humanity. Trying to make the world a place where people can live with dignity, strive with respect and live their best life without irony is what motivates me to teach, practice and – as it is here – shine a light on those instances where we as a collective fall short of serving others.

As such, it is my hope that, as you read through these pages and hear the stories of those who struggle against incredible odds, their truths provide you with some insight into how businesses and humanity often intersect – with the goal of helping you find your way.

Or your why.

ACKNOWLEDGEMENTS

The editors are incredibly grateful for the effort, work and dedication that the UN Working Group for Business and Human Rights has undertaken since its mandate began in 2011. In particular, the editors wish to thank Michael Addo (Working Group member from 2011 to 2019), Surya Deva (Working Group member from 2016 to present) and Anita Ramasastry (Working Group member from 2016 to present) for the guidance, support and mentorship they have provided to the editors, both individually and collectively. Their willingness to participate in conferences that discuss these important issues and their tireless efforts to advance the cause of business and human rights remain an inspiration to us. The conference that gave rise to this volume was hosted by the Aarhus University Department of Law (Denmark) and was generously funded by the Max Sørenson Mindefond (Denmark) and the INTRAlaw Centre at Aarhus University. For their support in finding money for this conference and organizing it, we are deeply indebted to Jens Vedsted Hansen, Ellen Margrethe Basse, Bettina Lemann Kristiansen, Hans Henrik Edlund, Ann-Dorte Bruun Nielsen, Tine Sommer, Kirsten Jakobsen, Tinna Meyer and Inger Krog Nyholm.

Karen Bravo's Acknowledgements

I am grateful to Jena Martin and Tara Van Ho, both of whom were essential to transforming this project from idea to reality. I am also grateful to all the contributors and narrators for their courage in sharing their experiences and perceptions. Funding from the Indiana University Robert H. McKinney School of Law has enabled me to work on this project.

Jena Martin's Acknowledgements

Jena's role in the conference and the edited volume was made possible, in part, thanks to funding from West Virginia University's Office of Global Affairs. Jena also owes a long overdue debt of gratitude to the WVU ADVANCE Center for providing her with an initial grant in 2012 that led to so much of her work in business and human rights. Jena is also grateful to the unending love, support and general cheerleading of her family, friends and, of course, the Scholarly Avengers. She remains forever grateful to her mother for constantly modelling goodness personified and for quickly becoming the 'conference mom' at the UN Forum for business and human rights. Most of all, Jena remains humbled by the bravery and courage that is reflected in the pages of this book.

Tara Van Ho's Acknowledgements

For invaluable support, Tara is grateful to Katerina Mitkidis, Fenella Billing, Lauren Neumann, Louise Halleskov Storgaard, Nikolas Feith Tan, Natalie Videbæk Munkholm, Viktoria Obolevich, Lærke Assenbjerg and Nana Amalie Harbo. Tara is also grateful, as always, to her biological family members – Kay, Greg, Adam, Tina, Valerie, Dan, Lizzy, Mikey and Ellie – who put up with her 'flittering around the world handing out hugs and rainbows' and then (wrongly) working through holidays to finish academic pieces. She also appreciates the support of her 'business and human rights family', whose members are too numerous to mention fully. She would be remiss, however, if she did not mention the other importance of the other core members of the Essex Business and Human Rights Project, most notably Sheldon Leader, Anil Yilmaz Vastardis and Luis Felipe Yanes as well as Chiara Macchi and Charline Daelman who helped organize other parts of the Aarhus conference.

INTRODUCTION

A few years ago, two of the editors of this volume were fortunate enough to have a book that we co-edited featured at the United Nations' Annual Forum on Business and Human Rights. Since 2012, the Forum has taken place every year in Geneva, Switzerland. It is free and open to anyone with an interest in business and human rights. Since its inception, the Forum's attendance has constantly exceeded expectations – growing exponentially in size and in importance to many in the field with each passing year. It has become a gathering of speakers from around the globe – a chance for people in civil society, businesses, governments and academics (like us) to gather and discuss the issues and challenges that arise when businesses and societies intertwine. There are plenary sessions, breakout sessions, parallel sessions and quite a bit of informal interactions by folks in between (or often during) all of the main events. In short, it is the premier event for people who work in this field.

The fact that our book was selected to be on the program was an incredible honour and Jena's mother, Pat (being the proud mother that she is), insisted on coming along. Pat has always been an independent woman, so the deal that they struck was as follows: apart from the book launch (where she was kind enough to take pictures), she would go her own way until the evening and then the two would reconvene to compare notes on what they saw and experienced during the Forum. At the end of the first night, they did just that: walking back to their hotel from the Forum, Jena asked her mother what she thought. Pat, keen as ever, went right to what was bothering her. 'Where are the communities?' she asked, 'I didn't really see them there.' She was right. Even though civil society often sits in to represent the voices of impacted communities during the Forum there is a dearth of actual, direct access to the Forum by the members of the communities themselves. It was something that many of us in the field acknowledged but in that way where you accept something as a *fait accompli* and try your best to find alternate solutions.

Jena patiently explained this to her mom: that it was a sad but unavoidable fact that the groups that are often hardest hit by negative business impacts are also the poorest communities on Earth. She pointed out that, even for people who have more income, Geneva is an incredibly expensive city and that, while the Forum itself is free, the cost of traveling there and finding lodging while there makes the journey a prohibitive one for most members of affected communities. And then Pat said something life changing for the second time that night.

'Then you should go to them.'

Jena can admit it now; her initial impulse was to dismiss her mother. But then she stopped. And she thought. And she realized Pat was right. What's more, every time we spoke with someone in the field about the issue, they reinforced the power of her mother's idea.

Because the truth of the matter is that, in the midst of all the policy discussions and legal analysis, it is *easy* to forget the why. In a room full of crowded suits and agendas (both the ones on paper and the ones unwritten), it's easy to forget the reason why we're engaged with business and human rights: to hear and respond to the stories of those most affected, to ensure that we let their words empower us and them to make changes.

The irony of this is one of many. For many of us, we have gone into this work to make a difference in the lives of people living in affected communities. But what sort of a difference can we really make if we don't talk to them about what we do? If we don't hear from them about what works and what doesn't?

This is what this book sets out to do. It is an attempt to go to the communities where these stories live and bring them back to share with the world. It is our hope that in doing so we shed light on some of the atrocities that can happen when businesses callously pursue profit without regard to the impact of their activities or profit seeking on communities or workers. We also hope it can provide some guidance for those businesses that would like to simultaneously do good and do well but may not understand how the latter impacts the former.

In some ways, these stories are our stories – they are the stories of those who understand the impact businesses have on our lives and who have responded by challenging the *status quo* and *fait accompli* that too often impact our communities without consequence. In these pages, you'll meet a farmer from Cameroon who was first accused by a Fairtrade company of taking building materials – then later arrested for the crime. You'll hear the story of a trade unionist from Colombia who was kidnapped, tortured and held for 42 days, allegedly for his role in campaigning against the privatization of ECOPETROL, a large Colombian oil company. You'll hear from coalminers in West Virginia – veterans who served their country and came back to work in an environment that wreaked havoc on their bodies with little hope for relief.

Human rights defenders and academics do not *always* have a personal motivation, but often they do. Those profiled in this book have taken up the call to protect human rights – sometimes their own, oftentimes others. Listening to – or reading – their stories can give us a clearer understanding of the challenges still facing the field of business and human rights; a reminder of why this field continues and needs to evolve further. To that end, while the chapters come with the authors' analysis of the situation, the heart of each chapter is the story itself.

We have tried to maintain a global perspective. You'll hear stories from North and South America (Brazil, Colombia and the United States); Asia (Turkey); and Africa (Cameroon, South Africa and Zimbabwe). In contrast, the types of companies spotlighted were rather similar. Most of the stories in this volume pertain to one of two industries, either the extractive industry (broadly defined) or the agricultural sector. This is, perhaps, not coincidental. As a recent report[1] suggests, the extractive sector, in particular, is at the top of the list for most reported business and human rights-related violations. This can be far better understood when you consider what it takes to make these sectors grow – both industries heavily rely on land and/or access to natural resources and the labour of human beings as their primary resource. As such, many companies face an uphill climb to make sure that they are compliant with national and international standards relating to human rights. Understanding the stories of those impacted within these sectors can go a long way to providing a more complete picture regarding how to address the challenges present in this field.

As much as possible, we have tried to use the words from the people directly affected – you will hear *their* stories, in *their* words, from *their* perspective. As academics, this can also raise challenges as we play the inescapable role of interpreters. What then of the stories from the other actors, the businesses who allegedly caused the harm and the governments that do not prevent it? Also, what if the stories of the communities and individuals who are affected are sometimes factually inconsistent or inaccurate, with perspectives that come from other sources? In Tara Van Ho's chapter on a community interrupted in Cajamarca Colombia, she does an excellent job of discussing these challenges and how she wrestles with them. Tara's conclusion – that these stories must nonetheless be rendered faithfully – is the same conclusion we reached when editing this book. Where we can, we will acknowledge that there are inconsistencies between their stories and the messages that have been delivered by the corporations involved or identified. We believe all of these stories are true, but as with anything, it is the truth, by and large, of a very specific perspective – those who have been impacted the most by the operations, actions or relationships of businesses within their communities – and as such the truth is not always the truth shared by all players.

Not every contributor to this edited volume has made the same choice regarding how to address conflicting narratives. For example, in their chapter depicting the human rights defender Maxima Acuna, authors Marianne Bertrand and Ariadna Tovar have made a point of explicitly detailing the position of the corporations that are involved. There are many reasons why an author might do this – for some it is an attempt to thwart the claims that are often levied against civil society and advocates in this area – that their advocacy is unbalanced and biased. For others, it is the acceptance of the new reality (detailed by members of the UN Working Group on Business and Human Rights)[2] that people who advocate for causes that clash with business – human rights defenders – are often subject to lawsuits and criminal prosecutions themselves. Claims can vary but defamation is a common tactic used. The report details the use of 'fraudulent or trumped up charges'[3] that are clearly without merit, but instituted anyway, often as part of a larger strategy to at once overwhelm and muzzle those with limited resources, in effect to take the one thing away from these individuals that they have left – their voice. We do not wish to ascribe motives to the choices of individual authors, but we are cognizant that in sharing these stories, there are risks for both the authors and the individuals they profile.

To better illuminate the issues that arise when human rights defenders challenge businesses, the arc of this book proceeds as follows: in the first section, you will hear the stories of individuals – tales told by one person who, in the author's mind, best exemplifies or highlights a particular issue that the author feels is significant. Madeline Hung's chapter, regarding the contradiction of a Fairtrade company that may be complicit in business and human rights violations, is one; Daysheelyn Brillo's analysis of the struggles of a Filipino farmer who attempts to get justice for sterilization, while being confounded with a corporation's litigation strategy, is another. In Rajiv Maher's and Adriana Bravin's chapter telling the story of a woman who must deal with the loss of her whole community when a corporation's dam bursts in Brazil, the anguish is easily felt.

The second section of the book highlights the stories of communities as a whole. Rather than focusing in on one voice, the authors in this section chose to lift up a series of voices, either connected by their occupation, for example, Jennifer Oliva's chapter on veteran coal miners in West Virginia and Cigdem Cimrin's and Yucel Demiral's chapter on the implications of working for a company in Turkey's free trade zone, or by their experience, for example, Tara Van Ho's chapter on a community fighting for justice in Colombia or Michael Clemens's and Maria Isabel Cubides's discussion on communities that must live in the shadow of abandoned mines.

There is a strong but often under-recognized tradition in the legal academy of using stories and personal narratives to inform more traditional legal analysis.[4] It has been happening in numerous areas of the law. For instance, survivors' stories have been used to push back on traditional (often male-dominated) policies underpinning sexual assault laws.[5] Even more relevant to this project, Mary Coombs, has discussed 'outsider scholarship' as a means of bringing personal narratives into the legal discourse.[6] According to Prof. Coombs,

> Outsider scholarship is created and defined, in part, by contrast to traditional legal scholarship, which adopts a prescriptive approach, is grounded on normative positions and is expressed in judicial discourse. Traditional scholarship assumes that neutrality and objectivity are achievable goals. The identity of the scholar should thus be irrelevant when assessing the work. In contrast, outsider scholarship is characterized by a commitment to the [others'] interests [...] by rejection of abstraction and dispassionate 'objectivity', and by a preference for narrative and other engaged forms of discourse.[7]

By using outsider scholarship, Prof. Coombs argues, the legal community can benefit from 'rethink[ing] what role law can play in liberation'[8] and by 'show[ing] the discontinuities between the experiences of outsiders and the law's rules and assumptions'.[9]

The intersectionality of experiences, and the emphasis on bringing affected individuals into the conversation, has happened in other fields as well. For instance, there is a field of study known as 'design justice' that provides for a more expansive view regarding who should be included in conversations regarding design.[10] According to Sasha Costanza-Choc, design justice is a field of theory and practice that is concerned with how the design of objects and systems influences the distribution of risks, harms and benefits among various groups of people.[11] Hallmarks of the system include the following:

(1) Using design to empower;
(2) Bringing marginalized voices to the centre;
(3) Understanding that community impact takes precedence over a designer's intent;
(4) Acknowledging that the designer is a facilitator rather than an expert; and
(5) Welcoming everyone's unique contributions.[12]

In line with this approach, this edited volume highlights the idea of community involvement in crafting remedies. Where possible, we have worked with contributors who are embedded in the community (or have long-standing relationships with individuals). We hope that these stories will provide a foundation for academics who are looking for qualitative research in the field to bolster their theories regarding business and human rights issues. To that end, we would like to emphasize that these chapters are not a unified depiction of a whole community but rather qualitative data points that can be used by others in understanding, analysing and ultimately crafting policy responses and solutions.

We hope that these narratives provide context to the lay reader who wants to understand the underlying issues that arise when, for example, a Brazilian dam bursts.[13] In addition, we hope that these chapters can serve as lessons for students and teachers alike who want to deepen their knowledge regarding the intersection of various academic areas of study such as law, anthropology, business and human rights. For us, the lessons that we learned are numerous; below are just a few worth highlighting.

Lesson 1: In Order to Provide Access to Remedies, You Need to be Accessible

In Chapter 3 of this volume, you'll meet Digong (Digong is not his real name). Digong was in his early twenties in the 1970s when he went to work as a banana farmer for Dole Philippines. As part of his job, he was assigned to inject a chemical called Fumazone into the roots of the banana plants in order to kill the worms. It worked. It killed the worms. It also allegedly killed Digong's sperm. Specifically, the chemical Fumazone is so toxic that, by 1979, it was banned in the United States. However, it was still used in other parts of the world for years afterwards. Specifically, many corporations continued to ship the chemical to other countries, where it was still legal. The problem with an effect like sterilization is that it takes years for the issues to manifest: it is only when the farmers noticed that they were producing less children than others in their communities (who did not work at the plantation) that they become alarmed. Workers heard that other farmers in Latin America were filing lawsuits against Dole, Dow and other companies (including manufacturing companies like Shell) for similar actions related to being exposed to the chemical.

As author Daysheelyn Brillo argues, what's particularly egregious about this legal saga is the argument that the corporations used to get the case dismissed in the United States – forum non conveniens. Claiming that the lawsuits would be more appropriate in home courts is a standard litigation tactic and a very effective technique for multinational corporations with many subsidiaries that have separate legal personalities. According to Daysheelyn, the US court agreed and dismissed the lawsuit but required the corporations to recognize the jurisdiction of the Philippines and appear there. However, when the case was refiled in the Philippines against the remaining corporations (including Dole and others), the remaining US corporations argued that they should not be summoned into the Philippines court because they had not done business in the Philippines. Once again, the Philippines Supreme Court agreed and dismissed the case, leaving the farmers without a significant remedy. The irony is that the tactics employed by the corporation and its lawyers were perfectly legal. However, from Digong's perspective, justice has yet to be served.

Lesson 2: Do What You Say You're Going to Do

There is a town in the south-eastern peninsula of Brazil called Bento Rodrigues. It's a tiny municipality that, until fairly recently, had enjoyed a quiet existence outside of the headlines. The town was next to a mine owned by the company Samarco (a joint venture between BHP Villton, an Australian company, and Vale, a Brazilian corporation). As part of its operations, Samarco was meant to monitor, and repair as needed, the Fundao tailings dam located a few short miles from the town. The company assured the community that the dam was safe and that they were continuously monitoring the dam for safety issues. However, as Rajiv Maher and Adriana Bravin report in Chapter 4 of the book, it seems likely that they weren't. On 5 November 2015 the dam burst, leaving the town of Bento Rodrigues destroyed, with members of that community unable to save their homes, their things or, in some cases, their lives. The stories in this chapter of the book concerns the *Atingidos* or the Affected, those people in the community affected by the dam disaster. Specifically, it follows the story of Monica dos Santos, a 31-year-old dental hygienist who had lived in that town all her life. She describes the terror of that day, not knowing who of her loved ones had survived the devastation. She describes how her life has been completely uprooted since she lost her home and all of her belongings. But she also describes the sense of hurt and betrayal she and other *Atingidos* feel from their relationship with the corporation. Specifically, how all of the corporation's assurances and corporate social initiatives were meaningless after the dam burst.

Lesson 3: When Crafting a Remedy, Bear in Mind Its Culture

There is a quote that is attributed to Napoleon Bonaparte that goes like this: 'Let her sleep. When the dragon awakes the world will tremble.' The quote relates to China and seems particularly appropriate for the story you'll read about in Chapter 5. In that chapter, author Belinda Chinowawa discusses the relationship between China and Zimbabwe and the challenges that can result when two countries with very different cultures interact around issues of business and social justice. When China awoke (in the words of Bonaparte), it started engaging with the world in an unprecedented way, particularly through the use of Chinese transnational corporations (TNCs) that have invested heavily in Zimbabwe and other African countries, specifically by establishing operations designed to extract the countries' natural resources. While the operations have been successful, Chinowawa notes that the corporations are often plagued by allegations of negative human rights impacts, including forced labour, extrajudicial killings and – relevant here – forced community displacement. For the people of Chiadzwa, this has been a particularly brutal phenomenon. The area is a diamond-rich resource that has been mined by many Chinese TNCs, including Anjin Investments (a joint venture between a Chinese construction firm and individuals from the Zimbabwe National Army and Ministers of Defence).

Anjin, and other companies like it, was given the authority to relocate Chiadzwa community members to make way for mining operations in the area. This can be brutal under any circumstance, but now imagine this:

Your name is Phillimon Jowani Kayiboni and you are the 92-year-old patriarch of a family that includes 14 wives, 70 children and an unknown number of grandchildren. You are part of a Christian-oriented apostolic sect known as the Johanne Marnage group, a group that encourages polygamy. To house your very large family you have a large compound, with enough land for every one of your wives to have their own home and space for 14 kitchen thatches, 21 herds of cattle, 14 vegetable gardens, plus an additional 30 acres of cultivated land, enough to grow crops like maize and cotton for the family to sell and maintain a decent standard of living. Now, as part of your forced displacement, you are moved to a dilapidated three-room farm house with leaky roofs, poor ventilation and little space for everyone to live.

Even after several rounds of negotiations, the cultural significance of the move seems lost on the Chinese TNC. For instance, Anjin offered Kayiboni a 14-bedroom house, thinking having a bedroom for each wife was sufficient. It wasn't, and the offer was rejected. Eventually, the company capitulated and gave each wife her own home. The struggle took six years and, in the words of one of the wives, was a hollow victory. Crafting a remedy with the local culture in mind would have allowed for a more expeditious, and good-willed conclusion to this move.

Lesson 4: One Man's Villain Is Another One's Avenger

In Chapter 6, you'll meet Maxima Acuna. That *is* her real name. She is a Peruvian *campesina* (a peasant farmer). She is also considered a human rights defender, attempting to defend her land from the incursions of various mining companies, most recently Yanacocha, a joint venture that has the US-based mining company Newmont as a majority owner. Maxima and her husband Jaime live in the high Andes region of Peru. As authors Ariadna Tovar and Marianne Bertrand describe, *campesino* communities are specifically protected by Peruvian legislation that recognizes communal property; members of that community collectively own the land and must, collectively, determine its fate. Maxima claims that the mining company has attempted to circumvent that process by only dealing with some members of the community, leaving others stranded. As a result, she has undertaken significant struggles to try and rectify this injustice, including lawsuits, protests and petitions. This has resulted in a delay in the mine's operations.

In most human rights circles Maxima is looked at as a hero; she has even received awards from, among others, the Goldman Environmental Foundation. However, in her own community, many see Maxima as the villain in the story – holding up much needed developments and jobs. The company, in public, has played a role in the portrayal of Maxima. This highlights a problem that has plagued the business and human rights world almost since its inception. Human rights defenders are going against some very powerful corporate opponents. In addition to launching aggressive public campaigns against anyone who challenges their operations, corporations often file strategic lawsuits against public participation (SLAPPs) to, in the words of Annalisa Ciampi (UN Special Rapporteur on the Rights to Freedom of Peaceful Assembly and Association), 'exhaust resources, campaign capacity and morale […] They often target individual campaigners, as well as the organizations they work for, to maximize the SLAPP's capacity to intimidate.' As a by-product, it often turns communities against each other, and leads advocates to become guarded, if not entirely silenced in their quest for justice.

Lesson 5: When Devising Remedies, Consider the Whole Life

In Chapter 7, you'll hear of the city of Cajamarca Colombia. It is a place filled with a diverse community of doctors, journalists, forest engineers and farmers. But, for many, their lives have been interrupted as they have banded together to mobilize against AngloGold Ashanti and their building of La Colosa mine (the Colossal mine). As author (and co-editor) Tara Van Ho writes,

> The name 'La Colosa', seems to highlight the disconnect between the company and the community over the promise of the mine. In anthropology, the notion of 'equivocation' is sometimes used to refer to an error in cultural translation that comes about when two individuals use the same word to express their own realities, without realizing that they are actually discussing two different realities specifically because each understands the word through their own worldview. The naming of La Colosa seems to be the embodiment of such equivocations: the company did not seem to understand that its approach to, and excitement over, the 'colossal' (gigantic, extraordinary, impressive, profitable) gold reserve would

> be deemed a threat by those who would be impacted by the 'colossal' (gigantic, consuming, looming, aggressive) mine.

As such, the community has spent a large portion of their time mobilizing against the mine. It's worked. In late 2018, the company said that it was suspending all operations in that area. But at what cost? Individual lives and the community at large have been irreversibly altered, even though the mine has yet to be developed. Many have argued that the reason why the community was forced to organize was because the state failed in its duty to protect. Now, will the state provide an effective remedy to redress this failure? And will it include not just quantifiable costs (loss of income, tangible revenue, etc.) but also the recognition of other impacts, like the time spent being diverted from their original 'life project?'

There are other stories that you'll read about in these pages, with lessons too numerous to summarize. Some stories you may feel that you know. For instance, Jennifer Oliva's depiction of coal miners in West Virginia seems particularly timely given the spotlight that the region of Appalachia has had in the US news. Others you might have less familiarity with, such as Cigdem Cimrin's and Yucel Demiral's chapter discussing occupational health in a free trade zone in Turkey.

However, the single unifying theme of the stories is that, in all likelihood, you have never heard *these* particular stories before, told primarily from their point of view. These are not the stories that have made the headlines (the dam bursting in Brazil is perhaps the single biggest exception – the story of Gilberto Torres perhaps being another). These are not the stories of Flint, Michigan; Rana Plaza; or Bhopal, India. At first glance, this might seem a shortcoming for a book of this sort. Throughout the years, stories of how businesses have intersected with communities – oftentimes with disastrous results – have dominated headlines around the globe. But what this book highlights is that there are many *more* stories that *never* make the news cycle but are nonetheless equally compelling. They are stories of people you have never heard of but, hopefully by the end of this book, will care deeply about. Although we have captured some of these stories and specifically situated them within the context of business and human rights, there are many more untold stories like these happening everywhere: in Twilight, West Virginia, and Chiadzwa, Zimbabwe.

There are stories of people who have faced businesses that have created incredible difficulties for the world where they live – either intentionally or not. Stories of callous executives and negligent employees who seem to have forgotten that at the heart of business is humanity and that humanity is the driver for enterprise. The stories we present here are not comprehensive, not representative and they might not even be the most important stories out there. Instead, they are a symbolic sampling of the various challenges that communities, victims and survivors face in working with (or sometimes in spite of) a business to achieve the goal of bettering their lives.

We hope that in reviewing these stories you will develop a deeper understanding of what we face in this world. For all of the differences in these stories, what unifies them is their voices. They all come from the perspective of an affected individual or community in the most unfiltered way we could provide.

In the end, the focal point of the business and human rights movement should always stay with the human beings. Their stories should power us, motivate us and enlighten us.

Here are their stories.

Notes

1 Menno Kamminga, 'Company Responses to Human Rights Reports: An Empirical Analysis', *Business and Human Rights Journal* (Cambridge University Press) vol. 1, no. 1 (June 2016), 95–110.

2 See UN Working Group on Business and Human Rights, 'Informal Background Note: Human rights Defenders and Civic Space – the Business and Human Rights Dimension', December 2017, available at https://www.ohchr.org/Documents/Issues/Business/ForumSession6/UNWG_ProjectHRDsBackgroundNote12052017.pdf.

3 Ibid., 5.

4 For a recent example of the use of story, see James Freidberg, 'Yitz and Ishmael: 'A Drama in One Very Long Act', 28 Minn. *Journal of International Law* vol. 55 (2019) (analyzing the Palestinian–Israeli conflict through the use of a play).

5 See, e.g., Haley Clark, '"What Is the Justice System Willing to Offer?": Understanding Sexual Assault Victim/Survivors' Criminal Justice Needs' [online], *Family Matters*, no. 85 (2010), 28–37.

6 Mary Coombs, *Outsider Scholarship: The Law Review Stories*, 63 U. Col. L. Rev. 684 (1992).

7 Ibid., 684–85.

8 Ibid., 688.

9 Ibid., 700.

10 Sasha Costanza-Chock, 'Design Justice: Towards an Intersectional Feminist Framework for Design Theory and Practice', *Proceedings of the Design Research Society*, 2018. Available at SSRN: https://ssrn.com/abstract=3189696 (accessed 3 July 2018).

11 Ibid.

12 Ibid.

13 This is particularly timely given that another dam burst in a mining area in Brazil in early 2019, with reportedly the same devastating impact.

Chapter 1

COMPLICITY IN FALSE ARREST, IMPRISONMENT AND THEFT BY A FAIRTRADE-CERTIFIED COMPANY

Madeline Hung

Introduction

The town of Njombe-Penja is located in Cameroon's Moungo Division in the Littoral Region. With a nutrient-rich volcanic subsoil, tropical climate and deeply rooted plantation economy, Njombe-Penja is one of the banana production capitals of Cameroon. Indeed, Njombe-Penja is home to the largest private banana production company in the country, Société des Plantations du Haut Penja (PHP).[1] PHP accounts for nearly 50 per cent of all banana production in Cameroon and is owned by the French multinational company Compagnie Fruitière de Marseille ('Compagnie Fruitière').

There has been significant conflict between PHP and the local population of Njombe-Penja almost since PHP's arrival in the region in 1990, when Compagnie Fruitière was able to acquire a majority stake in the now defunct state-owned Cameroonian Banana Organization (CBO).[2] Early allegations against the company included land grabbing, soil, water and air pollution and egregious labour rights violations – including the routine spraying of pesticides on field workers and the violent suppression of unionized workers in 1991 and 1992.[3] Conflict with the company came to a head in 2007 when Njombe-Penja's former mayor Paul Eric Kingue publicly accused the company of, among other things, failing to pay taxes to the local authority during its near 20 years of operation – thus depriving the town of much-needed funds for development.[4] Kingue was subsequently jailed in 2008 on what are widely believed to be trumped-up charges and was only released in 2015 after interventions by multiple UN bodies.[5]

Despite these controversies, PHP became Fairtrade-certified in 2013. Fairtrade International ('Fairtrade') is an international standard-setting body that works to 'connect disadvantaged producers and consumers, promote fairer trading conditions and empower producers to combat poverty, strengthen their position and take more control over their lives'.[6] Fairtrade works by auditing and certifying producers, traders and companies for compliance with standards around terms of trade, labour rights, health and safety standards and environmental protections. As noted on the Fairtrade International website, 'When a product carries the FAIRTRADE Mark it means the producers and traders have met Fairtrade Standards [...] designed to address the imbalance of power in trading relationships, unstable markets and the injustices of conventional trade.'[7] Such marks, labels or logos then also represent the business opportunity to sell products in new 'ethical markets' or to mainstream consumers more expensively.

This chapter raises questions around PHP's participation in Fairtrade certification given the company's long history of abuses and continued conflict with the local community. Specifically, this chapter documents the impacts of PHP on Mr Youpa Ngameni Pierre ('Mr Youpa') – a 62-year-old plantain and papaya farmer who experienced land grabs, false imprisonment and loss of personal property at the hands of PHP – and uses Mr Youpa's testimony as a starting point for inquiry into whether voluntary accountability mechanisms within initiatives like Fairtrade are likely to overcome structural barriers to justice in Njombe-Penja.

This chapter draws on interview-based research conducted by the Institute for Multi-Stakeholder Initiative Integrity (MSI Integrity) and the Network for the Fight against Hunger (RELUFA) in Cameroon from May to June 2017. Researchers set out to understand the extent to which Fairtrade certification holds companies accountable to workers, farmers and local communities and confronted the challenges multi-stakeholder initiatives (MSIs) face in acting as accountability and assurance mechanisms when operating in weak legal environments. Conversations with Mr Youpa point to two principal findings:

1. MSIs, given their limited scope, are particularly vulnerable to infiltration by companies that seek credit for a narrow set of good practices despite generally poor behaviour when operating in environments where the rule of law is weak.
2. As such, it is unclear if MSIs should be rightly understood as tools to fill 'governance gaps' when cases like that of Mr Youpa suggest that MSIs often have little power to improve upon local governance and law enforcement practices or supplement them with independent accountability mechanisms.

To begin, this chapter considers Cameroon's present-day political context and ongoing challenges related to the enforcement of local and national laws, including instances of arbitrary arrest and detention and failure to follow legal arrest procedures. From here, Mr Youpa describes the challenges he has faced in holding a Fairtrade-certified company to account for its crimes, even when the company has been certified as meeting good practice standards by an international standard-setting body. Finally, this chapter highlights the limitations of MSIs in providing broad-based assurances about a businesses' operations and raises questions about the ability of voluntary standard-setting initiatives to surmount governance failures. Although MSIs are often developed in attempts to close governance gaps, Mr Youpa's case raises questions around the baseline social and political conditions voluntary accountability mechanisms may in fact rely upon to effectively stop corporate impunity.

Political Context and the Rule of Law

The Republic of Cameroon is a Central African nation bordering the Bight of Biafra between Equatorial Guinea and Nigeria. Cameroon has been an independent nation since 1972. Although Cameroon is a presidential republic, there are no term limits for the president and President Paul Biya has been in power since 6 November 1982. In practice, the president retains the power to control legislation, maintains strong control of security forces – including the gendarmerie, army and the army's military security unit – and has strong personal ties to the private sector.[8] For years many sources have alleged that Biya is a shareholder of PHP – an allegation the company has repeatedly denied.

Arbitrary arrest and detention and a general failure to follow proper arrest procedures remain significant problems in the country. Cameroon's constitution and law prohibit arbitrary arrest and detention and provide that 'accused persons shall be given reasonable access to contact their family, obtain legal advice and arrange for their defense'.[9] However in both its 2016/17 and 2017/18 annual Cameroon country reports, Amnesty International noted that 'security forces continued to arbitrarily arrest individuals accused of supporting Boko Haram, often with little or no evidence' and that 'hundreds of suspects were held in unofficial detention centres [...] without access to a lawyer or their families'.[10] Other groups particularly vulnerable to arbitrary arrest included political opponents, peaceful protesters, particularly those from Anglophone-speaking regions, journalists, civil society activists and LGBTI people.[11] There is also precedent for the arbitrary arrest and detention of individuals opposing corporate or private land grabbing.[12] Amnesty

International's 2017/2018 annual Cameroon country report noted additionally that 'unfair trials continued before military courts, which were often marred by irregularities'.[13]

Arbitrary arrests are usually conducted by the police, gendarmerie and local government authorities who may then hold detainees for 'prolonged periods without charge or trial and at times incommunicado'.[14] The US State Department notes that both the Ministry of Defence – which includes the gendarmerie, army and the army's military security unit – and the national police – which includes the public security force, judicial police, territorial security forces and frontier police – both report to an office of the presidency, 'resulting in strong presidential control of security forces'.[15] Moreover, 'the gendarmerie alone has responsibility in rural areas', leaving rural populations particularly vulnerable to manipulation by local security forces that may use arrest and detention for personal gain and may otherwise use personal discretion in executing arrest procedures. For example, although the law requires police to obtain a warrant before making an arrest, except when a person is caught in the act of committing a crime, 'police often did not respect this requirement'.[16] Again such a provision may be particularly difficult to enforce in rural areas where witnesses or external accountability are limited.

Police and gendarmes often violate arrest procedures by failing to bring detainees before a magistrate, exceeding detention periods (48 hours for common crimes) and denying detainees access to legal counsel and family members. Moreover, though 'the law permits bail, allows citizens the right to appeal and provides the right to sue for unlawful arrest […] these rights were seldom respected'.[17] Ultimately, the police and gendarmes are 'ineffective, poorly trained and corrupt' and therefore highly vulnerable to persuasion and dealmaking with strong corporate or government powers.[18]

Testimony of Mr Youpa Ngameni Pierre

> PHP sent me to prison in 2001 for three months and three weeks […] Now I have lost my materials, my liberty, everything […] Now, I just suffer.[19]

Mr Youpa is a 62-year-old papaya farmer living in Njombe-Penja, Cameroon. MSI Integrity and RELUFA researchers spoke with him in May 2017 as part of a research project to understand the extent to which Fairtrade certification holds companies accountable to workers, farmers and local communities. He was identified as a relevant interviewee by RELUFA staff who had previously assisted him in claiming compensation from PHP for land he lost to the company in a fraudulent land acquisition deal.

Several concerning allegations arose during two days of interviews with Mr Youpa – including a detailed account of PHP's aggressive land grabs from local farmers. Such allegations are included in this testimony to provide context to the nature of his relationship with PHP. However, when asked if there was a particular part of his story that he would like to tell, he explained that it would be most important for him to share his experience of theft and his false imprisonment. As such, his testimony is weighted towards these allegations.

Land Grabs in Njombe-Penja: A History of Conflict

Originally from Bafang in the West province of Cameroon, Mr Youpa came to Njombe in the late 1980s to seek work when his family was unable to further support his education. He established his first papaya farm in 1991 – a one-hectare plot in the middle of the fertile Njombe-Penja subdivision. His first interaction with PHP came shortly thereafter when, in his own words, 'PHP destroyed this plantation' by tilling over his plants and offered him $1.5 million CFA (approximately US$2,700) in compensation. Mr Youpa explains that he willingly accepted PHP's offer and had no conflict with the company at this time.

In 1992, Mr Youpa then joined the local farmer's association, Common Initiative Group (CIG) 'Groupement des Petits Planteurs et Autres Fruits de Njombe-Penja' (GPPAF) (Association of Small Planters and Other Fruits of Njombe-Penja). The group rented a 63-hectare plot of land from the Bonandam indigenous community cooperative called SOPRABO and successfully cultivated plantain, papaya, macabo and other crops on the land for six years. Mr Youpa personally cultivated five hectares of the plantation. He recounts that GPPAF was regularly paying the necessary land rents but that in 1998 PHP's external relations officer ordered the farmers to leave their land by order of the agriculture authorities of the Njombe-Penja subdivision.

As documented by Transparency International Cameroon, the GPPAF land dispute began when the association's 63 hectares – part of a bigger 175-hectare plot leased to the Bonandam community – were transferred to PHP by the regional senior divisional officer on a long-term basis.[20] From here,

> In a bid to avoid direct conflict with the population, [PHP] signed a memorandum of understanding with the Bonandam community in which SOPRABO received 63 hectares on the condition that it would settle any existing disputes in the community and would also take part in the expulsion of 'foreigners' who occupied these lands. Consequently, in 1995 SOPRABO attempted to evict GPPAF CIG from this plot of land through a bailiff, but ultimately failed. The matter was taken to court, but SOPRABO's claims were rejected. It was

> at this stage that PHP intervened by trying to persuade the GPPAF CIG to leave through the offer of compensation, the terms of which were accepted by the CIG.[21]

As Mr Youpa remembers, the farmers were initially offered a compensation package of $600,000 CFA (approximately US$1,000) per hectare, an amount 'that we couldn't accept [...] and which wasn't based off a proper evaluation of the plants and value of the agriculture'. He estimates that GPPAF was earning close to $140,000 CFA per week from just one hectare of its papaya crop, highlighting the gross inadequacy of the original compensation offer. As such 'the planters rejected PHP's offer, considering it inadequate and proposed instead to be compensated $600 million CFA (approximately US$1,084,000), the amount which they themselves considered equal to the value of their crops'.[22]

GPPAF first wrote to the senior divisional officer to seek assistance in negotiating a fair compensation price, but the farmers found that the officer was 'already working with the company'. Mr Youpa recalls that they then wrote to the regional delegate of agriculture. She agreed to meet with the farmers and all convened at a local hotel. The meeting, though originally promising, turned south. Mr Youpa describes how 'this lady told us that the fight between us and the company was like an elephant fighting an insect. [She] suggested that we bring in an expert to conduct an evaluation of the value of the land, and so we gave her $600,000 CFA (approximately US$1,000) to hire an expert to conduct the evaluation. But the evaluation never happened, and we don't know where the money went.'

Given the farmers' continued inability to obtain a proper land evaluation, and thus, to negotiate a fair compensation price, the farmers sued PHP in the Court of First Instance in 1998. Mr Youpa notes that the farmers had to pay $1.5 million CFA to file their case and that while awaiting the inspection of their land, PHP had already begun clearing the land for its own use. The case was then transferred to the subdivisional Mbanga Magistrates Court, where the farmers were required to pay an additional $300,000 CFA as case-filing fees (approximately 1.5× Mr Youpa's average weekly wage at that time). Shortly thereafter, the court president called in the farmers and PHP management to schedule a site visit to the plantation to evaluate the value of the existing crops. However, as Mr Youpa recalls, 'The moment we were leaving the president's office, the [PHP representative] called to have the entire plantation destroyed', thus destroying all evidence that the farmers had cultivated the land and therefore deserved compensation.

With limited options remaining, the farmers began negotiation with PHP to adjust their compensation. PHP then committed to paying the farmers a total of $11 million CFA (approximately US$19,800) in compensation but claimed that they would pay the amount in three instalments. The first instalment of $1.9 million CFA was paid, as agreed, in December 1999. The second instalment of $1.28 million CFA was paid in 2013 after significant pressure and legal aid from civil society groups RELUFA and CED (Centre pour l'Environnement et le Développement). The final instalment, ultimately negotiated down to $2.5 million CFA, has yet to be paid. Mr Youpa laments, 'Today, we are doing everything possible to make sure that the Director General [of PHP] pays the third part of the money, but he doesn't want to.' Though the farmers have attempted to claim the full amount of their compensation through various means, including appealing to the Littoral Court of Appeal in Douala, they have been turned down at almost every turn and suspect that those they recruited to defend their case were ultimately bought off by the company.

Indeed, it seems that there is little that can be done to influence or override the company's will. As corroborated by Transparency International Cameroon, 'forged compensation forms were brandished during the case, supposedly indicating that the planters received twice the amount they received in reality [...] This shows how the members of GIC-GPPAF [...] became victims of embezzlement, and proves that the compensation process, the general principles they accepted, was not carried out on the basis of honesty and integrity.'[23] Mr Youpa notes, 'We have spent so much money following up on this whole thing that any offer PHP gives us, we will have to take. Surely, the company will still owe us money and the struggle will continue. But we can't refuse any money they offer us at this point because we are so in debt.'

When asked what might have prevented PHP's conflict with the local population to begin with, Mr Youpa explained that if PHP had continued to provide fair compensation for the land they acquired, as they did in their first two years of operation, there would not have been a problem. He notes that the company provided him with $1.5 million CFA for his original, one-hectare farm, which he accepted without complaint and moved on to cultivate new land. He provided another example where the company acquired land from a women's farming collective and paid each farmer fair compensation at $28,000 CFA, which they also accepted without complaint. Rather, the problem Mr Youpa identified is that the company became increasingly aggressive in its land acquisition and began to take advantage of the local population by coercing farmers into accepting compensation deals well below their land's value. Mr Youpa explained that a given papaya plant might produce 70 fruits in a year, with each fruit sold for at least $200 CFA. Mr Youpa's five-hectare plot within GPPAF was valued at $3 million CFA, meaning that 'PHP was buying each plant for less than $600 CFA. So, you can see how it was under-evaluated. My five-hectare plot should have been valued at least at $48 million CFA. Instead, PHP estimated its value to be $3 million CFA.'

The details of GPPAF's land conflict with PHP have been well-documented by both RELUFA and Transparency International Cameroon, and the farmers of GPPAF continue to be supported by RELUFA staff. Although there has still been no progress in securing the farmers' third compensation payment, several farmers interviewed noted attempts to involve the UN High Commissioner for Human Rights in an investigation on the issue.

False Arrest, Imprisonment and Theft of Personal Property

Amidst his near 20-year land conflict with PHP, Mr Youpa claims that PHP issued false charges against him that led to his false arrest, imprisonment and the theft of his personal property in 2001. As Mr Youpa describes,

> What happened was that I was living with a neighbour who was driving a tractor for PHP. At the time, I had just begun building my house on an empty plot next door, and so I needed a place to stay. Soon after, my neighbour was fired from the company, as it appeared that he may have been collaborating with thieves who were stealing things from the company by allowing them to keep the stolen materials in his house. I was not aware of this at the time.
>
> One day, I was coming back from the farm and went to the bar where I saw two PHP security guards wandering around the premises of my property. I noticed that the security guards slept on my property that night, though I went back to sleep in my neighbour's house. The next day, the gendarmerie arrived and invaded both my neighbour's house and my house even though it was still under construction. I was on my farm at the time, but when I came back home at the end of the day, I saw that my property had been raided and that all the materials I had stored in my house had been removed. All my building materials and material possessions were gone – the zinc, ties, windows, iron doors I had bought to build my house, and even my Suzuki bike. Without explanation, the gendarmerie ordered me to climb into a tractor, and they took me straight to the jail cell.[24]

Mr Youpa described how he arrived at the jail house, intimidated and confused:

> I was waiting for someone to explain the charges against me, but nothing happened. So, I went up to the gendarmerie commander and asked him 'Why am I here?' The commander just yelled, 'Go back in the cell! This is someone who belongs inside the cell!'

> At first, they locked me up for 21 days. It was horrible – I didn't even bathe during this time. Then they let me out, but they asked me to sign a paper. I refused because I said that I had to read the paper first. I didn't understand what they were asking me to sign. Instead of explaining the paper, they said that, just for refusing to sign, I had to go back to prison. That is how I ended up in prison for three months and three weeks.[25]

Mr Youpa suspects that the paper was intended to document the reasons for his imprisonment, similar to a paper he was asked to sign without reading when he was admitted to the prison. However, he remains uncertain as to the reasons why he was readmitted. He then describes how, after two months in prison, a newly appointed 'investigating magistrate' came to the jail.

> The new magistrate was there examining the case files of all the inmates. And then one day, he called me in saying 'Why are you here? There is no case file for you!'[26]

Mr Youpa explained the circumstances of his arrest to the magistrate and the two of them pieced together that PHP had likely alleged that Mr Youpa had stolen company property – 'conflating' his own personal property with the items supposedly stolen by his neighbour and his accomplices. Neither his neighbour nor any of his collaborators were ever found. He was finally permitted to contact his wife who then brought receipts for all the materials in question to the prison, clearly demonstrating that he had purchased the building materials himself. He and the general prosecutor learned that PHP had seized the building materials and put them in storage in their own warehouse. As such, the two went to PHP to locate the materials and then matched Mr Youpa's receipts to the materials seized. Mr Youpa recounts,

> The magistrate wrote a paper ordering for my immediate release [from prison] and saying that the materials should be refunded. But PHP never refunded the materials to me.
>
> There was one time that PHP's former Director of External Affairs called me to bring in the receipts. I brought them in and they did an evaluation which placed the value of the materials at $3.99 million CFA [approximately $7,000 USD]. At this point, I thought they would issue me a check, but nothing was done after the evaluation. I was really surprised by this.[27]
>
> After reaching out to PHP several times requesting that my materials be refunded, PHP's Director of External Affairs [...] told me directly that this case would never be ruled in my favour. Now I have lost my materials, my liberty,

> everything. I had to buy some old sheets of zinc to build my roof and now when it rains, we get wet.

To make matters worse, Mr Youpa's case was revived before the Court of First Instance in Mbanga in February 2005 given that the case had never been formally tried. Having thought that his theft charges were behind him, Mr Youpa recalls receiving his court notice thinking it was a bad dream. He was found 'not guilty' in these proceedings. However he describes the costs that were associated with his court appearance, including the necessary payments to hire a lawyer and the emotional toll of being made to testify and prove his innocence once again.

Living in the Aftermath

As Mr Youpa describes, the combined physical and emotional impact of GPPAF's ongoing land battle with PHP, his imprisonment, trial and loss of property, 'has really been horrible'. He has five children and became a single parent in 2009 when his wife left him due to the family's financial hardship. He continues to struggle in supporting his children.

> My first daughter was studying at an advanced level and went through four years of schooling. But now she can't continue her education because I have no money. Similarly, my second son was supposed to be playing on the national football team because he was a really good player. The team asked me to pay $300,000 CFA to allow my son to play (because one must pay small bribes for all of these things in Cameroon), but I could not even pay this small sum.[28]

To make ends meet, Mr Youpa continues to farm a small two-hectare plot of land 12 km from town. He explains that he struggled to acquire this land as there are few remaining farms that haven't been absorbed into PHP. He gets to the farm on his motorbike but must ride there standing up as severe scoliosis and back pain doesn't allow him to sit down on the bike. In general, he feels that the money he makes from his produce on the farm is insufficient to meet his basic needs. 'At least when I had five-hectares of land, I knew that I would get at least $200,000 CFA a week. Now, I just suffer.'

Mr Youpa added that as recently as 2016 he again requested audience with the director general of PHP to discuss reimbursement for his stolen property. The director general refused to see him and referred him to PHP's administrative office. The administrative office, in turn, refused to see him and referred him to a secretary. The secretary told him that this case would never be ruled in his favour and that he should give up. Though laughing, he lamented, 'I have never seen a company as bad as PHP […] They are just being wicked.'

Voluntary Standard-Setting Initiatives: Assurances and Limitations of Accountability Mechanisms

Unfortunately, Mr Youpa's story is not unique. Farmers and communities in Cameroon and around the world are experiencing similar threats to their land, livelihoods and freedom from governments and powerful companies on an almost daily basis.[29] However, one thing that does set Mr Youpa's circumstances apart from many others is that the company involved has been certified as meeting certain good practice standards for operation and production by an international standard-setting body – Fairtrade International. In a follow-up interview held by the author in June 2017, Njombe-Penja's former mayor Paul Eric Kingue expressed, 'How could a company such as PHP *ever* become Fairtrade certified?' Indeed, although Mr Youpa's testimony is anecdotal and therefore cannot speak to PHP's compliance with Fairtrade standards or the initiative's overall effectiveness, it raises questions around the effectiveness and impact of Fairtrade-like initiatives operating across a range of industries.

Fairtrade is one of many MSIs and other voluntary standard-setting initiatives and schemes that have flooded the business and human rights space over the past 25 years. MSIs can generally be understood as collaborations between businesses, civil society and other stakeholders that seek to address issues of mutual concern, including human rights and sustainability. To do so, initiatives may work to facilitate dialogue across stakeholder groups, foster cross-sector engagement or develop and apply standards for corporate or government conduct.

Many MSIs also provide assurances that participating companies, or sometimes governments, are complying with certain standards for responsible conduct or else are exceeding ordinary business practices. These assurances are perhaps most explicit for initiatives with certification or labelling schemes, like Fairtrade International, which allows companies certified as having met Fairtrade standards to use the 'FAIRTRADE' mark on their products.

Standard-setting MSIs are by no means *required* to assure the public that their members are exceeding ordinary business practices and that they are working to ensure that their members are in fact meeting initiative standards or taking steps to come into compliance.[30] Nevertheless, if an MSI *does* make claims or public assurances that its members are meeting a set of standards or taking steps to come into compliance over time, it must follow through on these commitments. Where companies or governments egregiously violate an

MSI's standards, they should be publicly held to account, such as through suspension or expulsion from the initiative or through requirements to provide a remedy to address any harm caused.

What then if a company complies with the letter of an initiative's standards but not its spirit?

Transparency International Cameroon has investigated a range of allegations against PHP through its Anti-Corruption and Legal Advice Centre since 2014. In November 2014, Transparency International Cameroon sent a formal complaint to Fairtrade International questioning PHP's certification status and shared Fairtrade's response – a commitment to 'undertake a further investigation into the practices at the Mantem and PHP2 plantations' in Njombe-Penja.[31] However, as Fairtrade does not publicly disclose the status of individual complaints, it remains unknown whether Fairtrade has followed up on its commitment to conduct further investigations. As of January 2019, PHP remained Fairtrade-certified as per the register of Fairtrade-certified companies available on the FLO-cert website.[32] Fairtrade's lack of transparency around how the complaint was resolved thus inevitably sends the message that Fairtrade condones PHP's continued use of the Fairtrade ethical mark and that PHP has been permitted to proceed with business as usual.

Many MSIs do not require 100 per cent compliance with initiative standards for members to be awarded certification or otherwise participate in initiative activities and decision-making processes. And while most standard-setting MSIs delineate some non-negotiable standards for regulated members, many utilize a 'staged' compliance model where companies or governments are only required to make progress towards 100 per cent compliance over time or else allow members to maintain their status in the initiative so long as a certain minimum percentage of standards are met. Such is the case with Fairtrade which both stages compliance with initiative standards over several years and allows participating producers, traders and companies to maintain certification so long as they meet the initiative's 'core requirements' and evidence 'continuous improvements' in complying with the initiative's 'development requirements'. These strategies may have benefits, such as lowering barriers to entry for participating companies and thus broadening the initiative's reach. However, they also open opportunities for some participants to take advantage of the system by complying with the minimum set of standards for certification or inclusion while continuing to fall short of critical obligations for extended periods of time. In this way, MSIs may be limited in their ability to hold companies or governments accountable for their misdeeds which, though noncompliant with the initiative's standards, are 'outweighed' by the actor's 'good practices'.

It is also important to note that most MSIs are simply limited in their scope, meaning that a participating company or government may be fully compliant with the initiative's standards while committing egregious rights abuses in other aspects of their operations. Some may argue that it is both unreasonable and impractical for initiatives to assume responsibility for holding participating companies or governments accountable to the full range of relevant human rights. And yet it is disconcerting that companies could be benefiting from such schemes while simultaneously committing abuses – outside of the initiative's scope – against the same beneficiaries the MSI is intended to benefit and protect. Such scenarios become even more likely when initiatives operate in environments with a weak rule of law where corporate abuses may frequently go undocumented or are committed with impunity, thus posing challenges to MSIs in both assessing and addressing corporate misconduct.

As such, there is some irony in the common understanding that MSIs 'were generally developed at the behest of NGOs, unions, companies and/or governments with the aim, in part, of filling the regulatory lacuna that emerged from the inability or unwillingness of many states to protect human rights in the workplace'.[33] While many MSIs were conceived as means to supplement weak laws around corporate conduct, filling 'governance gaps', in some ways they have also created the potential to layer on opportunities for or to reinforce local governance failures in weak or non-existent corporate regulatory environments. In other words, companies that have successfully manipulated local laws and law enforcement practices to their advantage may attempt to do the same with voluntary standard-setting initiatives. This makes accountability mechanisms within MSIs all the more critical as weak or non-existent mechanisms – such as sanctioning or grievance mechanisms – could 'risk compounding a sense of grievance amongst affected stakeholders by heightening their sense of disempowerment', especially for those who have already been failed by legal processes.[34]

More generally, the relationship between voluntary standard-setting initiatives, such as MSIs, and both national and international law enforcement and lawmaking remains unknown. Additional research is needed to understand whether MSIs, overall, result in better corporate conduct above and beyond the law, or whether these initiatives result in the creation of more robust laws. In the interim, where initiatives do provide assurances around corporate conduct and operate in weak states, they should: (a) be particularly wary of participating companies that may attempt to comply with the initiative's minimum standards for inclusion while carrying on abuses and misconduct in adjacent arenas; and (b) implement robust accountability mechanisms.[35]

Mr Youpa's testimony highlights the many struggles experienced by individuals who seek to challenge corporate power and gain access to remedy in Njombe-Penja, Cameroon. By comparison to the plights of many other individuals in Njombe-Penja and beyond, Mr Youpa's story has garnered appreciable attention through the documentary film *Big Banana* and the advocacy work of RELUFA and others.[36] And yet Mr Youpa has still not received any judicial or non-judicial remedy for his experiences of theft and false imprisonment at the hands of PHP. Mr Youpa remains both physically and mentally burdened by these experiences and agreed to use his personal identifying information in this testimony as he feels that he has 'nothing left to lose'. Such is to show the formidable power wielded by PHP in Njombe-Penja, which raises questions around the additional barriers to accessing remedy for those whose cases are not as well documented and who lack support services and advocates.

Though Mr Youpa's testimony cannot speak to the overall impact of PHP's participation in Fairtrade certification, it highlights the complexity of the initiative's value proposition in a weak legal environment like Njombe-Penja. Undoubtedly Fairtrade provides some benefits to the local community and PHP's workers such as the assurance of the Fairtrade minimum price and premium. However, it is important to consider how this benefit weighs against the legitimizing power Fairtrade has given to a company like PHP which continues to negatively impact and abuse the rights of the local population in other areas both inside and outside the initiative's scope. To date, Fairtrade has demonstrated little power to drive PHP to remedy its previous abuses against its workers and the local population since the company's certification. As such, it remains disconcerting that PHP both acquired and has maintained its certification status.

As compared to many MSIs, Fairtrade's standards are quite comprehensive. And yet it is important to recognize that the initiative's scope is still ultimately limited, thus making Fairtrade vulnerable to bad actors who seek to comply with the initiative's minimum standards for inclusion while carrying on abuses and misconduct in adjacent arenas – and particularly in a place like Njombe-Penja where there is precedent for impunity. Ultimately, additional research is needed to understand the extent to which voluntary mechanisms have been successful in supplementing or overcoming governance failures and whether, in some cases, MSIs may in fact create additional opportunities for governance failures within a voluntary standard-setting framework. Mr Youpa's case challenges aspects of the traditional framing of MSIs as tools to fill 'governance gaps' and rather encourages us to consider whether voluntary standard-setting initiatives may in fact rely upon certain baseline social and political conditions to effectively stop corporate impunity.

Notes

1 'In Cameroon, Compagnie Fruitière de Marseille Aims for a Production of 230,000 Tons of Bananas by 2020', *Business in Cameroon*, 31 August 2016, http://www.businessincameroon.com/agro-industry/3108-6476-in-cameroon-compagnie-fruitiere-de-marseille-aims-for-a-production-of-230-000-tons-of-bananas-by-2020.

2 Transparency International Cameroon, *Banana Report: The Bone of Contention and Its Acid Political Taste (English version)* (2014) at 16.

3 The term 'land grabbing' is most often used to describe land acquisition deals in which the land purchaser uses corrupt or coercive means to acquire a large plot of land. In a Declaration adopted at its 2011 General Assembly, the International Land Coalition (ILC) defined large-scale land grabs as '[land] acquisitions or concessions that are one or more of the following: (i) in violation of human rights, particularly the equal rights of women; (ii) not based on free, prior and informed consent of the affected land-users; (iii) not based on a thorough assessment, or are in disregard of social, economic and environmental impacts, including the way they are gendered; (iv) not based on transparent contracts that specify clear and binding commitments about activities, employment and benefits sharing and; (v) not based on effective democratic planning, independent oversight and meaningful participation'. International Land Coalition, *Tirana Declaration* (2011), principle 4 at 2, accessed 19 December 2017, http://www.landcoalition.org/sites/default/files/documents/resources/tiranadeclaration.pdf.

4 Transparency International, 'Slippery Justice: The Travails of a Whistleblower in Cameroon', 24 November 2014, https://www.transparency.org/news/feature/slippery_justice_the_travails_of_a_whistleblower_in_cameroon.

5 Evidence gathered by Transparency International Cameroon, Amnesty International and Fédération internationale des ligues des droits de l'homme (FIDH) among others shows that the judicial process that put Kingue behind bars was severely flawed. In 2014, the United Nations Working Group on Arbitrary Detention, the United Nations Human Rights Commission and the Special Rapporteur on the Independence of Judges and Lawyers released public statements and opinions stating that the arrest and judicial proceedings of Kingue's case were 'arbitrary' and 'a number of procedural guarantees were not applied'. Only after continued urging 'to ensure the release and compensation of Kingue' did the public prosecutor drop the charges against him. Kingue was ultimately released from prison in 2015 after seven years of incarceration in the Nkongsamba and Douala prisons. See: Transparency International, 'Cameroonian Corruption Fighter Paul Eric Kingue Is Free!' 17 July 2015, https://www.transparency.org/news/feature/cameroonian_corruption_fighter_paul_eric_kingue_is_free.

6 Fairtrade International, 'What Is Fairtrade?' accessed 22 September 2017, https://www.fairtrade.net/about-fairtrade/what-is-fairtrade.html.

7 Ibid.

8 US Department of State – Bureau of Democracy, Human Rights and Labor, *Cameroon 2016 Human Rights Report* (2016) at 1, 7.

9 US Department of State at 7.

10 Amnesty International, *Amnesty International Report 2016/17 – Cameroon*, 22 February 2017, http://www.refworld.org/docid/58b0341213.html. A range of public security forces conduct arrests in Cameroon, including arms of the Ministry of Defence – which includes the gendarmerie – and the national police – which includes the public security force, judicial police, territorial security forces and frontier police.

11 See, for example. FIDH, 'Cameroon: Arbitrary Detention, Judicial Harassment and Ill Treatments Inflicted on Mr. Franklin Mowha', 29 June 2014, https://www.fidh.org/en/region/Africa/cameroon/15830-cameroon-arbitrary-detention-judicial-harassment-and-ill-treatments; Human Rights Watch, 'Guilty by Association: Human Rights Violations in the Enforcement of Cameroon's Anti-Homosexuality Law', 2013, https://www.hrw.org/report/2013/03/21/guilty-association/human-rights-violations-enforcement-cameroons-anti; FIDH, 'Cameroon: Arbitrary Detention and Judicial Harassment of Mr. Alain Patrice Nganang', 18 December 2017, https://www.fidh.org/en/issues/human-rights-defenders/cameroon-arbitrary-detention-and-judicial-harassment-of-mr-alain.

12 See, for example, FIDH, 'Cameroon: Arbitrary Detention of Five Members of the Esu Youth Development Association (EYDA)', 8 July 2016, https://www.fidh.org/en/issues/human-rights-defenders/cameroon-arbitrary-detention-of-five-members-of-the-esu-youth. In Cameroon, land grabbing has been associated with many agro-industries and especially palm oil. See, for example, Greenpeace, *Herakles Farms in Cameroon: A Showcase in Bad Palm Oil Production*, 2013, http://www.greenpeace.org/usa/wp-content/uploads/legacy/Global/usa/planet3/PDFs/HeraklesCrimeFile.pdf.

13 Amnesty International, *Amnesty International Report 2017/18 – Cameroon* at 11, https://www.amnesty.org/en/countries/africa/cameroon/report-cameroon/ (accessed 13 November 2019).

14 US Department of State at 9.

15 Ibid., 8.

16 Ibid., 9.

17 Ibid.

18 Ibid., 8.

19 Pierre Youpa, personal interview with Madeline Hung, May 2017.

20 Cameroon is divided into 10 semi-autonomous regions, each governed by a presidentially appointed governor. Each region is further divided into divisions (*départements*) and then subdivisions (*arrondissements*). A senior divisional officer (*préfet*) is one of 58 presidentially appointed officers charged with carrying out the governor's duties on a smaller scale within a division.

21 Transparency International Cameroon, *Banana Report*, 33.

22 Ibid., 34.

23 Ibid., 35.

24 Pierre Youpa, personal interview with Madeline Hung, May 2017.

25 Ibid.

26 Ibid.

27 Ibid.

28 Ibid.

29 See, for example, Oxfam International, *Custodians of the Land, Defenders of Our Future* (2016), https://oi-files-d8-prod.s3.eu-west-2.amazonaws.com/s3fs-public/file_attachments/land_rights_en_final.pdf (accessed 13 November 2019).

30 The Global Reporting Initiative, for example, is a multi-stakeholder initiative that provides a standardized framework for sustainability reporting but does not obligate a group of participating companies or governments to follow this standard. In this way, the initiative does not attempt to uphold a standard but rather to disseminate and diffuse a standard.

31 Transparency International, 'Slippery Justice: The Travails of a Whistleblower in Cameroon', 24 November 2014, https://www.transparency.org/news/feature/slippery_justice_the_travails_of_a_whistleblower_in_cameroon.

32 FLOCERT, 'Fairtrade customer search', 22 September 2017, http://www.flocert.net/fairtrade-services/fairtrade-certification/fairtrade-customer-search/.

33 Dorothée Baumann-Pauly and Justine Nolan, *Business and Human Rights: From Principles to Practice* (United Kingdom: Routledge, 2016), 44–45.

34 UN Office of the High Commissioner on Human Rights, 'Guiding Principles on Business and Human Rights: Implementing the United Nations "Protect, Respect and Remedy" Framework', HR/PUB/11/04 (2011), 34, http:// www.ohchr.org/Documents/Publications/GuidingPrinciplesBusinessHR_EN.pdf (accessed 13 November 2019).

35 For more information on the qualities of effective MSI accountability mechanisms, see MSI Integrity & International Human Rights Clinic at Harvard Law School, *MSI Evaluation Tool*, v.1.0 (2017).

36 In 2011, the documentary film *Big Banana*, produced by Cameroonian filmmaker, Frank Bieuleu, documented the impact of PHP on the local population of Njombe-Penja – highlighting the company's impact on the environment, its land grabbing practices and Mr Kingue's imprisonment. However, the film was later banned in Cameroon, reportedly 'because the filmmaker did not have the correct permits'. See: Transparency International, 'Slippery Justice: The Travails of a Whistleblower in Cameroon', 24 November 2014, https://www.transparency.org/news/feature/slippery_justice_the_travails_of_a_whistleblower_in_cameroon.

Chapter 2

HINDRANCES TO ACCESS TO A REMEDY IN BUSINESS-RELATED CASES IN COLOMBIA: THE CASE OF GILBERTO TORRES[1]

Piergiuseppe Parisi and Gareth Sims

At the end of 2015, the Colombian government launched its *Plan de Acción de Derechos Humanos y Empresa*, designed to domesticate the international standards on business and human rights. It took partial inspiration from the UN Guiding Principles on Business and Human Rights, which, among other things, demand that states implement effective remedies for business-related human rights abuses, in particular through judicial avenues. Moreover, states should actively endeavour to remove barriers to the access to judicial remedies.

In its 10 years of operation, the Colombian Caravana, a London-based charity,[2] has conducted advocacy work in relation to human rights lawyers and defenders at risk because of their work. In some cases, the Caravana has intervened in support of individuals whose right to access remedies, as posited by the UN Guiding Principles, was not implemented effectively, therefore endangering the safety of petitioners claiming redress for or protection from business-related human rights violations. One case in particular has made the front page of several newspapers not only in Colombia but also worldwide. That is the case of Gilberto Torres Martinez.[3] We met Gilberto in 2016 through his attorneys Sue Willman and Daniel Carey, at the UK law firm Deighton Pierce Glynn, while he was on a speaking tour around the UK. At that time, Gilberto was living in exile, first in Spain and then in the Dominican Republic, having fled Colombia in 2002 after he had been kidnapped by the paramilitary group *Autodefensas Unidas de Colombia* and, in an almost unprecedented way, released after 42 days of captivity as a result of intense pressure from the international community.

Gilberto Torres Martinez is a former leader of *Unión Sindical Obrera* (USO), a leading trade union in the Colombian oil industry. USO has campaigned against the privatization of ECOPETROL, the major Colombian oil company and one of the largest oil companies in the Americas.

Oil explorations in the region of Casanare, where Gilberto was based, began in 1987 under the lead of BP, the most prominent British oil company, through its subsidiary companies, BP Exploration Company (Colombia) Limited ('BP Exploration Colombia'), now Equion Energia Limited ('Equion Energia'), and BP Colombia Pipelines Limited ('BP Colombia Pipelines'), the latter subsidiary being controlled by the former company pursuant to a series of association contracts with ECOPETROL. Since then, thousands of people have been either killed or disappeared, allegedly at the hands of governmental forces or right-wing paramilitary groups. BP Exploration Colombia controlled operations, activities and facilities in the area. Between 1995 and 1997, a pipeline was built to transport the oil to the Caribbean coast. According to a prior agreement, the pipeline was owned and operated by Oleuducto Central ('OCENSA'), a company whose shareholders include ECOPETROL and BP Colombia Pipelines.[4]

At the time, it was well known that guerrilla groups such as the FARC and the ELN would target oil infrastructures in Colombia.[5] For years the Colombian National Army had been engaged with these groups in a bloody and violent conflict. Thus, BP Exploration Colombia entered into agreements to have the Colombian army and the local police provide security services to the company's installations. BP also employed private security. On 7 November 1995, BP Exploration Colombia signed a three-year collaborative agreement with the Colombian government whereby the company paid roughly US$2 million to the Ministry of Defence, in addition to a 'war tax' on oil barrels to finance such security services. Over the three years, and with the approval of BP, BP Exploration Company paid over US$54 million to the Ministry of Defence. BP continued to pay the Ministry of Defence for several years. According to Human Rights Watch, BP benefitted in particular from the security services of the XVI Brigade of the Colombian National Army, which was created pursuant to the agreement between BP Exploration Colombia and the Colombian government and numbered approximately 3,000 soldiers based in the capital of Casanare, Yopal.

The Colombian army was known to have worked closely with paramilitaries. The presence of these groups in Colombia was facilitated by the Colombian government which, unable to defeat the guerrillas, decided to first allow the creation of paramilitary forces not bound by the rules of engagement applicable to the army and second, pass legislation that would legalize their funding. As a result, several private landowners and companies made payments to paramilitary groups for the provision of security services for the benefit of their properties. In Casanare, the paramilitary group *Autodefensas Unidas de Colombia* was integrated into the Colombian army. This strategy allowed BP to suppress social movements protesting the exploitation of their land. Following some scandals, BP attempted to distance themselves from the exploration projects by agreeing to the incorporation of the company OCENSA but, through its subsidiary BP Colombia Pipelines which held shares in the newly incorporated company, managed to shield its continuing involvement and control of the operations of its subsidiary.[6]

Since oil explorations and extraction began in Casanare, thousands of people have been killed or 'disappeared'. In a letter to BP,[7] Human Rights Watch noted that paramilitaries were used to intimidate critics of the oil company and that the presence of such groups was at least tolerated by BP. Human Rights Watch noted that on several occasions paramilitaries had been seen carrying heavy weapons and responding to Colombian military commanders while being dressed in civilian clothing. Similar reports were also compiled by other organizations such as World in Action, which released a documentary titled *BP's Secret Soldiers*. These allegations prompted the Colombian government to launch inquiries into the conduct of BP in Casanare. The investigations confirmed that BP had contracted with the Ministry of Defence and that additional payments had been made to bring in elite anti-guerrilla forces. In addition, it emerged that BP had provided the XVI Brigade with intelligence and military equipment. Finally, it appears that BP had also contracted with the Colombian subsidiary of a London-based security company and had considered entering into an agreement with an Israeli private security company.[8] Even the CEO of BP Exploration Company admitted that the company had been involved in human rights abuses[9] but while BP officials were paying lip service to following up on the allegations formulated by Human Rights Watch, little seemed to be changing.

Gilberto had worked for ECOPETROL since the late 1980s. In 1997 he was elected local union leader for the Los Llanos area, and in 2001 he was voted the representative for the National Petroleum Forum (*Foro Petrolero Nacional*). Gilberto's duties included visiting the three pumping stations in Los Llanos in order to receive the workers' complaints and report them to the management. He was successful in negotiating with ECOPETROL on behalf of the workers and managed to reach several agreements that were favourable to the workforce. In his position, Gilberto attempted to introduce the issue of the impact of oil extractions on human rights in oil-rich regions of Colombia, paving the way for unprecedented discussions between the USO and the state.

Gilberto was also successful in his direct negotiations with BP, whose representatives he met with on several occasions in the company's offices in

Yopal. He would report breaches of contractual or security regulations to the Colombian BP officers or protest the company's delays in paying workers. In October 2001 Gilberto complained about the training of Colombian soldiers, funded by BP, in the pumping station of El Porvenir since this was in breach of agreements. He voiced his concerns to active members of the Colombian army. Gilberto also organized a strike over the disappearance and murder of a fellow trade unionist, Aury Sará Marrugo, on 30 November 2001. The strike had a dramatic impact on the pumping of oil in Colombia over the course of several days, in particular on the OCENSA pipeline operations, effectively bringing oil production to a standstill.

While on the one hand Gilberto's successes benefitted the position of workers, they also put him in the spotlight as a prominent leader of the labour rights movement. As a result, between 2001 and 2002, Gilberto started to receive threatening phone calls from unidentified men who accused him of being a 'communist' or 'guerrilla' member. Gilberto wrote a letter to the chief of corporate security in ECOPETROL asking for protection measures but never received a reply. The USO also requested protection on his behalf but was informed that Gilberto was not in immediate danger and there was not a sufficient basis to grant the protection requested. Finally, in early February 2002, Gilberto filed a complaint with the authorities.

After the murder of Aury Sará Marrugo, Gilberto raised concerns over his threatened personal situation and the risk posed to the local community and the oil installation by the nearby presence of the FARC in a meeting organized by BP Exploration Colombia in which the head of security of ECOPETROL, an OCENSA representative and a major of the army participated.

On 25 February 2002, on his way home from El Porvenir pumping station, after passing through OCENSA security, Gilberto was abducted by unknown men driving a van that, according to Gilberto, was clearly recognizable as the OCENSA security vehicle. He was kept as a handcuffed prisoner in a rain-filled pit, full of insects that bit him repeatedly, for 10 days then periodically moved to other sites and tortured for a total of 42 days by the *Autodefensas Campesinas de Casanare*, a paramilitary group originally opposed to the *Autodefensas Unidas de Colombia* but which later joined them. Gilberto suffered both physical and psychological torture and was even forced to watch the dismemberment of another kidnapped activist. His captors led him to believe that they had his wife and son. During Gilberto's captivity, he was interrogated several times by his captors who accused him of having ties with the guerrillas. The individuals who interrogated Gilberto asked him how he knew that the FARC were in the vicinity of the oil facilities, a detail that he had only disclosed during the private meeting he had had with the head of security of ECOPETROL prior to his capture, pointing, according to Gilberto, to the involvement of ECOPETROL in his abduction. Thanks to the strenuous support of his trade union and the pressure of the international community,[10] Gilberto was freed in April 2002. Gilberto reported that over the course of his release, his captors transferred him to the custody of a Colombian army officer, whom the paramilitaries addressed as *mi comandante* (my commander) and who told Gilberto that he would have to share his story publicly and show his wounds without naming any names as a lesson to other trade unionists. He was then handed over to the International Red Cross.

Shortly after his kidnapping, Gilberto was moved to Bogotá with his family and assigned security guards by USO and ECOPETROL. When he was informed that a paramilitary commando in Bogotá had intended to murder him, Gilberto decided that remaining in Colombia would constitute too great a risk to his life and that of his family and so decided that the best course of action would be to leave the country. On 4 June 2002, Gilberto fled Colombia with his family to seek asylum in Spain. He remained in exile for almost 15 years, only returning briefly during the recent peace negotiations.

In the meantime, criminal proceedings were initiated in Colombia against paramilitary leaders who had taken part in Gilberto's kidnapping. It emerged from their testimonies that the companies ECOPETROL and OCENSA were in some way involved in Torres's abduction. Some of the responsible paramilitaries declared explicitly that both companies 'had sent for' Gilberto Torres and that his kidnapping was politically motivated.[11] A USO leader testified that Gilberto had become 'a thorn in their sides' because of the frequent strikes he had been organizing. The judge who found the four paramilitaries guilty of Gilberto's kidnapping concluded that there were elements, including documentary evidence of contacts between the multinational company (MNC) OCENSA and the paramilitary group, that warranted a criminal investigation. In one of the judgments, it was stated,

> There are enough elements that point to the participation of the multinational company OCENSA in the kidnapping [...] Consequently, [...] the motives behind the kidnapping and the other related offences emerge clearly; it was [Gilberto's] activism in his capacity of trade union leader, which affected the companies involved in the oil extraction process, that [...] led them to consider necessary the removal of whoever was jeopardising their economic interests.[12]

Yet the Colombian authorities failed to act on these leads.

Aside from criminal action, Gilberto reported that the Colombian legal system offers few avenues to seek redress against the masterminds behind his abduction. In particular, there exists no civil action that could be brought against BP in Colombia. While administrative claims could be filed against government officials and a governmental compensation scheme was available for victims of the *Autodefensas Unidas de Colombia*, Gilberto could hardly avail himself of these remedies while being in exile. Moreover, returning to Colombia would have meant risking his life. Human Rights Watch reported that the Colombian government's collusion with paramilitary violence, manifested through the 'legalization' of the funding of certain paramilitary groups, ensured that violence perpetrated at the hands of these groups would mostly go unpunished.[13] Nonetheless, Gilberto stated that the evidence which emerged during the trials of the four paramilitaries allowed him to file an administrative complaint in the Colombian administrative court.

Proceedings under US and Colombian tort law were initiated first in the United States and later in the UK against oil giant BP but both cases were later dropped. The case filed in the United States under the Alien Tort Statute (ATS) was dropped after the Supreme Court determined the limits to the extraterritorial application of the ATS in the leading case *Kiobel*.[14]

Significant efforts were put into fighting Gilbertos's case in the UK; however, it faced a number of obstacles common in this type of litigation which are predominantly related to overcoming resource constraints and navigating a complicated and cumbersome process involved in bringing cross-jurisdictional claims. The case was plagued by mainly evidentiary problems that made it difficult to establish a liaison between the paramilitary group and BP, which ultimately led to Mr Torres deciding to withdraw the case. These problems were exacerbated by a number of practical problems including that several years had passed since the incident occurred, his legal team was based far away in the UK and there was a clear inequality of arms between an impecunious Colombian trade unionist with no legal aid and oil corporations retaining corporate law firms.

At the invitation of USO, Gilberto returned very briefly to Colombia in 2015 for the presentation of his biography written by Vladimir Carrillo Rozo and titled *En el Tiempo de la Bala y la Salamandra*.[15] He reported that during the presentation of the book somebody from the audience implied that neither he nor the presentation of the book was welcome in Colombia. Hence, Gilberto resolved to not stay in Colombia.

Eventually, in 2016, Gilberto decided to go back to Colombia. He resumed his work for civil society by training trade unionists around the country. He is currently a member of the *Mesa Social Minero Energética por la Paz* established by the *Asamblea Nacional de la Sociedad Civil por la Paz* in November 2015 and has participated in the national peace talks as a delegate of the Human Rights Commission of USO. Since his return to Colombia, however, Gilberto has been the victim of a series of suspicious security incidents. He has been regularly followed by unknown men with military characteristics who would quickly disappear if he attempted to take pictures of them.

In August 2016, Gilberto's brother Jorge Andrés Torres Martínez was attacked by unknown men while he was leaving the garage where he worked. He was beaten and stabbed several times but luckily survived the assault. On another occasion, in March 2017, Gilberto took part in a roundtable organized by SUNCOPETRANSCO (*Sindicato Único de Conductores y Pequeños Proprietarios de Colombia*)[16] and other organizations in the transport sector. During the meeting, Gilberto reported that a man known to be a paramilitary commander in the area of Casanare revealed that the gathering had been infiltrated and that photos had been taken and sent to the police.

Notwithstanding the high risk that Gilberto is facing, the Colombian state provided him with only a bulletproof jacket and an emergency mobile phone, which in Gilberto and the *Colombian Caravana*'s views are patently inadequate to protect his life. In early 2017, Gilberto applied to the National Protection Unit (*Unidad Nacional de Protección* – UNP) for protective measures. In accordance with its usual practice, the UNP referred the case to the risk assessment unit (*Comité de Evaluación de Riesgo y Recomendación de Medidas* – CERREM) entrusted with determining the risk level for threatened individuals and with formulating recommendations directed at the UNP as to what protective measures should be implemented in the specific case. In July 2017, the CERREM recommended that Gilberto be assigned two bodyguards and a vehicle, in addition to the protective measures already in place to guarantee his safety. However, the UNP upon notification of the recommendations decided to disregard them and remit the case to the National Prosecutor Office (*Fiscalía General de la Nación*). Gilberto, supported by the Colombian Caravana and other organizations, has appealed the decision of the UNP with no success. Thus, in December 2017, he decided he had no option but to leave Colombia again and, at the time of this writing, is again in exile.

Gilberto's case is exemplary of the many hurdles that plague access to justice for business-related human rights violations in Colombia. Endemic corruption affecting institutions at all levels, a lack of support for victims of human rights abuses, a lack of resources and insufficient protection schemes for claimants dramatically diminish the opportunities for victims to access legal remedies. The complex corporate structure of BP and its subsidiaries constitutes a substantial hurdle to tracing the attributability of the conducts described. Moreover, while they undeniably offered a platform to elicit the attention of the international community, the unsuccessful litigation attempts both in the United States and in the UK demonstrate the paucity and inefficacy of the legal instruments available, the imbalance between claimants and respondent enterprises and the lack of country-specific expertise in the host country.

Due to a lack of human rights obligations on corporations in the UK, such cases need to use the common law of tort to bring civil cases to claim damages for personal injury. Two of the main legal challenges of bringing such cases are establishing jurisdiction and determining the applicable law. The Brussels Regulation I[17] provides that persons domiciled in a member state can be sued in the courts of that state. Therefore, as BP is a UK-registered company, it enabled Mr Torres to bring his claim under the jurisdiction of the English and Welsh Courts. Under Article 4 of the Rome II Regulations,[18] the applicable law is the law of the country in which the damage occurred. Thus, Mr Torres's case was brought in the Courts of England and Wales applying Colombian law.

The main challenges in bringing such cases are the need to appoint experts in Colombian law to assist the court; substantial litigation costs; geographical and language barriers; and the risk of large costs to claimants. This means that only a small number of victims are able to bring these types of claims and only a handful of legal firms are willing to take instructions on such cases, often on a pro bono basis and at a great cost risk. Group actions are possible but very difficult.

For instance, one of the main issues in Mr Torres's case was establishing the rule that determined the statute of limitations period for bringing his claim. The applicable rule would have been derived from Colombian law; however, there were differing opinions as to what this period would be under Colombian law and whether his claim was time-barred. Of course getting to the bottom of this issue required identifying and instructing expensive experts in Colombian law with the appropriate knowledge and experience, adding to the risks of the claim.

Mr Torres was unable to obtain legal aid in the UK to fund his case, so paying for his case was the first obstacle that he had to overcome. The vast majority of these types of cases fall at this first hurdle as victims are often some of the poorest people in society or at least do not have the funds to finance a legal battle that will easily run into tens if not hundreds of thousands of pounds. Victims therefore need to find lawyers who are willing to conduct the case on either a pro bono basis or under a Conditional Fee Agreement (CFA). Mr Torres case proceeded under a CFA. A CFA is a contract which establishes that the client does not need to pay for the services of their legal representatives until they win the case and upon their lawyers being able to recover their fees on their behalf from the other side.

In the UK, contingency style agreements, where the lawyers can take a cut of the compensation, are expressly prohibited, therefore further limiting the options for representation. However, due to the complex and often very lengthy nature of litigation in these matters, legal costs are likely to be substantially higher than compensation.

Such cases carry highly significant costs and cash flow implications for claimants' lawyers. This is because these cases are highly complex, hard-fought, risky, uncertain, very expensive, potentially very lengthy and resource intensive.[19] Much time and effort can be spent on dealing with and fighting over procedural matters rather than the legal merits of the cases themselves. Indeed, these are all issues that Mr Torres's team had to grapple with over the course of his claim.

Due to the unusual and complex nature of these claims, large legal teams need to be assembled which recruit the highly specialized expertise of lawyers with knowledge and experience in litigating cross-jurisdictional tort and human rights matters. This requires very skilled and senior counsel who are able to assist with navigating the tricky procedural and legal terrain, which can often give rise to uncharted territory on questions of law and procedure and which are yet to be tested and resolved by the courts. This of course also requires the recruitment of lawyers in the jurisdiction where the act was committed.

Legal advice needs to be passed from lawyers in different jurisdictions and language barriers need to be overcome. For instance, in this case, there were thousands of pages of documents which needed to be translated. There was also satellite litigation in Colombia when OCENSA refused to accept service of the claim. This all adds to the cost, time and effort required.

For example, some cases have spent years moving up and down through the legal system in an attempt to establish jurisdiction in the MNC's home state. Until recently in the UK, courts would dismiss these cases on the basis that there was a more appropriate forum in a non-European Union state. However, the European Court of Justice has since ruled that courts in the European Union (EU) member states did not have the authority to dismiss proceedings on this basis in cases brought against EU-domiciled defendants.[20] Brexit obviously presents a further future layer of complexity for claims brought in the UK which are currently governed by EU law.

While the matter of jurisdiction in Gilberto's case did not arise in this sense, it was a matter that needed to be addressed at the outset. As is common with MNC operational structures, BP had set up a number of subsidiaries to conduct operations in Colombia in which their ownership investment varied over time. Therefore, the level of investment and operational control at the time of Gilberto's abduction needed to be established. The claim was initially brought against a number of companies that were BP subsidiaries at the time of the incident.

Although the case did not get to the stage where this became an issue for opposing sides to dispute with one another before the court, the question of the applicable period of limitation for Gilberto's case may have raised the type of issue that would have been contested by both sides and would have needed to be tested by the courts.

Further practical issues, which are not insignificant in themselves, revolve around gathering and transporting large volumes of evidence and gathering a team with the requisite language skills to analyse them. Also interviewing witnesses in Colombia would either require using interpreters or recruiting lawyers fluent in the Spanish language while also navigating different time zones.

Gilberto's is not an isolated case. Over the last 15 years, over 4,000 trade union leaders have been assassinated in Colombia.[21] The high-profile case of Mr Sará Marrugo, for example, has not resulted in any prosecution as the alleged perpetrators are currently serving prison time in the United States for drug trafficking offences. Mr Torres reported that most of the USO leaders are currently the beneficiaries of protection measures from the Colombian state due to the threats posed against them. In fact, the USO has been relentless in its fight against the adverse environmental impact of fracking and hydrocarbons, which threatens the economic interests of multinational oil companies. However, the Colombian Caravana found that most of the times the measures assigned to individuals are insufficient to provide effective protection.

In the course of the 2016 regional consultation for Latin America and the Caribbean, held by the UN Working Group on Business and Human Rights, the Colombian representative pointed to the progresses made within the country in implementing the UN Guiding Principles on Business and Human Rights through the country's National Action Plan. Nonetheless, he also noted that the third pillar on remedies was, at that moment, the weakest. Furthermore, the peace process has diverted much of the attention to issues related to the negotiations between the guerrilla groups and the government. However this has left human rights defenders in the industry sector vulnerable, especially in light of the political unwillingness to acknowledge the resilience of paramilitary groups that often act as the long arm of MNCs.[22]

Thus, it seems that systematic hindrances to access to justice for victims of business-related human rights violations should be tackled by (a) the adoption of more favourable provisions that make enterprises accountable both in their home countries and in host countries; (b) international regulations that inform the content of governments-enterprises contracts rendering human rights provisions non-negotiable; (c) enhancing protection schemes for victims; (d) addressing the resource imbalance between parties; (e) breaking the exploitative cycle that link non-state armed groups to MNCs; and (f) a legal regime that is able to effectively pierce the corporate veil, with provision for stricter liability applicable to corporations.

Having these systems in place could have acted as a deterrent to the human rights abuses suffered by Gilberto and the many others in the region or at least provided access to a remedy. They would have ensured that any MNCs operating in Colombia would have had to abide by a normative framework for the compliance with strict human rights obligations. They could have prevented the destructive operational links between the oil companies and the paramilitary groups in the region. Furthermore, the operating oil companies would likely have conducted their operations with much greater caution and respect for human and environmental rights in the knowledge that effective mechanisms were in place for holding them accountable for any abuses. As it stands, MNCs are acutely aware that the risks of being held accountable for abuses conducted within their overseas operations is extremely low and that they are easily able to escape liability behind the corporate veil. Such a framework would have allowed Gilberto and others to have overcome the many obstacles that they faced in accessing justice, such as the substantial litigation costs and navigating the highly complex and cumbersome litigation processes for bringing cross-jurisdictional claims.

Notes

1 This piece is the result of extensive research on the case of Gilberto Torres Martinez, an in-depth interview with him and his UK-based lawyer, Sue Willman of Deighton Pierce Glynn (www.dpgalw.co.uk). Our most heartfelt thanks go to both of them for the time they have dedicated to speaking with us about the case. We would also like to thank them individually. Gilberto, for his incredible resilience and determination and for agreeing to speak with us about his case despite the pain involved in remembering such a traumatic and tragic experience. Sue, for her invaluable assistance in the revision of early drafts of this piece and for assisting in gathering the material necessary to extrapolate the information needed for this piece.

2 Colombia Caravana UK Lawyers Group: Promoting Access to Justice and Protecting Human Rights, http://www.colombiancaravana.org.uk/ (accessed 4 November 2019).

3 See, for example, Michael Gillard, 'BP Is Accused over Kidnap of Union Leader', *Sunday Times*, 9 November 2014; Michael Gillard, '"If You Speak Out You Die" Say Villagers Struggling to Fend Off Death Squads and Oil Giants', *Scotsman*, 28 June 2016; Wilfredo Oseguera, '"En el Tiempo de la Bala y la Salamandra": Una historia que clama justiciar', *expressnews*, 27 October–2 November 2015; Mary Carso et al., 'Gilberto Torres Survived Colombia's Death Squads. Now He Wants Justice', *Guardian*, 22 May 2015.

4 An outline of the corporate structure can be found in *Arroyo v Equion Energia Ltd* (formerly BP Exploration Co (Colombia) Ltd) [2016] EWHC 1699 (TCC) paras 253–85, 27 July 2016.

5 The FARC-EP (*Fuerzas Armadas Revolucionarias de Colombia – Ejército del Pueblo*) and the ELN (*Ejército de Liberación Nacional*) are the two main armed groups involved in the Colombian armed conflict. Both groups were founded in 1964 in Colombia in response to a prolonged period of political violence known as *La Violencia*, which lasted from 1948 to 1958. Both groups were inspired by Communist ideology, although their composition was different in that the FARC included mainly militant communists and organizations of peasants who joined forces to defend themselves, while the ELN was mostly formed of left-wing intellectuals and students. The identities of both groups rest upon the purported defence of rural communities and the fight against the privatization of natural resources. Both groups have employed violence and kidnappings. In addition, the FARC exploited the production of illicit narcotics to generate revenues. Because of their activities, the US State Department has backlisted both groups as foreign terrorist organizations (US Department of State, 'Foreign Terrorist Organizations', https://fas.org/sgp/crs/terror/IF10613.pdf, accessed 4 November 2019). With the aid of the United States, which invested several billions of dollars in what was known as the *Plan Colombia*, the Colombian government inflicted a severe blow to the FARC and the ELN, during the presidency of Alvaro Uribe Vélez. However, domestic and international human rights groups documented systematic human rights and humanitarian law violations during this period. The Colombian judiciary has been investigating, among other things, allegations of complicity between then President Uribe and right-wing paramilitary groups. Under the presidency of Uribe's successor Juan Manuel Santos, the government and the FARC reached a peace agreement that, after being rejected by a narrow majority in a plebiscite in October 2016, was finally signed by the parties in November 2016 in an amended version and ratified by the Colombian Congress in December 2016. Since then the government and the ELN have been engaged in peace talks which, unfortunately, halted in August 2018, when President Santos terminated his office and newly elected president Iván Duque Márquez took office. Among the many texts on the two armed groups, see Mario Aguilera Peña, *Guerrilla y Población Civil: Trayectoria de las FARC 1949–2013* (Bogotá: Centro Nacional de Memoria Histórica, 2014); Alejo Vargas Velásquez, *Guerra o solución negociada: ELN: origen, evolución y procesos de paz* (Bogotá: Intermedio, 2006).

6 While most of the information provided in the last two paragraphs is common knowledge (see, e.g., Diana Jean Schemo, 'Oil Companies Buying an Army to Ward Off Rebels in Colombia', *New York Times*, 22 August 1996; Michael Gillard, Ignacio Gomez and Melissa Jones, 'BP Hands "Tarred in Pipeline Dirty War"', *Guardian*, 17 October 1998; PLATFORM, Unravelling the Carbon Web, 'Line of Fire: BP and Human Rights Abuses in Colombia', October 2002, http://www.carbonweb.org/documents/chapter11.pdf, accessed 31 January 2018), the exposition follows the complaint filed by Gilberto Torres against BP PLC before a US district court in the District of Columbia Complaint. *Gilberto Edgar Torres Martínez v BP P.L.C.*, D.D.C., filed on 24 February 2012 (on file with authors).

7 Human Rights Watch, 'Colombia: Human Rights Concerns Raised by the Security Arrangements of Transnational Oil Companies', Letter to President Ernesto Samper (April 1998).

8 Gillard, Gomez and Jones, 'BP Hands "Tarred in Pipeline Dirty War"'.

9 *Gilberto Edgar Torres Martínez v BP P.L.C.*

10 See, for example, USO, 'Colombian Oilworkers Strike as Pipeline Union Leader Disappears', *Report*, 27 February 2002, http://www.labournet.net/world/0202/colomb4.html (accessed 6 December 2018).

11 Case No. 110013107011-2009-00054-00, Juzgado Once Penal del Circuito Especializado de Bogotà (15 December 2011), 9.

12 The original text reads, 'se cuenta con suficientes elementos de juicio, que fueron decantando la participación de la multinacional OCENSA en el rapto, [...] Por consiguiente, [...] emerge de manera diamantina el motivo del secuestro y los delitos relacionados con éste; no fue otro que el activismo sindical que libraba desde su condición de dirigente, y que por lo tanto afectaba a las empresas beneficiadas con el proceso normal de bombeo del petróleo, [...] consideraron necesario quitar del camino a quien ponía en riesgo sus intereses económicos.' Ibid. at 11 (translated by author).

13 Human Rights Watch, *War without Quarter: Colombia and International Humanitarian Law* (New York: Human Rights Watch, October 1998).

14 *Kiobel v. Royal Dutch Petroleum Co.*, 569 U.S. 108 (2013).

15 *In the Time of the Bullet and the Salamander* (translated by author).

16 SUNCOPETRANSCO is an umbrella trade union organization that groups workers in the transport sector.

17 Brussels Regulation on Jurisdiction and the Recognition and Enforcement of Judgments in Civil and Commercial Matters (Brussels I Regulation), Council Regulation (EC) No 44/2001 of 22 December 2000.

18 Rome II Regulation on the Law Applicable to Non-Contractual Obligations, No 864/2007.

19 Richard Meeran, 'Tort Litigation against Multinational Corporations for Violation of Human Rights: An Overview of the Position Outside of the Unites States', *City University of Hong Kong Law Review* vol. 3, no. 1 (2011), 1–41.

20 See ECJ case of *Owusu v Jackson* [2005] ECR 1383 (the ECJ is the highest court in the European Union).

21 Kuehnert, Daniel Richard, 'The International Labor Organization and a Possible End to Violence against Union Members in Colombia', *Washington University Global Studies Law Review* vol. 7, no. 3 (2008), 593–618, 593.

22 UNHRC, Informe del Grupo de Trabajo sobre la cuestión de los derechos humanos y las empresas transnacionales y otras empresas sobre la 'Consulta regional para América Latina y el Caribe: Políticas públicas para la implementación de los Principios Rectores de las Naciones Unidas sobre Empresas y Derechos Humanos, en el marco de la Agenda 2030 para el Desarrollo Sostenible', UN Doc A/HRC/32/45/Add.4, specifically at para 15, 9 June 2016.

Chapter 3

THE GLOBAL PURSUIT FOR JUSTICE FOR DBCP-EXPOSED BANANA FARMERS

Daysheelyn Anne P. Brillo

Introduction

Almost four decades ago, thousands of Filipino banana plantation workers were exposed to a sterility-inducing nematicide called dibromochloropropane (DBCP) used by the subsidiaries of transnational corporations (TNCs) operating in the Philippines. This chemical was employed in the farms by these corporations even though it was already banned in the United States. As a result, those plantation workers filed several lawsuits against the nematicide manufacturers and the TNCs before Philippine and US courts. While a few of them were able to obtain out-of-court settlements, the majority remain uncompensated for the injuries that they have sustained. The chapter takes us to the experiences of Digong who is one of the numerous former plantation farmers rendered sterile by DBCP and narrates the legal battles of ex-farmers like him against these huge fruit corporations and chemical manufacturers.

These TNCs take advantage of the failure of the domestic legal regimes, both in the United States and the Philippines, to provide an effective judicial remedy to these farmers. The callousness of these TNCs is manifested by their refusal to recognize and appear before Philippine courts while at the same time advocating for these same trials to be removed to Philippine courts when the farmers sued them in US courts. The legal manoeuvres employed by these corporations means that the farmers would have to shell out significant litigation expenses and exhaust their precious time – making it practically impossible to obtain relief for their injuries.

By having the cases referred back to the Philippines, these corporations already won half the battle. First, the Philippine judiciary has been marred by widespread corruption and suffered from debilitating inefficiency. Second, it is more difficult to impute liability on the parent corporation for the acts of its subsidiary since Philippine case law has a higher threshold before the courts to 'pierce the corporate veil' so to speak. Third, even if the farmers win the case the amount of damages to be awarded would most likely be minimal since it would be based on the average compensation of a Filipino farmer.

With the current legal framework in the Philippines, the plaintiffs would be better off initiating the action before the courts of the country of origin of the parent corporation rather than before Philippine courts. The chapter uses Digong's story to urge the Philippines to be at the forefront in protecting the interest of these farmers, as in theory the Philippines has the capacity in patching these loopholes by providing a nonjudicial mechanism for compensation of TNC's toxic tort victims.

Use of DBCP in the Philippines

'Digong' was in his early twenties when he started working for Stanfilco, a division of Dole Philippines, Inc., in 1975.[1] It was his lucky break. After leaving behind a life of armed struggle as a member of a secessionist group in Mindanao, the southernmost part of the Philippines, most employers would not accept former rebels, not to mention illiterates. Since Digong badly needed the money, as he was just starting a quiet family life with two kids, he grabbed the opportunity.[2]

Initially assigned to cleaning the drainage in one of the company's farms in Davao, he was made a Fumazone[3] injector two years later in 1977. The Fumazone chemical kills the worms eating the roots of the banana plants and thus makes the plants more resilient to strong winds. That practice resulted in improved production rates in Dole's banana farms. Dole's competitors, Chiquita and Del Monte, also started using the same substance.

But the so-called productive substance had its secrets. Digong said he and the other farmers noticed that all the insects, frogs and small animals would always die the day after it was introduced to the soil. It was also packed in containers with labels that Digong did not understand. He barely knows how to read and understand Filipino; how much more could he understand if it's a foreign language?[4] He attended primary school but had to drop out by the age of 10. Back then his family could not afford to send him to school. Even his supervisors were not aware of any potential adverse effects; they merely instructed him to inject the substance near the roots of the banana plants and said nothing about undertaking precautions. Furthermore, the company did not issue any protective equipment or clothing for the farmers. He recounted that he merely wore a T-shirt, jeans and rubber slippers whenever he went to work.[5]

What Digong and the other farmers did not know is that Fumazone[6] had been banned in the United States as early as 1979 for causing male sterility,[7] although the prohibition covered only domestic application and not exportation. For its part, Dole claimed it 'halted all purchases of DBCP' the same year it was banned by the United States.[8] But DBCP was neither banned nor regulated in the Philippines at the time.[9] Thus, it was just a rational business decision on the part of Dole to ship its remaining stocks and to continue its use in Third World countries like the Philippines until the early 1980s.[10]

It would take years before Fumazone's toll on Digong and the other Dole farmers would manifest. Only during the 1990s when Digong and his co-workers noticed they were having 'a very hard time producing children'[11] did they become alarmed. In an agricultural community like Digong's, it is desirable and sought for to have as many children as one family could practically have as many hands would make farm work easier and more efficient. Thus, an issue of impotency would certainly be a concern among families, not to mention the subject of gossip among neighbours. Digong himself was 'confused' about why his brother had nine children while he could only have two. 'I really, really wanted to have more kids, aside from my two', he stated.[12]

Digong learned from his workmates that they were planning to file a legal action against their employers. The workers also heard that cases were being filed by plantation workers from Latin America. Believing that his work handling Fumazone contributed to his inability to conceive more children with his wife, Digong joined one of the workers' organizations, Baog-baog, named after a local word for infertile.[13] Baog-baog earlier conducted sperm count tests among its members – the results showed that most of them were sterile. As a result, Baog-baog petitioned Dole Philippines for monetary claims for the sterile farmers. In response, the company claimed that it was also not aware of the adverse effects of DBCP and directed them to sue the US-based manufacturers instead.[14]

Going all the way to the United States to file their case against the manufacturers,[15] the farmers of Baog-baog joined farmers from Latin American countries who were also filing cases based on the same underlying facts in Texas.[16] Together, these DBCP-affected farmers filed suits against other fruit growers which used the substance, like Del Monte Fruit and Chiquita Brands, along with the DBCP manufacturers, which included Dow Chemical, Shell Oil and Occidental Petroleum.[17] Buttressing their case were reports from the US Environmental Protection Agency based on medical examinations showing that approximately 6 out of 10 banana workers were sterile[18] and that 1 out of 5 women who've worked in the banana farms had a damaged uterus.[19]

The DBCP Litigation History of Filipino Toxic Tort Victims

Delgado v. Shell Oil Co. (1995) and Navida et al. v. RTC J. Dizon et al. (2011)

The case of *Delgado v. Shell*[20] is highlighted in the following story. Since 1993, thousands of banana workers from several countries, including the Philippines (as well as many Latin American countries),[21] have filed cases before the Texas courts against the DBCP manufacturers and the fruit corporations. The TNCs countered that it would be more convenient for the parties to litigate in the courts of their respective countries rather than in US courts, arguing that much of the testimony and evidence would be available in the countries where the farmers were based. The American courts agreed with the TNCs but ordered them to recognize the jurisdiction of and appear before the Philippine courts.

In 1995, months after the dismissal of their case in the United States, around 500 farmers brought their case before the trial courts of Davao and General Santos City, Philippines.[22] The plaintiffs sought to recover around $2.7 million PHP (US$53,000) each,[23] pointing out that the fruit companies failed to provide them proper protective equipment and supervision regarding how to safely apply nematicides with DBCP. Furthermore, the plaintiffs alleged that the manufacturers failed to include warnings regarding the product's hazardous effects.[24] But a year later, the Philippine trial courts dismissed their case citing a lack of personal jurisdiction over the TNCs.[25] The Philippine courts ruled that foreign corporations cannot be sued in the Philippines unless they (a) are 'doing business'[26] in the country or (b) have consented to appear before the Philippine courts.[27]

In 1997, while the case was pending before the Philippine Supreme Court, a majority of the plaintiffs in the *Navida* case settled with the chemical manufacturers, including Shell Oil, Dow and Occidental.[28] This was after the manufacturers offered to pay the plaintiffs but without admitting liability; instead, they insisted that it was the fault of the fruit corporations for not using the product properly.[29] The manufacturers paid US$41.5 million,[30] half of which went to the claimants' lawyers[31] who promised that those who became sterile and had no children would receive at least US$4,000 as full compensation.[32] In that payout scheme, the amount to be received by each claimant would depend on their sperm count results and their number of children.[33]

As one of the plaintiff-farmers, Digong received approximately $50,000 PHP (US$1,000 USD).[34] But Digong lamented that 'it was not enough to cover the medical bills' for the ailments that he believed to be caused by DBCP.[35] Worse, the settlement excluded other claimants who developed other illnesses.[36] Afterwards, the manufacturers requested that they be dropped from the case, which was opposed by the fruit corporations. The Philippine Supreme Court denied their request and ruled that the trial courts should decide on this matter.[37]

Fortunately, in 2011 the Philippine Supreme Court decided that the Philippine courts could hear the case since the corporations 'voluntarily' accepted the court's jurisdiction, as mandated by the US courts. Even though the case remained pending, the banana farmers who had waited for 15 long years for justice breathed a sigh of relief that the Philippine Supreme Court had sided with them.

Macasa v. Dole Food Co. (2014)

In 1998, members of Davao Banana Plantation Workers Association of Tiburcia, Inc. (DBPWATI) filed their claims before the Philippine courts against the American fruit corporations and manufacturers. Initially, there were 20,981 claimants but that number increased to 34,868 in an amended complaint filed in 2000. The US-based corporations countered that they could not be summoned before the Philippine courts since they were not doing business in the Philippines. The Philippine Supreme Court agreed with the American corporations and dismissed the DBPWATI complaint on 13 April 2009.[38]

Undaunted, 2,432 Filipino claimants led by Roque Macasa, Jr, filed an action in the Los Angeles Superior Court two years and four months later, with another 504 Filipino claimants joining their fight in 2012.[39] But the action was dismissed by the Los Angeles Superior Court, ruling that the complaint was filed four months late and thus already time-barred under California law.[40] The Filipino farmers appealed, arguing that they had no way of discovering the adverse effects of the *nematicide* since sterility is not an apparent injury. However, the Los Angeles appellate court reasoned that the farmers must have been aware of their injuries by the time they filed the suits before the Philippine courts in 1998. At the very least, the appellate court said they should have filed their cases before 13 April 2011 – two years after the Philippine Supreme Court dismissed their claims.

The Los Angeles appellate court also denied the farmers' request to apply the four-year time-bar under Philippine law. The court argued that it had an interest to apply its own law to protect Dole, a California-based corporation, from 'litigating claims that accrued decades ago'.[41] In a very pro-business ruling, the California-based court extended the same protection to the manufacturers, reasoning that the state has a 'legitimate interest' in attracting business and eventually collecting 'taxes and other revenues'.[42]

After the case's dismissal, Dole released a statement claiming that the case 'should never have been brought in the first place'.[43] The company went further and stated that Macasa group's claims were 'all fraudulent anyway'.[44] But Dole's press release omitted the fact that the case never went to trial since the company refused to participate in the trials before the Philippine courts.

One of the leaders in the Macasa group confided that it was very difficult for them to comply with the statute of limitations imposed by the US court. 'We have to compile thousands of documents, the medical reports of our members and proofs of employment from the fruit corporations', he lamented. 'We must make sure that no one will be left behind'. Also the lawsuit has exhausted their financial resources of the farmers. 'I had to shell out around $1 million php (US$20,000) to pursue the case and fly back and forth to the United States to meet with the lawyers and prepare the documents', he added. Sadly, Macasa group's loss decimated the morale and faith of the members in their leaders.[45]

The Macasa group appealed the dismissal of their case to the California Supreme Court. Their petition for review was denied the same year that it was appealed.[46]

Philippine Pioneer Banana Plantation Workers, Inc. v. Shell Oil Co., et al. (2015)

For their part, Philippine Pioneer Banana Plantation Workers, Inc. (PPBPWI) filed their cases directly before the Philippine courts. But this proved fatal to their case as most of the corporations refused to participate in the cases before the Philippine courts, saying the latter had no jurisdiction over them which eventually led to the dismissal of their suits before the Philippine courts.

Similar to Baog-baog, former banana workers banded together to form the PPBPWI to file their claims. The huge amount in filling fees was a big problem for the workers. As they were demanding a total of $6 million PHP (US$1.1 million) individually from their former employers and the DBCP manufacturers, they had to prove that they were indigents in order to be exempt from the filling fees, which amounted to $60,000 PHP (US$1,100) – or around seven times the minimum monthly salary in the Philippines.

While the corporations could call upon large law firms to represent them, most of these farmers could not afford lawyers. To have a fighting chance, the farmers decided to pool their resources and form PPBPWI to represent them before the courts. PPBPWI is composed of former employees of the fruit corporations. They appointed officers who would be in charge of collecting monthly fees from their members. In this manner, they would be able to afford lawyers.

PPBPWI filed their case in the Philippine courts against the fruit companies and the manufacturers in 2010.[47] But most of them feared that the lawsuit would be fruitless as the plaintiffs were all aging. They felt as if this case was their last chance for justice. As in other cases, the corporations refused to recognize or appear before the Philippine courts. Specifically, the fruit corporations and the manufacturers pushed forward the argument that they have never done business in the Philippines and thus may not be summoned before the country's courts.[48] They also raised as a defence that the plaintiffs failed to pay the proper filing fees and that their action was time-barred.

Siding with the corporations the trial court dismissed the suit, which was affirmed by the Court of Appeals for two reasons. First, the Court of Appeals held that PPBPWI had no legal interest in the case.[49] The board resolution authorizing the president to sue and represent its members was not enough for the appellate court; each of its thousand members should have executed an individual authorization in favour of PPBPWI. The appellate court likewise ruled out the possibility of filing the action as a class suit explaining that each member of PPBPWI has a distinct cause of action against the corporation. Second, PPBPWI failed to show that the companies engaged in business in the Philippines;[50] thus, they may not be sued in the Philippine courts. The appellate court's dismissal was affirmed by the Philippine Supreme Court in a resolution in 2016.[51]

Canales Martinez v. Dow Chemical Co., 219 F. Supp. 2d 719 (E.D. La. 2002)

The *Canales* case is one of the few, small victories claimed by the DBCP-affected farmers. In this case, the corporations invoked their usual defence that litigation will be more convenient if done in the farmers' own countries and that the case has been already decided in their favour in *Delgado*.[52]

But the American court expressed its qualms regarding the adequacy of the Philippine justice system to accord redress to the DBCP claimants. That court observed that the unwarranted delays and corruption that plagued the Philippine judiciary would affect the chance that the plaintiffs will be accorded with 'basic fairness in the prosecution of their claims'.[53] Furthermore, the Louisiana court pointed out that the financial disparity between the farmers and the corporations also threatened the chance of the claimants to a fair trial, citing rampant 'reports of improper relationships between the Philippine courts and corporate litigants'.[54]

Enduring the Protracted DBCP Litigation

Now in their twilight years, most of the affected farmers remain uncompensated.[55] In an interview with the author, one of them summed up the doubts lingering among the group: 'Do you think we still have a fighting chance? We're dying out here – a fourth of us in our group are already in their graves.' One of the farmer-leaders said the majority of the farmers have already given up their pursuit for justice against the fruit corporations and the manufacturers. They have been in this battle for decades now – their pockets and patience are nearly empty.

The multinationals' legal strategy has been consistent – if a case has been filed before the United States, they would request for its dismissal and removal to the farmer's home country. By having the cases referred back to the Philippines, these corporations already won half the battle. It took 15 years for the Philippine Supreme Court to decide that the Philippine courts have jurisdiction over the *Navida* case which has been pending for more than two decades now.

Furthermore, when a trial on the merits is imminent, the corporations would pre-empt it by offering out-of-court settlements, just like in *Navida*. These settlements would include requirements that the claimants admit that there were 'no causal connection' between DBCP and their injuries.[56] This ensures that no judicial decision is promulgated establishing a causality between DBCP and their injuries as a proven fact. Unlike out-of-court settlements, a judicial decision creates precedential value and thus would deal a major blow to the corporations as other claimants might use the same arguments for their own cases. (For example, a decision in favour of the *Navida* claimants means that other farmer groups need not prove the causality between DBCP and sterility).

Meanwhile, if a case has been filed before the Philippine courts, the corporations would simply refuse to recognize the legal authority of such judicial bodies. While they consistently requested the cases removed back to the Philippine courts whenever the farmers would sue them in US courts, as in *Delgado*, these same corporations nevertheless refused to voluntarily appear before the Philippine courts, just as in *Macasa* and *PPBPWI*.

The financial capacity and the solid foundation of these corporations allows them to prolong this legal battle. In contrast, the plaintiff-farmers have few financial resources and limited time; they are being buried in legal fees, paperwork and literally in their own graves. DBCP attacks the reproductive system of a person, with many of the claimants failing to have children. This was why the plaintiff-farmers fear that once they die they would have no one else to carry on their cause.

As Digong stored the court papers hidden inside their cabinet, he lamented the sorry state of their quest for justice. 'It has been more than a decade since I opened them', he said. With a sardonic laugh, he quipped that it was impossible to win the fight since the pleadings were signed by the most prestigious law firms in the country. However, his mood turned sombre upon seeing the list of the claimants, pointing out the names of his co-workers who already died.

Digong's story is just one of the thousands of names waiting for their own day in court. It was a David versus Goliath story – except theirs doesn't have a happy ending. Not yet.

Notes

1 Anonymous, personal interview with retired plantation worker of Dole in Tagum City, 4 March 2017. Interviewee wished to be renamed as 'Digong'.

2 Ibid.

3 Fumazone is a brand of a nematicide manufactured by Dow Chemical and used by Dole. Its active ingredient is 1,2-dibromo-3-chloropropance (DBCP).

4 Anonymous, personal interview with retired plantation worker of Dole in Tagum City, 4 March 2017.

5 Ibid.

6 As mentioned, previously, Dole Food was one of the companies that used the chemical. Dole Food Company, Inc, Quarterly Reports for the quarterly period ended 24 March 2012. *Dole Food Company Inc. Quarterly Reports*, 24 March 2012 (hereinafter 'Dole Quarterly Reports'). Other manufacturers include Shell Oil and Occidental Petroleum. According to Digong, other fruit growers followed Dole in using DBCP, including Del Monte Fruit and Chiquita Brand. Anonymous, personal interview with retired plantation worker of Dole in Tagum City, 4 March 2017.

7 Eula Bingham and Celeste Monforton, *Late Lessons from Early Warnings: Science, Precaution, Innovation: Late Lessons II Chapter 9 – the Pesticide DBCP and Male Infertility* (European Environment Agency, 2017).

8 Dole Quarterly Reports, 24 March 2012.

9 Until the early 1980s, Dole allegedly continued to ship and use DBCP in its farms in Third World countries like the Philippines. The regulation of fertilizers and pesticides in the Philippines was still in its early stages in the 1970s – the Fertilizer Industry Authority was established on 22 February 1973 through Presidential Decree No. 135. However, its primary purpose was to regulate the prices and volume of production of the fertilizers. The Fertilizer and Pesticide Authority, the government office with the authority to regulate pesticides based on its health hazard effects, was not established until 30 May 1977. However, Dole was still able to use the product until the early 1980s. Jim Gomez, 'Filipinos Seek Claims against U.S. Firms in Pesticide Case", *Los Angeles Times*, 23 November 1997, http://articles.latimes.com/1997/nov/23/news/mn-56736.

10 This information was also confirmed by Digong during the interview. See also Diana Jean Schemo, 'U.S. Pesticide Kills Foreign Fruit Pickers' Hopes', *New York Times*, 5 December 1995, https://www.nytimes.com/1995/12/06/world/us-pesticide-kills-foreign-fruit-pickers-hopes.html; Bingham and Monforton, *Late Lessons from Early Warnings*.

11 Anonymous, personal interview with retired plantation worker of Dole in Tagum City, 4 March 2017.

12 Ibid.

13 Ibid.

14 Ibid.
15 Ibid.
16 *Delgado v. Shell Oil Co.*, 890 F. Supp. 1324 (S. D. Tex. 1995).
17 Schemo, 'U.S. Pesticide Kills Foreign Fruit Pickers' Hopes'.
18 'Running Amok: Landlord Lawlessness and Impunity in the Philippines', *FIAN International*, 19 June 2006, https://www.fian.org/library/publication/running_amok_landlord_lawlessness_and_impunity_in_the_philippines/.
19 Ibid.
20 *Delgado v. Shell Oil Co.*, 890 F. Supp. 1324 (S. D. Tex. 1995).
21 Plantation workers from Burkina Faso, Costa Rica, Dominica, Ecuador, Guatemala, Honduras, Ivory Coast, Nicaragua, Panama, Saint Lucia and Saint Vincent filed several complaints in various Texas courts. The cases were eventually consolidated and heard in Houston, Texas. See ibid.
22 *Navida et al. v. RTC J. Dizon et al.* (2011)
23 Ibid.
24 Ibid.
25 Ibid.
26 The Congress adopted the case law definition of 'doing business' into the Foreign Investments Act of 1991:

> The phrase 'doing business' shall include soliciting orders, service contracts, opening offices, whether called 'liaison' offices or branches; appointing representatives or distributors domiciled in the Philippines or who in any calendar year stay in the country for a period or periods totalling 180 days or more; participating in the management, supervision or control of any domestic business, firm, entity or corporation in the Philippines; and any other act or acts that imply a continuity of commercial dealings or arrangements, and contemplate to that extent the performance of acts or works, or the exercise of some of the functions normally incident to, and in progressive prosecution of, commercial gain or of the purpose and object of the business organization: Provided, however, That the phrase 'doing business: shall not be deemed to include mere investment as a shareholder by a foreign entity in domestic corporations duly registered to do business, and/or the exercise of rights as such investor; nor having a nominee director or officer to represent its interests in such corporation; nor appointing a representative or distributor domiciled in the Philippines which transacts business in its own name and for its own account.

27 *Asiavest Ltd. v. CA*, G. R. No. 128803 (1998). In an *in personam* action against a non-resident, personal jurisdiction may only be acquired through the voluntary appearance of the defendant or through personal service of summons if the defendant is 'physically present in the country'. The courts cannot acquire jurisdiction over a non-resident defendant if the action is *in personam* even if extraterritorial summons was served.
28 Jim Gomez, 'Filipinos Seek Claim against U.S. Firms in Pesticide Case', *Los Angeles Times*, 23 November 1997, http://articles.latimes.com/1997/nov/23/news/mn-56736.
29 Ibid.
30 Ibid.

31 Ibid.
32 Ibid.
33 Ibid.
34 Anonymous, personal interview with retired plantation worker of Dole in Tagum City, 4 March 2017.
35 Ibid.
36 Gomez, 'Filipinos Seek Claim against U.S. Firms in Pesticide Case'.
37 Ibid.
38 *Macasa v. Dole Food Co.* (2014) CA2/2, B245138 (Cal. Ct. App.) [Unpublished].
39 Ibid.
40 Ibid.
41 Ibid.
42 Ibid.
43 'DBCP Facts', *Dole.* http://www.dole.com/AboutDole/DBCP-Facts (accessed 14 November 2019).
44 Ibid.
45 Anonymous, personal interview with retired plantation worker of Dole in Tagum City, 4 March 2017.
46 *Macasa v. Dole Food Co., Inc.*, No. S218425, 2014 Cal. LEXIS 3844 (11 June 2014)
47 *Philippine Pioneer Banana Plantation Workers, Inc. v. Shell Oil Co. et al.* (2015). CA-G.R. CV NO. 02695-MIN.
48 Ibid. The court, through the Philippine Department of Foreign Affairs, served extra-territorial summons on the foreign corporations involved.
49 Ibid. The Rules of Court requires that the action be pursued by a real party in interest or a representative on behalf of a beneficiary. PPBPWI presented a board resolution authorizing its president to file a complaint on behalf of the corporation. This was not accepted by the Court of Appeals. It ruled that the authorization must emanate from the members itself as the real party in interest. The appellate court likewise ruled out the possibility of filing the action as a class suit. It explained that each member of PPBPWI has a distinct cause of action against the corporation.
50 Ibid.
51 *Philippine Pioneer Banana Plantation Workers, Inc. v. Shell Oil Co. et al.* (2015).
52 Ibid.
53 Ibid, citing the US Department of State, Country Report on Human Rights Practices, Philippines (2001)
54 Ibid.
55 Anonymous, personal interview with one of the farmer leaders in *Macasa* case by author in Davao City, 5 March 2017.
56 'Dole Begins Payments to Central American Banana Workers | Banana Link', *Banana Link*, 18 September 2012, www.bananalink.org.uk/Dole%20begins%20payments.

Chapter 4

THE RUPTURING OF THE DAM AND THE COMMUNITY'S SOCIAL FABRIC: A TESTIMONY FROM AN 'ATINGIDO' FROM BENTO RODRIGUES, BRAZIL

Rajiv Maher and Adriana Bravin

This chapter will cover the life stories of 'Atingidos', or those 'victims' of the Bento Rodrigues dam disaster, owned by Samarco mining company in south-eastern Brazil. Samarco is a joint venture between the world's largest mining company BHP Billiton (headquartered in Australia) and Vale, another one of the largest mining companies in the world (headquartered in Brazil). Both multinationals are members of prestigious corporate social responsibility initiatives such as the United Nations Global Compact initiative and the International Council for Mining and Metal (ICMM). BHP is currently ranked third by the Corporate Human Rights Benchmark (CHRB),[1] while Vale was ranked in sixth place until 28 January 2019[2] after its second fatal dam collapse in Brumadinho also in Minas Gerais state, Brazil, where 249 fatalities had been recorded by end of August 2019.[3]

The bursting of the Fundão dam has been described as the worst environmental disaster in Brazil's history. The disaster occurred on 5 November 2015, when the Fundão tailings dam in Bento Rodrigues (a village located within the municipality of Mariana, Brazil) broke. Within 60 minutes of the collapse, 35 billion tonnes of iron-ore reject and mud had engulfed and destroyed the nearby village; the devastation continued for the next 668 km, sweeping away everything in its path until it reached the Atlantic Ocean coast. All told, the disaster took the lives of 19 people[4] and negatively impacted 23,000 other families.[5]

Scientific studies claim that 90 per cent of the Doce River basin that was affected by the dam burst was still contaminated two years later.[6]

The company denies responsibility for the collapse of the dam despite a 2013 report from the Brazilian authorities stating that there were structural weaknesses in the dam. According to a *Wall Street Journal* report, the company had been warned in 2014 about the severe structural cracks to the dam, which the company claims it had addressed.[7] Regional and national Brazilian courts are attempting to prosecute 21 Samarco executives for homicide related to the rupture of the Fundão dam. Originally, the Brazilian government stated that it would fine Samarco R $250 million (US$66.3 million) for the incident. In January 2016, the Brazilian government and Samarco reached an agreement where the company paid a fine of R $20 billion (US$4.8 billion). The fine does not include any compensation to the people affected by the disaster, nor the cost of cleaning the polluted area. The fine also seems relatively low when compared to the fines levied against corporations that have left similar devastation in their wake. For instance, the US government fined BP US$65 billion for its responsibility in the horizon deepwater disaster in the Gulf of Mexico that took place in 2010.

Under pressure, in March 2016 (five months post-disaster), Samarco together with the Brazilian state decided the best way to deal with remediation and compensation would be through the creation of a private foundation, arguing that a mining company was not best equipped for the task. In August 2016 Fundação (foundation) Renova began operating with a budget of R $11.6 billion (US$2.87 billion).[8] The foundation continually stresses that it is not a mining company and operates with a multi-stakeholder governance model despite being 100 percent financed by BHP and Vale with both these firms representing six of the seven members on its board of governors.[9] According to its website, dialogue with impacted communities is central to its method for resolving grievances.[10] As part of its work, the foundation reports on a series of social responsibility and development initiatives it funds and implements locally in addition to the compensation payments it provides. However, from the perspective of many *Atingidos*, the foundation is just a smokescreen to protect the images and reputations of Samarco (and BHP and Vale) and therefore terms such as 'togetherness' and 'dialogue' with the company responsible for the dam collapse are unlikely to be so welcoming or reassuring. As one anonymous interviewee explained, the foundation 'has an incredible capacity to manipulate and strike fear into the community, let alone telling lies' (resident, Bento Rodrigues).

As of August 2019, Renova has reported that compensation and financial aid paid to the 'atingidos' totalled R $1.61 billion (US$388 million)[11]. They claim this aid has benefited more than 250,000 people, with more than 7,000 instances of compensation being given as of August 2018. The foundation also claims to have attended to 10,906 families for 'damages incurred'. The emergency financial aid program currently assists 9,579 families, representing more than 22,700 people affected (Fundaçao Renova).[12] The main response by *Atingidos* during fieldwork in August 2019 is one of lament, that they have not seen the benefits of this generous spending in terms of being permanently resettled. Many also decry not having received any indemnification for lost livelihoods such as fishing.[13]

On 1 October 2018, the state prosecutor of Minas Gerais came to an agreement with BHP Billiton and Vale (known as Samarco) on the terms of conditions of the process for paying compensation to each registered 'Atingido'. This was regarded as a victory for the affected community members from Mariana.[14] A month later, on the three-year anniversary of the tragedy, the state prosecutor Guilherme Meneghin lamented that no definitive solutions had been finalized and some *Atingidos* were still homeless. Meneghin was also critical of the silence by politicians and the absence of measures that guaranteed rights in legislation to the *Atingidos*.[15]

As a result of this very slow and cumbersome legal process in Brazil, the US-UK law firm Sanders Phillips Grossman Law commenced legal collective action in November 2018 against Samarco's parent company BHP Billiton, which is headquartered in London. This collective lawsuit represents 240,000 individuals, 24 municipal governments, 11,000 businesses, a Catholic archdiocese and about 200 members of the Krenak indigenous community affected by the dam burst. The lawsuit is suing for £5 billion (US$6.5 billion), with the lawyers expecting an out-of-court settlement payment that is much more generous than what the corporation has paid out to date via the Renova foundation.[16]

The chapter provides the perceptions of those *Atingidos* hurt by the dam collapse from the small village of Bento Rodrigues in relation to how their lives and relations with Samarco and relevant authorities have evolved from pre-dam collapse to post-dam disaster. The chapter also focuses on community perceptions of Samarco's corporate social responsibility, respect for human rights, community relations and a United Nations Working Group on and Business Human Rights visit to the community in December 2015 just after the dam disaster. Overall, this chapter provides readers with an insight into how top-down CSR and human rights-related corporate policies are perceived by the *Atingidos*. Key issues highlighted include power asymmetries between community and corporation and the importance of the independent state actor of the Public Prosecution office, who our interviewee describes as the community's 'guardian angel'.

For this chapter we provide the life story as told, in the first person, by Monica dos Santos, a 32-year-old who is one of the *Atingidos* from Bento

Rodrigues.[17] Specifically, Monica provides the following account of the disaster and life before and after the dam collapse:

> The disaster […] it destroyed everything, community life. We left home at 6 am to go to work one morning and some of us just didn't make it back home alive. We had 10 minutes to run away from death. Imagine if you had lost your mum, a son of 7 and daughter of 5 all of this because of irresponsibility and greed for profit?
>
> The relationship with Samarco before the dam ruptured was good, they used to help us a lot with the kids at school and for parties, mostly social things. They only had one employee from our Bento community [an] employee who worked directly at Samarco. They held direct meetings with the community to discuss their social investment projects and where we also questioned the possible rupture of the dam. They told us they were super sure, that we could sleep carefree – that such a disaster would never happen. The company always told us we could sleep safely.
>
> They explained that the dam was monitored 24 hours a day, it had the best standards, best professionals working there. Of course we believed them! What choice did we have? They were the experts, well at least that's what they said, that they knew what they were doing.

On the Day of the Disaster

> The day [of the disaster] I left the house at six in the morning to come to work, my boss was not there, so I could leave early in the afternoon. When it was, I think, about ten to four (in the afternoon) my phone rang and I was closing the office to leave. It was a cousin of mine asking, 'Monica, have you heard the dam has broken? I'm trying to call the people there at Bento and I can't get hold of anyone.' And I was like […] 'Oh no! Let me try to call!' I tried to call my aunts, my cousins and I could not get through, I thought, then I called my mother, I called my aunt who works here in Mariana I said: 'Oh, aunt, have you heard the news?' She replied 'no, I haven't heard anything'. Then I told her that I would call my aunt Zizi who lives in Santa Rita, she was closer to Bento to see what was happening, if it was really happening. Then I tried to call my uncles and I could not get through, then I said, 'Ah, I'll send a WhatsApp that everyone can see, nobody answered their phone, but everyone sees a message.' So I sent it and thought, I have a cousin and my sister-in-law who worked in the area of the dam, so I thought 'no! I'll call them instead as they are by the dam, they must know something. I picked up the phone and called them. I asked them did you know the dam broke? And she said 'Oh Monica, I just tried to call you and yes it's true.'

I immediately switched off my phone, finished closing the office, got the car keys, called my aunt and mother and I said 'I'm coming to pick you up because the dam has burst', so we could go to Bento, to see how I could help, what I could save, something like that, because until then, I thought it was just water that had leaked, and gone into the houses, so maybe I could save something. I went to my aunt's workplace, which was on the way, I took her, I then stopped at my mother's work, she was at the door of her work and she went back in to clock off with her card, the car was in motion with the door open for her to enter, she was still clocking off inside in order not to lose her day's pay.

A neighbour of ours asked for a ride as her daughters were there [in Bento] and she had come to Mariana to get paid, she was very desperate because she had heard that all the students at the school had died, and I tried to go there, trying, thinking that I was accelerating the car, but I couldn't go faster than 40 km per hour, we were all anxious, I was crying, I remembered my things, people, my mother cursing at us all the time, being quite tough.

We got to a certain point on the road where [we] encountered significant amounts of mud and there were some residents of Bento who were on the way also trying to get to the village, they said that 'you can not go any further!' Some friends of ours had come down from the bush screaming 'Let's go, let's go the mud is coming and will hit us!!!' Looking ahead where I had stopped the car all you could see was mud and destruction. I do not know how, [but] I managed to turn the car in a matter of seconds and we left, then we went to the village, but on the way you looked to the left side, and could no longer see the river as there were so many fallen trees, and the mud [was] approaching us, we had to cross a bridge, I said 'guys, we are going to die now.' It was unexplainable how the mud had not reached that bridge – we were very fortunate, we crossed it and stopped at Vila Samarco, to get more information, and to be honest I don't know why we stopped at Vila Samarco, the lady that was with us began to feel ill, that's when I saw a group of men, Samarco employees huddled in a circle and one in the middle passed a list to see which employees were counted for, I thought to myself, well, if they're here they can give me some more concrete news.

I got between the employees and looked at the young man who was in the centre and asked him, 'Do you have any information about how Bento is, what really happened?' He turned to me and said, 'Look, you'll have to excuse me our priority now is to look for our employees!' He still told me that God would allow everyone to be there, because my family is there and I am here without any news. No concrete news, nothing. Until we decided to go to Santa Rita, as Bento is closer to Santa Rita and was where more information coming out from there and also because my aunt lived there we would get more information.

At the time I was in tears we stayed about an hour and a half in the village without any news, you know? It was almost nine o'clock at night when I had contact with my first relatives, [it] was my aunt Sandra, and her three year old daughter, Anamélia, so they were safe, my Aunt Ana, she went to the Santa Barbara hospital because they had to go through the woods to escape the mud. My aunt managed to get through the bush, they were in Bento at the time of the rupture, they managed to save themselves, walking through the bush. My aunt said that there were people in the upper part of the Bento where there was no mud that they were well, but that they would have to spend the night there because there was no way out and said that until then I could not tell how many people had died [from] this kind of thing, we just got that information the next day when we were missing people, but I was not sure if anybody had really died, if they were going to find someone alive.

Returning Home

I only got to see Bento on the 6th [of] November, in the morning, from afar; we stood at a high point far away where we could see everything. You could only see a few pieces of roofing and nothing else, and the two mango trees that survived, you could not identify anything else. You only saw mud, and more mud, and destruction. My mother and I only got to enter Bento, on December 20, with the Globo Network news reporter, that's when we got there. It was the worst feeling, because it was much worse than we had seen on television. Wow, it was very sad! It was horrible! And also having to deal with seeing all the houses that are left standing in ruins and having been looted as well.

A lot of people were taken to spend a night at the Mariana Gymnasium during the first night of the dam rupture, my mother and I stayed in a hotel, separated from my aunts, everyone [was] separated. We stayed almost a month in the hotel, and then went to a house rented by Samarco, which is where we are today.

The Struggle for Justice

We know our struggle will not be easy but as long as we have strength we will resist and fight for our lands because that's not something we will compromise on ever. Thank God we have the public prosecutor Dr. Guillherme and Dr Nivea who have always helped us fight for our rights – they are our guardian angels.

Everything we've achieved so far is thanks to the intervention by the Public Prosecutor's office […] the benefits we got, it's all due to public hearings we had, since these two hearings we haven't obtained a single benefit from the mining company, we only get promises […] which they change all the time […]. The Public Prosecutor's office has been our guardian angel […] the company has not been responsible, they haven't had any love for their neighbour, they didn't even have any for their own employees.[18]

Community Divisions and Conflicts

In regard to discrimination, we have heard so much. Not [by] all the people, all the residents of Mariana, but there is a very large prejudiced group that thinks we are guilty for what happened, as now there will be some layoffs (in Samarco), they think it's our fault […] because Samarco's operations have been suspended, they think it's our fault.

What have I heard? That Bento's people are taking advantage of Samarco; That Bento's residents are receiving perks and benefits, that they are having all the good and the best while employees are losing their jobs; That the whole city is turning against us in Bento. This kind of thing! It's a bad feeling, because it seems like we are invading a space that is not ours, it's more or less like that.

Our Present Struggle

They have divided us into three groups to discuss our expectations, but all groups have the same goal, which is for that the new Bento to be the way it used to be. Our current struggle? For us to have the reconstruction as soon as possible. Because there are a lot of people who say they will not get to see it, they are very old in the community and they say that their fear is not being able to see the new Bento and even for us youngsters it is very difficult to live in Mariana, very difficult because there in Bento we had a routine and everyone was close to one another and here everyone is separated. There are neighbours of mine who used to live nearby, which I have not been able to see for months. My life is at a standstill. I work, but I do not have the courage to leave the house, I do not feel like doing anything, just working to see if time goes by faster. But that lust for life will only come back once I'm in my own house.

The land, the place. My house does not have anything, not a piece of wall remaining, but I know where my house was, so that piece of land there is still ours. Even if the company will indemnify us it will continue being ours, because it was not for sale. Whatever they compensate, they will be compensating for their mistake, a mistake that they made, an error that Samarco committed. Our land will not be for sale, it will not be [that] because they compensated that they will be able to do whatever they want there.

We really don't want for our land to be converted into yet another dam and lose this history, the archaeologists are digging and still finding some things there, they already found two baptismal fonts, they already found a piece of the floor of the central altar [of the local church].

Look, I still do not know how to tell you exactly what it's going to be, if it's really going to be a museum territory. But the intention of the majority of the community is that we get the permission to preserve Bento, the way it is, without touching anything. Let people go and see what really happened.

Unfortunately we do depend on the company! We are fighting for our rights, but at no time do we trust them, just like when they repeat 'you will be compensated' 'you will be compensated' 'you will have your house back' I only believe it after it is done, and completed. Our trust in the company ended on November 5 at 4:00 PM, when the mud destroyed everything we had. From that point on, there was no longer any trust!

Those who had a house and spent only the weekends in Bento, they are considered as 'Weekend Atingidos'. These people are not entitled to a rent compensation, these people are not entitled to the new furniture, as we who lived there had. That person only has the right in the amount of 10,000 reais and [should] not receive the 10,000 reais extra payment, these people do not have the right to social benefits card, that kind of thing. Whoever had a car, had to prove they had a car, how are you going to prove that you had a car if the document left? Then you had to go to the Detran [Transport authorities], get the history of the car, that sort of thing. If you haven't registered your name properly you do not get the compensation, they do not want to pay, because the car is not in [your] name.

The company created a register of all homes but without any [community] participation without knowing for certain what we really had. They're not giving us back the possession we had in our homes. In other words, it took just ten minutes for the company to destroy everything but for us it's an eternity to get our lives sorted out. It's now been two years since the disaster and the land hasn't been cleaned up still. They [the company] forbid us from re-entering our land and property and are forcing us to be resettled and keep our land for themselves. We don't find this to be fair and will continue resisting this.

Before the dam broke, as is coming out in reports, Samarco had knowledge of the problem even when they built the Fundão dam, that they altered the project, they could already predict that something in the future, in the distant future or in a future could happen. And if they knew it was in trouble, they might as well have tried to get us out of there. I assure you that if they had a meeting with the community and talked about the problem and what could happen to everyone,

everyone would prefer to leave without losing anything, without losing life the way it was.

The day the dam burst at four o'clock in the afternoon, I saw a report just then, which they later took off from Facebook that said at three o'clock in the afternoon the President of Samarco was in meeting in the state capital of Belo Horizonte, where he learned of the dam bursting around three in the afternoon, if at three o'clock in the afternoon they knew of the problem, they could have telephoned people in Bento, which would have at least given the people a dignified exit without anyone having lost their lives.

Everything hurts, the photographs I had of my father, my grandparent's things. Everything hurts, even small things like a needle I need. I know, my mother says that we should not be attached to material possessions. Even after you've lost everything I could not change my way of thinking, my taste. I miss everything, even clothes I had, I miss it all! It makes me feel very bad, remembering things, knowing that it does not exist anymore, that we cannot go back, that there is no way to recover. Actually, in the beginning when we got to go to Bento, I still had a lot of hope of finding at least a third of my grandmother's things. I still hoped to find things but every day that passes, you do not see a trace of anything, you do not know in what direction your things went, where they went. It's so bad.

Life before the disaster? Oh! It was so great there! I was born and raised there. I spent the best years of my life there, and now we don't have a thing left anymore, and we're in another city [Mariana] where the locals are turning on us Atingidos, blaming us for the unemployment, blaming us for everything that's happening.

My dream? My dream is to have the house built as soon as possible. For us to try to rebuild, to try to start again, it will be to start over, we will start from scratch, it will be like this, we will start over when the house is ready, turn around and say 'it's your house, here's the key'. Then I think it will feel some relief.

Being Labelled an Atingido?

No, no! It's the worst feeling in the world. Like that, we've already lost everything, we have nothing, we have to start over and it's not easy to keep talking, to be called an Atingido. I think, from my point of view, I find it very humiliating. But Bento, if we could, if I could go back, rebuild, redo my life, I would prefer it to anywhere else.

In September 2016 the government authorized Samarco to construct a new dam called S4 to contain the mud and waste from the previous dam. We were against this new dam and have never given our consent to it. The company has promised to compensate us but we have seen nothing so far. Samarco is trying to do everything it can to get our land. The company has put us into rented accommodation and provided us with social assistance and it only does this because of the legal defence actions by the Public Prosecutor. It is not a nice kind hearted company, it does what it does for us simply due to judicial decisions made by the courts.

We have a relationship of hate, fear and lots and lots of anger and lots of resentment with the company. After everything that came out in the press around the phone hacking, leaked emails etc that proved the company knew about the risks and dangers of the tailings dam rupture they could have done something about it and saved us. In August 2017 a Federal Judge even suspended the case for homicide against 22 officials from Samarco.[19]

How are we going to have a good relation with the company after everything it has done? After the fact [that] we are living in hell? You can visit the community members in their new homes in the city. None of them are happy. All the elder people are getting ill and weaker by the day. Everyone is anxious as everything takes time and it's delayed. We've also lost community members since the dam collapse due to depression and sadness.

It was a company versus 600 residents, it was the voice of a company against ours. Who would win? Do you think we would win? […] This is all about power. What power do we have? Sometimes I think we have power and other times we don't. But if we really had power I think things would be moving along much quicker.

Human rights? I think it means the right to life, a dignified life, but to be honest I'd say everything we have lost due to the disaster is linked to human rights […] we lost material goods, history, things you can't put a price on […] and it also means respect for human beings. They should respect human rights, right? Despite the company speaking a lot about this since the disaster[20] they should be forced to respect our rights, but they – the company – have the power.

My dream was that the rest of my life would be in Bento. My plan was, I was born and raised there, if I ever get married it would be there in the church next to my house, if I would have children they would be raised there and when I died I would be buried there. I don't think we can recuperate our old life so, I used to be so hopeful but since each day that passes with everything so slow, so many meetings everyday and nothing resulting from them I don't think we'll get anything out of them. I fear they won't even return us our homes that's my fear.

Final Reflections

What can Monica's story teach us within the larger narrative of Samarco's Fundão dam's collapse? Monica's frustrations at the excruciatingly slow speed of justice from corporate and state actors echo those from the state prosecutor. These frustrations eventually resulted in the collective action lawsuit against BHP Billiton in London by an Anglo-American law firm. This story bares the stark limitations of providing access to justice to victims of environmental disasters via private arrangements, albeit with the involvement of state and civil society actors in its governance. By comparing the overlaps between Monica's narrative and the facts of the Fundão dam collapse, we can also question private self-regulated initiatives such as the CHRB which ranked BHP as the third best corporation for its human rights performance.[21] Perhaps on the basis of internal policies, processes and controls, BHP has much to impress in terms of human rights. However, comparing this with the outcomes of Samarco's Fundão dam collapse and Monica's retelling of how the disaster impacted her life calls into question the credibility of self-regulated business and human rights or corporate responsibility initiatives.

In December 2015, a month after the dam collapse, the UN Working Group on Business and Human Rights conducted a two-week visit to Brazil that included a stop in Mariana to meet with Samarco, community victims, state and civil society actors. While the Working Group's statement initially questions Samarco for its lethargic communication with the community on several issues, it largely 'appreciated the efforts taken by the company to take action after the disaster. The fact that the CEO himself took a lead in the company's response, and the willingness to consult with communities were important steps to finding solutions together with the affected communities'.[22] The Working Group finalizes its section on Mariana by reminding the Brazilian state that it has a duty to protect the human rights of the victims of the tragedy. Monica's retelling of events since the tragedy of November 2015 contrasts with that of the Working Group since she affirms that everything the community has gained in terms of reparations is thanks to the public prosecutor, who is very much a state justice actor. The actions of Samarco and the private foundation Renova to repair the damage seem to have caused more grievances than satisfaction among many of the *Atingidos*.

Beyond the devastation caused by such a corporate environmental disaster at an individual level to their life, livelihood, culture and dreams, the impact is also being felt at a collective level. The corporate disaster has led to the tearing up of the community's social fabric, social ties and community kinship. The *Atingidos* now feel persecuted and discriminated by their fellow neighbours, those with a vested economic interest (e.g. jobs and business) in Samarco. These neighbours blame the *Atingidos* for the termination of their own jobs and business relations with Samarco, since the company stopped operating. In addition, the *Atingidos* are vilified as scheming people who are looking to make a quick profit from the disaster. *Atingidos* often wonder how they became to be seen as the villains in this tragedy. In short, though Samarco may at some point reconstruct Bento Rodrigues as Nova (New) Bento with new houses elsewhere, it will be nearly impossible to reconstruct the social fabric and ties which had been built up over generations. The latter cannot be materially remedied or compensated.

Notes

1 Corporate Human Rights Benchmark, www.corporatebenchmark.org (accessed 14 November 2019).

2 'CHRB Response to Brumadinho Dam Disaster – Vale Suspension from Human Rights Benchmark' (2019), https://www.corporatebenchmark.org/sites/default/files/CHRB%20Response%20to%20Brumadinho%20Dam%20Disaster%20 29Jan2019.pdf (accessed 29 January 2019).

3 Brumadinho: Sobe para 249 o número de mortos no rompimento de barragem, https://www.cenariomt.com.br/2019/08/31/brumadinho-sobe-para-249-o-numero-de-mortos-no-rompimento-de-barragem/ (accessed 14 November 2019).

4 Many *Atingidos* argue in person that the death total is 20 as one pregnant woman had a miscarriage when she was trying to escape the flooding.

5 Vale prevê mais dois anos para reparar danos do desastre da Samarco, diz presidente, https://g1.globo.com/economia/noticia/vale-preve-mais-dois-anos-para-reparar-danos-do-desastre-da-samarco-diz-presidente.ghtml (accessed 14 November 2019).

6 C. Linhares, 'Rivers Contaminated with Waste from Mining Company Samarco Are in Poor Condition, Says NGO', http://www1.folha.uol.com.br/internacional/en/brazil/2017/11/1933768-rivers-contaminated-with-waste-from-mining-company-samarco-are-in-poor-condition-says-ngo.shtml (accessed 14 November 2019).

7 Paul Kiernan (2016-01-17). 'Samarco Warned of Problems at Dam, Engineer Says', *Wall Street Journal*, 17 January 2016.

8 Fundaçao Renova, 'Who We Are', https://www.fundacaorenova.org/en/the-foundation/ (accessed 1 September 2019).

9 Fundaçao Renova Participating parties, https://www.fundacaorenova.org/en/participating-parties/ (accessed 1 September 2019).

10 'We believe that no challenge can be overcome without adding one single word: together. Dialogue unites us and makes collective construction of the future possible. When getting together, each party becomes stronger. Our role, somehow, is this: to promote coming together and creating connections.' (Fundaçao Renova website, https://www.fundacaorenova.org/en/the-foundation/, accessed 3 January 2019).

11 Renova, 'Who We Are'.

12 M. Parreiras, 'Advogados apostam em acordo na ação internacional pela tragédia de Mariana', https://www.em.com.br/app/noticia/gerais/2018/09/25/interna_gerais,991417/advogados-apostam-em-acordo-na-acao-internacional-por-mariana.shtml (accessed 14 November 2019).

13 Views also expressed by *Atingidos* in Minas Gerais State Assembly on Human Rights video from 26 August, Assemblea de Minas Gerais. Comissão de Direitos Humanos, 26 August 2019, https://www.youtube.com/watch?v=dnwHWRTGfEc&t=3178s (accessed 1 September 2019).

14 Flávia Christini, 'Acordo de indenização final para atingidos de Mariana é fechado após quase 3 anos do desastre, diz MP-MG', https://g1.globo.com/mg/minas-gerais/noticia/2018/10/02/acordo-de-indenizacao-final-para-atingidos-de-mariana-e-fechado-apos-quase-3-anos-do-desastre-diz-mp-mg.ghtml (accessed 14 November 2019).

15 R. Freitas, 'Mariana: apesar de acordo para indenização e obras, promotor não vê o que comemorar', https://g1.globo.com/mg/minas-gerais/noticia/2018/11/06/mariana-apesar-de-acordo-para-indenizacao-e-obras-promotor-nao-ve-o-que-comemorar.ghtml (accessed 14 November 2019).

16 J. Watts, 'BHP Billiton Facing £5bn Lawsuit from Brazilian Victims of Dam Disaster', https://www.theguardian.com/environment/2018/nov/06/bhp-billiton-facing-5bn-lawsuit-from-brazilian-victims-of-dam-disaster (accessed 14 November 2019).

17 Interviews were conducted on three separate occasions between July and September 2016 and in October 2018.

18 It is worth noting that there have been small gains for the community in terms of reparations, but that, by and large, it has been insufficient as noted by the prosecutor and Mónica.

19 A federal regional court of the First Region in Brazil reduced the charges against the executives and blocked criminal charges against them, effectively providing them with a loophole as reported in the Brazilian press on 9 October 2018. https://www1.folha.uol.com.br/cotidiano/2018/10/justica-abre-brecha-para-livrar-executivos-da-samarco-da-acusacao-de-homicidio.shtml (accessed 14 November 2019).

20 In references to the UN Working Group on Business and Human Rights visit to the community in December 2015.

21 https://www.corporatebenchmark.org/sites/default/files/documents/CHRBKeyFindings2018.pdf (accessed 19 November 2019).

22 https://www.ohchr.org/EN/NewsEvents/Pages/DisplayNews.aspx?NewsID=16891&LangID=E (Accessed 19 November 2019).

Chapter 5

TAMING THE DRAGON, UNPACKING OPTIONS FOR ACCESS TO REMEDY FOR VIOLATIONS BY CHINESE MULTINATIONAL CORPORATIONS OPERATING IN CHIADZWA, ZIMBABWE

Bellinda Chinowawa

> Let her sleep. When the dragon awakes, the world will tremble.
>
> –Napoleon Bonaparte[1]

When Bonaparte made this proclamation in the eighteenth century, he may well have been envisioning the current global economy. Since the People's Republic of China (China) opened its doors to the West 30 years ago, there has been a dramatic change in its economic fortunes.[2] China is now a formidable global economic player and was the top exporter of the world with the value of its exports in 2012 being 1.4 times the value of exports of the United States, the second largest exporter.[3] The economic transformation of China has required, and will continue to demand, massive quantities of resources, and akin to other major powers in modern history, China is looking outward to find them. Africa, with its abundant natural resources, provides a natural location in this quest and the figures speak for themselves.[4]

While China's interest in Africa is hardly new, the scope and scale of the burgeoning Sino-African trade is unprecedented.[5] To a large degree, China pursues its global acquisition strategy through multinational corporations (MNCs).[6] The marked presence of Chinese MNCs on the global stage is changing the landscape of international business and politics. Highly competitive and strongly supported by the state, Chinese MNCs are embarking on an acquisition drive that is capturing key resources and market share across the continent.[7] Western firms, which once had virtually undisputed command over international financial resources and the requisite political and historical ties to dominate global business, are now being challenged.[8] Nowhere is this trend more evident than in Zimbabwe where trade with China has steadily risen due to various factors, including the imposition of sanctions and trade restrictions by the European Union (EU)[9] and the United States.[10]

However, many Chinese corporations are tainted by allegations of persistent abuses, including, poor health and safety conditions, regular 12-hour and 18-hour shifts involving arduous labour and anti-union activities, all in violation of national laws or international labour standards.[11] This is despite the fact that, globally, a number of MNCs have sought to align their activities with the UN Guiding Principles on Business and Human Rights (UNGPs). However, the fatal flaw in the design of the UNGPs is that they are premised on the assumption that corporations and states are willing to provide a framework for access to remedy where there has been a violation. Thus, in instances where there is a breakdown in the rule of law coupled with weak home state regulation, victims are left in a remediless limbo, unable to secure remedies for abuses perpetrated against them.

This is particularly true for the people of Chiadzwa in Eastern Zimbabwe where security forces committed heinous acts of cruelty as documented in Human Rights Watch's report, False Dawn, dated 31 August 2009.[12] In the ultimate act of callousness in Marange, the government forcibly relocated villagers from their ancestral homes to a farm with an inadequate infrastructure and little ability to conduct any income-generating activities.[13] As diamond mining in Chiadzwa intensifies, the state has announced that there will be further relocations from Marange to Arda Transau.[14]

While some of the companies have provided some form of remedy, as will be shown below, this has proven to be both inadequate and insensitive to the cultural needs of many of the people of this community.

The Context

Diamonds were discovered in the Marange area of Eastern Zimbabwe in June 2006. This was not the first time that diamonds had been found in Zimbabwe,[15] but the Marange discovery was unique in that the Government of Zimbabwe (GoZ) effectively encouraged a diamond rush as there was no state presence or regulation at the site,[16] notwithstanding the provisions of mining legislation that vests dominium over the right to search, mine and dispose of all minerals exclusively in the president of Zimbabwe.[17] The GoZ attempted to correct the situation and in November 2006, the Zimbabwe Republic Police (ZRP) launched an operation to clamp down on illegal mining across the country, including in Marange. Police assumed control of the diamond fields but, rather than halt illegal mining and trade, they exacerbated and exploited the lawlessness on the diamond fields.[18] Locals were subjected to arbitrary arrests, beatings and general harassment. Thus, by May 2008 the result of the police operation was that the local remand prison had 1,600 inmates – 1,300 more than its carrying capacity.[19] With police presence disintegrating into anarchy, the Zimbabwe National Army (ZNA) was called in, both to restore a semblance of order and to allow key army units access to the diamonds to stave off discontent occasioned by rising inflation and general economic malaise. According to Human Rights Watch, military operations over a three-week period involved the indiscriminate shooting of both miners and local villagers. Between 1 and 12 November 2008, 107 bodies, many with visible bullet wounds, were brought from Marange to the morgue at nearby Mutare General Hospital. With control established, the army rapidly turned to forming syndicates, often using forced labour, including that of children, to mine for diamonds.[20] From 2009 however, the ZNA and the GoZ became more organized and partnered with Chinese multinational companies to formally exploit diamonds in the area. Inspiration for this model was drawn from China's People's Liberation Army (PLA) which owns and operates a number of enterprises that are involved in food production mining, services, among others.[21]

End of the Diamond Rush

When the GoZ provided licensing to companies to operate in Marange, it formalized diamond mining and ended the diamond rush of the years 2006–8. However, it did not bring about the structure and prosperity associated with the exploitation of high-value diamonds.[22] The nominal involvement of the army and the GoZ was simply to comply with the country's indigenization laws which stipulate that 51 per cent of any enterprise should be owned by 'indigenous Zimbabwean', but in reality the companies are controlled by their Chinese owners. Given how Chinese companies generally operate, this has grave implications for human rights infractions arising from weak local legislation combined with the standard business practices of Chinese corporations, as will be explored below.

The Nature of Chinese Venture Capitalism.

To properly understand the Chiadzwa situation, it is crucial to delve into the workings of Chinese operations. Studies on the foreign expansion of Chinese firms stress the peculiarity of Chinese MNCs, which are predominantly state-owned enterprises and whose investment decisions may reflect political objectives that are not necessarily consistent with the profit-maximizing strategies of private companies.[23]

This is an important distinction in understanding the Marange diamond tragedy. International relationships between Zimbabwe and China date back to the Cold War era, when communist China supported the black majority in the war of liberation from the white rule. Since then, the two countries have enjoyed good relations, and China is described by the political elite as 'an all-weather friend'. After the country's ostracization following a controversial land reform program, Zimbabwe espoused a 'look east policy' resulting in Chinese goods and corporations obtaining special treatment. The companies profiled below appeared unworried about the political and economic risk of investing in a country which has a history of non-respect for property rights and poor governance due to the preferential treatment accorded to Chinese investors by a country which had attained pariah status on the global stage.[24]

Who They Are

As stated above, the GoZ entered into joint ventures with a number of companies for the exploitation of diamonds in Chiadzwa. These include the following:

1. Anjin Investments Private Limited – A joint venture between Chinese construction firm, Anhui Foreign Economic Construction Group, and individuals from the Zimbabwe National Army through the Zimbabwe Defence Industries (ZDI).
2. Jianin Mining – A subsidiary of the Anhui Foreign Economic Construction Group, with the same shareholding.
3. Sino-Zimbabwe Development Private Limited – A company owned by China International Fund (CIF), whose diamond entity in Zimbabwe is known as Sino-Zimbabwe Development Private Limited.

Despite the secrecy surrounding the allocation of the mining claims from which to mine the diamonds, Global Witness unearthed documents revealing that Anjin was assigned mining claims, referred to as 'blocks'. These are blocks C, Lii, and E and Sino-Zimbabwe Development Limited (Sino-Zimbabwe) was allocated Marange blocks H and D61. The allocation process did not involve open bidding, hence the difficulties in verifying the allocation of claims. Even the Parliament of Zimbabwe which set up a Portfolio Committee on Mines and Energy on Diamond Mining noted that 'there was a contestation of power between the Executive and the Legislature over access to information and entry by the Committee to carry on site visits in Marange',[25] This chapter relates largely to the actions of Anjin, as the Kayiboni family, which is the subject of the case study, originally lived in the block allocated to Anjin and was relocated from Chiadzwa by that company. However, their experiences are not unique and the same model of relocations was utilized by all the diamond mining companies in Chiadzwa.

What They Did

The evictions and relocations

Each of the mining companies profiled above was given the responsibility to relocate the inhabitants of the area in which their claims were located in order to clear the land for mining to commence. From interviews conducted with Mr Kayiboni, the evictions were not conducted in conformity with international human rights standards. To incentivize villagers to leave, the companies' ring fenced the villages so that movement would be restricted and villagers would have to endure undue hardship from lack of access to their fields, wells and other amenities of life. Thereafter, the community was issued a 28-day ultimatum to leave the land before they would be forcibly evicted. After the expiry of the 28 days, authorities - acting in collusion with company officials - burnt houses and advised villagers to sell their cattle at lower prices as the smaller lots of land in the area they were being relocated would not be able to accommodate them.[26] The companies provided a 'remedy' for the majority of the Chiadzwa community by relocating them to the Arda Transau farm. Each displaced family in the community as a whole was allocated a three-bedroom house, one hectare of arable land and a one-time payment of US$1,000, which was far below the US$40,000 which the government's own evaluators had assessed as being adequate compensation.[27] As will be shown below, this remedy does not meet the threshold set out in the UNGPs.

Inadequate Remedy – Case Study: The Kayiboni Family

Before writing this paper, the author conducted interviews with members of the Kayiboni family who were relocated from Marange to Arda Transau farm in 2011. The account below is a summary of the meeting. Reliance is placed on interview notes made at this meeting and the interventions staged thereafter to analyse the adequacy of the remedy offered by the company and how it was culturally and socially ill-suited for the Kayiboni family and similarly placed families belonging to the apostolic sect.

Phillimon Jowani Kayiboni, aged 92, is a member of the Johanne Marange apostolic sect, a Christian-oriented religious group, which encourages polygamy among its members and shuns Western values. He has 14 wives, 70 children and an unknown number of grandchildren.

On 27 February 2011, he was relocated from his communal home in the Gamunorwa Village in the Chiadzwa area to what was called 'a temporary facility' at Arda Transau Farm in the Odzi district. During the relocation, he was told that he would be relocated to an equivalent or superior accommodation to that which he previously occupied. His compound in Chiadzwa comprised 17 three-roomed brick houses, 14 kitchens under thatch, a kraal with 21 herd of cattle, 14 vegetable gardens (measuring two acres each) and 30 acres of cultivated land. Kayiboni used the land, together with members of his family, to produce cotton, groundnuts, maize and other crops and thus was able to maintain an acceptable standard of living as well as send their children to school.

However, since his relocation to Arda Transau Farm, his family's quality of life has deteriorated rapidly. Mr Kayobini's new accommodations were markedly smaller than before. As a result what was once a well-knit family has now been scattered across the farm, with some family members inhabiting old barns and horse stables while others have been cramped into a dilapidated three-room farmhouse, with leaky roofs and poor ventilation.

After sustained pressure from lawyers and the family itself, Anjin constructed two standard three-bedroom houses as they had done for other polygamous men; but Mr Kayiboni refused to move into the house, stating that it was too small and could not possibly accommodate his wives, children and grandchildren. He argued that at the very least, the company ought to provide his family with the same model of houses as the ones he had constructed in Marange.

The space was also inappropriate for his 14 wives who had to share the same situation. In their own words, they said, 'As wives, we have no "kitchen" and we have to share an open space with our co-wives. We do not have a place for our children to sit and learn from their elders as we did in Marange'.[28] In a Shona setting,[29] the kitchen is more than just a place to prepare meals. It is a place for the family to gather and where values are passed down over generations. When visitors come, it is the first port of call and it is central to any household, which is why each wife has her own space.

In response to pressure, the company then built a single fourteen-room house, with a bedroom for each of his wives; however, this was also rejected, as each had previously occupied their own home and not a single room. Eight houses were then prepared and accepted. The remaining wives moved into houses which had been constructed for teachers working at Anjin Primary School. These wives were arrested and charged with criminal nuisance, and on their release on bail, they promptly went to erect shacks at the offices of the district administrator for Manicaland Province as they attributed their struggles to lies he had told. The minister of state for Manicaland Provincial

Affairs intervened and ensured that the remaining six wives were allocated individual houses.

Although each wife eventually received her own house, it was a hollow victory, and having spent six years struggling, with no means of production, the Kayiboni family is significantly poorer.

> When we finally got the houses, we no longer had anything, not even a goat. To worsen the situation, the land here is too small, so we can't even farm anything to sell. I wish the company would pay me and my wives enough compensation so that we can find a way to survive.[30]

International Law Framework

Zimbabwe is a state party to the International Covenant on Economic, Social and Cultural Rights (ICESCR), the International Covenant on Civil and Political Rights (ICCPR), the Convention on the Elimination on all Forms of Discrimination against Women (CEDAW) and the Convention on the Rights of the Child (CRC). At regional level, it is a state party to the African Charter on Human and Peoples Rights (ACHPR), the African Charter on the Rights and Welfare of the Child (ACRWC) and the Protocol to the African Charter on Human and Peoples' Rights on the Rights of Women in Africa (Maputo Protocol).

Zimbabwe also has a comprehensive Constitution,[31] with a justiciable bill of rights incorporating economic, social and cultural rights. However, the most pertinent legislation governing the prospecting and mining for minerals is the Mines and Minerals Act (MMAZ) as read with the Communal Lands Act and the Precious Stones Act (PSA). With specific relation to diamonds, in November 2012 the government promulgated a Diamond Policy (DP) whose main objective is 'to promote the sustainable development of the diamond industry for the benefit of all Zimbabweans'. However, the MMAZ is the only Act of Parliament under which the acquisition of the rights to minerals can be acquired.[32] The PSA only governs the administration of licences issued under the MMAZ as well as the granting of permits to possess, dispose and acquire precious stones for purposes other than trade.[33] As noted by Masiya et al., 'The Mines and Minerals Act was crafted in 1963, during the colonial era, in the context of repression and recognition of only white minority rights'.[34] To date, there have been no amendments to the Act to bring it in line with the new Constitution of Zimbabwe or international law. Thus, the MMA provides that all dominium in and rights to minerals are vested in the president.[35] The DP, while contemporary and progressive, has not been supported by the necessary institutional and legislative backing necessary to bring its protective provisions to fruition, with the result that many of its aspects remain unimplemented.[36] More importantly, communities residing on communal land such as the Chiadzwa community do not own the land they have occupied for generations due to the provisions of the Communal Land Act, which again vests all communal land in the president. Rural district councils (RDCs) are empowered to manage the land on the president's behalf by allocating users rights over the land with due regard for the traditional and customary use and allocation of such land. Thus, communities are given rights to use with respect to land for agriculture, housing and pasture but no title or ownership.

The combination of inadequate and inconsistent laws and policies has fuelled corruption and illicit financial flows in the diamond mining sector.[37] More importantly, there have been negative consequences for human rights and environmental rights as there is no scope or provision for free, prior and informed consent; community consultation; or the protection of cultural rights. Finally, there is very minimal consideration of environmental rights as the MMAZ overrides the Environmental Management Act.

The combined effect of this deadly cocktail of legislation is illustrated in the remedy offered by Anjin. Even though the corporation's resettlement of the Kayiboni family resulted in significantly smaller accommodations and an inadequate source of income, Anjin's acts actually exceeded the bounds of the law. Under current national law, communities are only compensated for 'improvements' made to communal land; there is no scope for assistance with relocation, or the erection of schools or houses, which the company also provided.

Inadequacy of the remedy

The Chiadzwa community consisted of communal peasant farmers relying on subsistence farming. There are very limited livelihood opportunities at Arda Transau apart from tilling the 70 m × 70 m of land allocated to each family. Informal promises to employ at least one person per family at the diamond mines were never fulfilled, heightening the sense of betrayal and the violations below.

The remedy had a negative and disproportionate effect on women and children

The vast majority of rural families in Zimbabwe are sustained by women.[38] The situation of women displaced from Marange mirrors this, and is compounded by the fact that the vast majority of people from this area are members of the Johanne Marange Apostolic Sect which encourages polygamy and prohibits the use of contraceptives, equating it to the murder of an unborn child. Thus, women are married early and face a myriad of religious and cultural barriers which impede access to education and medication. This religious aspect brings in other dimensions including that, even before the relocation, the right to education, especially for the female children, was already compromised, as children born to families in the Johanne Marange sect are unlikely to attain an education beyond primary school due to the practice of early child marriages. For instance, one of the key sources for this chapter was a 28-year-old woman, whose oldest child was 15.

However, even for those willing to send their children to school, the forced relocations were disruptive, as a number of families were moved between October and November 2010, which is the period in which final examination is written in Zimbabwe. No provisions were made to ensure that there was an examination centre on site. Schools were not immediately constructed and children had to learn in makeshift classrooms with no textbooks or furniture. Currently, there are only two primary schools in the area, Anjin Primary School and Wellington Primary school, constructed by Anjin and Mbada, respectively, but the infrastructure is still not adequate for the number of children going to school in the area. As such, children as young as six are walking long distances to attend school.[39]

Remedy negatively affected the right to health

There is one clinic that provides health services to the thousands of people resettled in Arda Transau. Only two nurses and one general hand are employed at the clinic, which has no electricity or running water. Patients requiring treatment after sunset have to bring their own candles and there are no functional life-saving machines and no doctor at the facility. This has obvious negative implications on the community which is forced to rely on traditional medicines or travel long distances to access doctors and hospitals. This situation is especially untenable for people living with HIV who require a sustained level of care and engagement with the health delivery system. The health situation in Arda Transau was described by one community leader as a 'time bomb'.[40] The Kayiboni family is fortunate that the clinic is close to their homesteads, but those resettled farther have to walk a long distance to access health services.

Remedy had negative effects on language and culture

The people of Chiadzwa left behind holy sites and other places of cultural and religious significance. In the flurry of the hurried relocations, there was no opportunity to exhume and rebury loved ones. Although the community in Arda Transau is also Shona-speaking and hence linguistically similar, there is a definite cultural disconnect due to the fact that those from Chiadzwa have their own traditions.[41]

Remedy resulted in conflict with the local community

The relocations also created conflict between the relocated families and the Odzi-Zimunya community where they were moved to. This is because the displaced villagers are seen as contemptuous of the existing leadership structures in the area in which they have been resettled. An issue that has come to the fore is that the community from Chiadzwa engages in mundane tasks such as cutting grass for thatching their huts and trees for firewood without the permission of the local chief, in violation of the custom and practices of the original Odzi community. While it was not possible to interview the original inhabitants of the area, it is unlikely that the GoZ consulted the people of Odzi before relocating the people of Chiadzwa to their area and this has certainly contributed to the conflict.

The new reality – prostitution, hunger, starvation

Without a source of livelihood, villagers are sliding deeper into the abyss of poverty and resultant social ills including prostitution, child marriages and an upsurge in HIV infections.[42] There are continuing violations of their socio-economic rights, specifically the right to health, education and cultural rights, as outlined above. It is arguable that this state of affairs is attributable to the fact that there was not enough thought or consultation with the communities by both the companies and the GoZ before the relocations were done.

What Should Remedies Have Looked Like in the Context of the UNGPs?

Access to remedy is a foundational principle of the UNGPs.[43] In the context of an asymmetry of power between people and corporations, it is crucial that communities receive adequate redress from corporations. Ensuring the legal accountability of business enterprises and access to effective remedy for persons affected by such abuses is a vital part of a state's duty to protect against business-related human rights abuse.[44] Thus, both states and corporations should take measures to provide recourse as the right to an effective remedy for harm is a core aspect of international human rights law.

In the case study above, the state was remiss in its duty to provide access to remedy as there was no accountability for the atrocities committed by the army and police in the era before mining operations were formalized in Chiadzwa; neither was there adequate support given once mining was formalized and families displaced, as the state relied on legislation which vests rights in communal land and minerals in the state itself.

Communities thus had to rely on the benevolence of the company which provided an operational-level grievance mechanism. Guiding Principle 31 sets out the criteria for operational-level grievance mechanisms, stating that they should be 'legitimate, accessible, predictable, equitable, transparent, rights-compatible, and a source of continuous learning: drawing on relevant measures to identify lessons for improving the mechanism and preventing future grievances and harms'.[45] More importantly, operational-level mechanisms should also be based on engagement and dialogue: consulting the stakeholder groups for whose use they are intended on their design and performance and focusing on dialogue as the means to address and resolve grievances.[46] This was not done in the Chiadzwa case, resulting in a remedy that was inadequate and culturally inappropriate. Had the company engaged with the community beforehand, it would have been possible to avoid the acrimony and bitterness which still hounds these communities due to the hardships of brutal displacement from their ancestral land.

Cultural Relativism and Human Rights

Extending from the scholarly developments of Franz Boas, cultural relativism has gained currency as both a principle for academic field research and as the cornerstone of various social ideologies.[47] Cultural relativism asserts that all truths are subject to the norms and expectations of a specific culture, and that neither liberties nor value claims should be considered to be fundamentally inherent to human nature.[48] As Melville Herskovits puts it, 'Judgments are based on experience, and experience is interpreted by each individual in terms of his [or her] own enculturation.' On its face, the remedy provided by the company appears adequate and generous. It exceeds the bounds of local legislation and with time and pressure the company responded to the circumstances of the Kayiboni family. However, such notions point to the fallacy of exporting a singular notion of human rights, which fails to take local context into account. The remedy offered was culturally insensitive, requiring 14 wives who previously owned and occupied individual homesteads to live under one roof with their husband, children and grandchildren. In this way, it completely failed to consider the nature of polygamous marriages and the accommodations which should be made for families in this situation, however repugnant it may be to some. The remedy also does not make provision for the allocation of adequate farm land, despite the fact that the community consisted exclusively of peasant farmers, reliant on farming for their daily sustenance, impoverishing many who do not have any other means of sustenance.

Conclusion

The third pillar of the UNGPs establishes that access to remedy should be provided for victims of rights violations. In providing remedies, it is crucial that any remedy be seen through the lens of the rights holder. In this case, it is clear that an attempt was made to provide remedy, but because there was no consultation with victims, the remedy has proven inadequate and inappropriate.

Notes

1 'China's Fitful Sleep', *Economist*, 17 July 1997, http://www.economist.com/node/151617.

2 Mary B. Teagarden and Dong Hong Cai, 'Learning from Dragons Who Are Learning from Us: Developmental Lessons from China's Global Companies', *Organizational Dynamics* vol. 38, no. 1 (March 2009), 73. https://www.researchgate.net/publication/256924110_Learning_from_Dragons_who_are_Learning_from_Us_Developmental_Lessons_from_China's_Global_Companies.

3 UN Comtrade, <http://comtrade.un.org/pb/FileFetch.aspx?docID=5253&type=country%20pages> (accessed 7 September 2017).

4 Elizabeth Economy and Michael Levi, *By All Means Necessary: How China's Resource Quest Is Changing the World* (Oxford: Oxford University Press, January 2017).

5 David Haroz, 'China in Africa: Symbiosis or Exploitation?' *Fletcher Forum of World Affairs*, http://www.fletcherforum.org/home/2016/8/12/china-in-africa-symbiosis-or-exploitation (last accessed 24 February 2019).

6 Peter Kragelund, 'Knocking on a Wide Open Door: Chinese Investments in Africa', *Danish Institute for International Studies*, http://gdex.dk/ofdi/24%20Kragelund%20Peter.pdf (last accessed 24 February 2019).

7 Chris Alden and Martyn Davies, 'Chinese Multinational Corporations in Africa', *ResearchGate*, https://www.researchgate.net/publication/265080340_Chinese_Multinational_Corporations_in_Africa (last accessed 24 February 2019).

8 Ping Deng, 'Outward Investment by Chinese MNCs: Motivations and Implications', *Business Horizons* vol. 47, no. 3 (May 2004), 8, http://www.sciencedirect.com/science/article/pii/S0007681304000230.

9 'European Union: Restrictive Measures (Sanctions) in Force', *European Commission Service for Foreign Policy Instruments*, 7 July 2016, http://eeas.europa.eu/cfsp/sanctions/docs/measures_en.pdf.

10 'Resource Center: Zimbabwe Sanctions', *U.S. Department of the Treasury*, http://www.treasury.gov/resource-center/sanctions/Programs/pages/zimb.aspx (last accessed 15 September 2017).

11 This is especially true in Zambia. See Human Rights Watch, 'You'll Be Fired if You Refuse: Labor Abuses in Zambia's Chinese State-Owned Copper Mines', https://www.hrw.org/report/2011/11/04/youll-, https://www.state.gov/documents/organization/252957.pdfbe-fired-if-you-refuse/labor-abuses-zambias-chinese-state-owned-copper-mines (last accessed 18 January 2018).

12 'False Dawn: The Zimbabwe Power-Sharing Government's Failure to Deliver Human Rights Improvements', *Human Rights Watch*, 31 August 2009, https://www.hrw.org/report/2009/08/31/false-dawn/zimbabwe-power-sharing-governments-failure-deliver-human-rights.

13 Centre for Natural Resource Development, 'Marange Relocations Lead to New Poverty', 2014, http://www.swradioafrica.com/Documents/Marange%20relocations%20lead%20to%20new%20 poverty.pdf.

14 'Country Reports on Human Rights Practices for 2015', *United States Department of State Bureau of Democracy, Human Rights and Labor*, https://www.state.gov/documents/organization/252957.pdf (last accessed 24 January 2019).

15 The country has two other diamond mines, namely, Murowa Diamond (Rio Tinto) and River Ranch Mines, which mine Kimberlite diamonds. See Rio Tinto, https://www.riotinto.com/copperanddiamonds/about-rio-tinto-diamonds-10527.aspx (last accessed 20 November 2019); AGD Diamonds, https://www.rough-polished.com/en/expertise/81069.html (accessed 20 November 2019).

16 Human Rights Watch, http://www.hrw.org/sites/default/files/reports/zimbabwe 0609web.pdf (last accessed 8 September 2017).

17 Section 3 of the Mines and Minerals Act (Chapter 21:05).

18 Human Rights Watch, http://www.hrw.org/sites/default/files/reports/zimbabwe 0609web.pdf.

19 Ibid.

20 Mutare, 'Soldiers are the new illegal diamond miners', *IRIN*, 20 January 2009, http://www.irinnews.org/report/82477/zimbabwe-soldiers-are-the-new-illegal-diamond-miners.

21 For a complete list of the types of businesses the post-Mao PLA is involved in, see Zhang Zhenlong, chief editor, *Jundui shengchan jingying guanli [Management of Military Production]* (Beijing: Jiefangjun chubanshe, October 1989), 15–16, quoted in 'The Chinese Military and Its Business Operations: The PLA as Entrepreneur', *Thomas J. Bickford Source: Asian Survey* vol. 34, no. 5 (May 1994), 460, https://www.jstor.org/stable/2645058.

22 For instance, Botswana has been transformed from a low- to middle-income country as a result of diamond mining. See 'Botswana Celebrates 50 Years of Independence & the Harnessing of Diamond Resources to Empower Youth', *Diamonds Do Good*, https://www.diamondsdogood.com/diamonds-transform-botswana-empower-youth/ (last accessed 25 February 2018).

23 John Child and Susan B. Rodrigues, 'The Internationalization of Chinese Firms: A Case for Theoretical Extension?' *Management and Organization Review* vol. 1, no. 3 (2005), 381, https://myweb.rollins.edu/tlairson/mba/chiglbization.pdf. In a 2014 paper, Amighini et al. empirically analysed the host-country determinants of Chinese outward direct investments (ODI). The results showed that the pattern of Chinese ODI differs from developed countries because of the peculiarity of China's institutional environment, which results in an attraction to countries with large endowments of natural resources and risky political environments. Diego Quer et al. 'Political Risk, Cultural Distance, and Outward Foreign Direct Investment: Empirical Evidence from Large Chinese firms', *Asia Pacific Journal of Management*, December 2011,

https://www.researchgate.net/publication/225400913_Political_risk_cultural_distance_and_outward_foreign_direct_investment_Empirical_evidence_from_large_Chinese_firms.

24 In 2003, Zimbabwe formally announced the Look East Policy (LEP) in the face of economic sanctions by the West. This, coupled with the Forum on China Africa Cooperation (FOCAC) of 2000, has strengthened trade and bilateral investments between Zimbabwe and China. China is increasingly involved in Zimbabwe's agriculture, mining, construction and tourism industries. Nusa Tukic and Felix Tombindo, 'Economic Repercussions of the Look East Policy in Zimbabwe', *Centre for Chinese Studies*, 2016, http://scholar.sun.ac.za/handle/10019.1/101548. In contrast, many Western countries including the United States, the UK and the European Union have maintained sanctions against Zimbabwe since 2002. See 'Financial Sanctions, Zimbabwe', *Gov.uk,* 16 February 2018, https://www.gov.uk/government/publications/financial-sanctions-zimbabwe; 'U.S. Relations with Zimbabwe', *U.S. Department of State*, 20 July 2018, https://www.state.gov/r/pa/ei/bgn/5479.htm.

25 'Chindori Report', http://petergodwin.com/wp-content/uploads/2013/06/Chininga-Parliament-Report-on-Marange-Diamond-Mining-June-2013.pdf (last accessed 14 December 2018).

26 This is corroborated in research conducted by the Centre for Natural Resource Governance Centre, 'Marange Relocations Lead to New Poverty', https://www.swradioafrica.com/Documents/Marange%20relocations%20lead%20to%20new%20poverty.pdf (last accessed 20 November 2019).

27 'Hope on the Horizon for Zimbabwe's Diamond Communities', <http://www.thezimbabwean.co/2017/08/hope-horizon-zimbabwes-diamond-communities/ (last accessed 26 January 2018).

28 Personal interview with Mrs Lucia Kayiboni, 5 February 2014.

29 The Shona are a Bantu ethnic group native to Zimbabwe and neighbouring countries. The Kayiboni family belongs to the Manyika tribe, which is a Shona tribe.

30 Personal interview with Mr Phillimon Jowani Kayiboni, 5 February 2014.

31 Constitution of Zimbabwe (2013).

32 Section 3 MMAZ.

33 Section of the Precious Stones Act.

34 T. Masiya, Y. D. Davids, S. Y. Ntola and N. Bohler-Muller, 'Zimbabwe's Minerals Amendment Bill (2015): Enhancing Natural Resource Governance?' Human Science Research Council, Policy Brief, March 2018.

35 Section 2 of the Mines and Minerals Act.

36 Selina Kudzai Zhuwarra, 'An Assessment of the Impact of Zimbabwe's Mining Policy, Legislative and Institutional Framework on Acquisition and Oversight of Diamond Mining Rights', *University Van Pretoria Faculty of Law Dissertation,* January 2017, https://repository.up.ac.za/bitstream/handle/2263/60116/Zhuwarara_Assessment_2017.pdf?sequence=1.

37 'An Analysis of Zimbabwe's Diamond Policy', *Centre for Natural Resource Governance*, http://www.eisourcebook.org/cms/Zimbabwe%20Diamond%20Policy%20Analysis%20-%20Centre%20for%20Natural%20Resource%20Governance.pdf (last accessed 18 December 2018).

38 'Poverty Assessment Study Survey (PASS)', *Zimbabwe National Statistics Agency*, http://www.zimstat.co.zw/sites/default/files/img/publications/Population/National_Report.pdf; 'Social Aspects of Sustainable Development in Zimbabwe', April 1997,

http://www.un.org/esa/agenda21/natlinfo/countr/zimbabwe/social.html (this information was provided by the Government of Zimbabwe to the Fifth Session of the United Nations Commission on Sustainable Development).

39 CNRG report.

40 Ibid.

41 Ibid.

42 See Rumbidzai Mutahwa, 'The Effects of Diamond Mining on the People of Bocha: A Case Study Of Chiadzwa from 2009–2016', *Midlands State University Faculty of Social Sciences Dissertation*, June 2016, http://ir.msu.ac.zw:8080/jspui/bitstream/11408/2707/1/RUMBIDZAI%20MUTAHWA.pdf.

43 See introductory note to Principle 31.

44 http://www.ohchr.org/Documents/Issues/Business/DomesticLawRemedies/A_HRC_32_19_AEV.pdf (accessed 8 February 2017).

45 UNGP Guiding Principle 22.

46 UNGP Principle 31(h).

47 A. Prasad, 'Cultural Relativism in Human Rights Discourse', https://doi.org/10.1080/10402650701681236 (last accessed 20 November 2019).

48 Ibid.

Chapter 6

MÁXIMA ACUÑA: THE STORY OF HOW A BUSINESS IMPACTED HUMAN RIGHTS DEFENDERS

Marianne Bertrand and Ariadna Tovar

Máxima Acuña is a Peruvian campesina ('female peasant farmer'). She is also a human rights defender. Specifically, she is part of a social movement defending and promoting human rights in the context of the Conga mining project to be developed in the Cajamarca region of northern Peru. The Conga mining project first belonged to Minas Conga Ltd, but was purchased in 2001 by Minera Yanacocha Ltd ('Yanacocha'). Yanacocha is a joint venture gold company founded in 1992 in Peru. It operates another mine in the region, also called Yanacocha, which is known to be the largest gold mine in South America. Yanacocha is majority owned by Newmont Mining Corporation ('Newmont'), a US-based company founded in 1921. Since 2011, Máxima Acuña, her husband Jaime Chaupe and their children have been involved in a legal dispute with Yanacocha regarding a parcel of land in an area known as Tragadero Grande, where she lives. Amnesty International has been in close contact with and has campaigned for Máxima Acuña since 2013.

This chapter aims to show, through Máxima's story, areas in which natural resource extraction projects may generate human rights risks, especially with respect to human rights defenders. The chapter makes recommendations to both governments and businesses on the basis of its findings. It does not pretend to determine who has the right to property or the possession of the land in dispute in the case under review, as this is a matter for Peru's judicial system. As of March 2018, the time of the writing of this chapter, the decision around the property of the portion of land was still pending.

The authors would like to thank the following people: Arjun Chaudhuri, Rodrigo Da Costa Sales Gabriela Quijano, Daniel Joloy, Maggie Maloney and Malavika Vartak. The information provided for this chapter was verified as of March 2018.

In October 2016 and March 2017, Amnesty International carried out several missions to Lima and Cajamarca in order to conduct interviews with civil society, government officials and Yanacocha representatives, as part of the organization's work in monitoring the situation of human rights defenders across the region. In writing this chapter, Amnesty International also took into account the conclusions published in September 2016 by an independent fact-finding mission commissioned by Newmont and conducted under the auspices of the organization RESOLVE.[1] In March 2018, Amnesty provided Newmont and Yanacocha with an early draft of the present chapter and took their comments into account in preparing the final version.

This document also takes into account the United Nations Working Group on Business and Human Rights' visit to Peru, which took place between 10 and 19 July 2017 and aimed to review efforts to implement the United Nations Guiding Principles on Business and Human Rights (UNGPs)[2] in the country.[3] Máxima Acuña's case was mentioned in the statement published at the end of this visit recognizing the 'steps taken by the company to establish an independent fact-finding mission about this land dispute and [encouraging] the company to learn from these findings for their current and future business activities'.[4] The Working Group observed a need for investment to be balanced with respect for and the protection of human rights in the pursuit of sustainable development, given a growing awareness of the human rights impact of certain natural resource extraction projects. The Working Group found that mining operations had been associated with conflicts over land and concerns about land acquisition through coercion or deception.

The structure of this chapter is as follows. First, Máxima's story is described, as closely as possible to how she tells it. Second, we will analyse Máxima Acuña's case to examine four different impacts that natural resource exploration and extraction projects have on human rights defenders. Finally, the paper makes recommendations to the state and businesses in Peru aimed at creating an enabling environment in which human rights defenders can work effectively.

Máxima Acuña's Case: A Campesino Struggle in Peru

The story of Máxima Acuña illustrates the different forms in which campesinos are targeted for defending human rights associated with the land,[5] territory[6] and a healthy environment.[7] These attacks include stigmatization, smear campaigns, threats, intimidation and unfair criminal prosecution, among others.

Máxima Acuña and her husband Jaime Chaupe live in Cajamarca, in the high Andes region of northern Peru on a parcel of land in an area known as Tragadero Grande. Tragadero Grande is located within the footprint of the Conga mining project, operated by the Yanacocha mining company.

Máxima and Jaime are part of the Sorochuco Campesino Community. In Peru, campesino communities are protected by specific legislation that recognizes communal property as pertaining to such communities.[8] Members of these communities collectively own the land upon which they live and work. Individual community members can purchase 'possessory rights'[9] from the community, that is, the right to live upon and cultivate specific plots of communal land. For the community to sell its ownership of the land, the decision must be taken by a qualified majority of its members.

Since 2011, the Chaupe-Acuña family and Yanacocha have been involved in a legal dispute regarding who owns rights over the portion of land known as Tragadero Grande. The protracted dispute has included several judicial complaints, including a seven-year long criminal case against Máxima and members of her family for *usurpación* ('land invasion'), of which the family was recently acquitted.[10] Two civil suits which seek to determine who has rights over the area in dispute are pending before the courts, leaving Máxima and her family in a state of anxiety and uncertainty.

This legal dispute has taken place in a context of heightened social opposition to the Conga mining project. Since 2004, Cajamarca has been the scene of strong social mobilization that aims to defend and protect the environment, the water and the very survival of campesino communities against the possible negative consequences of mining activities in the region.

Communities have opposed the Yanacocha gold mine and the company's intention to expand its activities as part of the Conga mining project. One of the main concerns of the local population is the potential pollution of the environment and the water.[11] According to interviews carried out by Amnesty International in 2016 and 2017, those opposed to the Conga mining project fear that the project will be located on wetlands, the origin of several sources of water for their communities.[12] They are also concerned that the project will lead to the contamination of several rivers with metals and chemicals, and that the Perol, Mala, Azul and Chica lakes will be utilized as part of the mining activities, potentially leading to their pollution and thus limiting their availability to the population as a water source. Communities rely on these water sources and lakes for agriculture, the breeding of livestock, the farming of fish and domestic uses.[13] Yanacocha has recognized that if the Conga project goes ahead, the aforementioned lakes will be drained.[14] Peru's Ministry of Environment has also pointed out that the project would 'significantly and irreversibly transform the water sources and lead to the disappearance of several ecosystems'.[15] Those opposing the project have additionally claimed that campesino communities have not been properly consulted with respect to the implementation of the project.[16]

The authorities have responded to social mobilization in a harsh way. People reported to Amnesty International that police used tear gas, fired bullets and arbitrarily arrested persons during massive demonstrations, sit-ins and encampments beside the aforementioned lakes that took place from 2011 to 2013 in opposition to the Conga mining project. Those interviewed also pointed out that confrontations between the police and certain demonstrators took place and that material damages were sustained, such as the burning of project offices. In 2011, three men who participated in a demonstration suffered serious injuries which they allege were a result of action taken by police. They eventually filed a criminal complaint against members of the Directorate of Special Operations (*Dirección de Operaciones Especiales* – DINOES, a police body) for excessive use of force.[17] On 4 December 2011, Peruvian authorities declared a 60-day state of emergency that suspended constitutional guarantees in relation to the rights to liberty, freedom of peaceful assembly and movement.[18] In July 2012, the government again declared a state of emergency which lasted for 30 days after five people were killed during another round of demonstrations.[19] Families of people killed filed a complaint before the Inter-American System of Human Rights denouncing the lack of genuine investigation into these killings.

On 5 May 2014, the Inter-American Commission on Human Rights granted precautionary measures to 46 social leaders and human rights defenders, including Máxima Acuña, ordering the state to implement measures to protect their lives and physical integrity.[20] The precautionary measures were granted based on allegations of harassment, intimidation and attacks suffered by these leaders. Their opposition to Yanacocha's expansion plans has placed Máxima Acuña and many others in the region at risk of victimization. Amnesty International has called on authorities on multiple occasions to ensure that she and her family are effectively protected.[21]

In the case of Máxima Acuña, there is a dispute regarding who has rights to the land upon which she and her family live. According to Máxima and Jaime, they purchased possessory rights over the parcel of communal land in Tragadero Grande in 1994 from Jaime's father's family and have lived there ever since. As a part of the Sorochuco campesino community, Máxima and Jaime also consider themselves to hold ownership of the land in question. In contrast, Yanacocha's representatives told Amnesty International that the company purchased the respective land in 2001 as a part of a larger land acquisition and has exercised possession since.

In 2015, Newmont commissioned a fact-finding investigation conducted under the auspices of RESOLVE.[22] The results of the investigation showed that the underlying sale at issue was poorly documented and, as a result, had contradictory information. Specifically, the investigation showed that Minas Conga, a now-defunct corporation, acquired Tragadero Grande in 1995 and 1996 when it purchased two larger parcels of communal land from the Sorochuco campesino community. According to RESOLVE, the process by which Minas Conga acquired the land was reasonable and complied with relevant legal and customary requirements. Minas Conga had legally negotiated the sale of the property with the community and followed the customary requirements to secure possession by negotiating with individual possessors.

However, the mission also observed that the Chaupe-Acuña family was in possession of a 'transfer domain of possession' document dating back to 1994. They themselves had not negotiated with Minas Congas regarding the possession of land. It was another individual from the Sorochuco campesino community who negotiated the sale in 1996. The fact-finding mission therefore concluded that information regarding the sale of possessory rights of the parcel of land to Minas Conga was contradictory and incomplete. Later, in 2001, these titles were transferred to Yanacocha when it acquired the assets of Minas Conga. In 2010, following exploration and project design, Yanacocha obtained the relevant permits to begin extracting gold there.

In 2011, and later in 2015 and 2016, Yanacocha security personnel carried out several 'defence of possession' actions against Máxima and her family. 'Defence of possession' is a legal mechanism contained in Peru's civil code that allows those who consider that someone has invaded their property to, within a specified time period, use force to repel the invasion. While Newmont sees these actions as lawful measures aimed at protecting their business interests, the family considers them to be attacks, sanctioned by authorities, which threaten their human rights.

Rights at Risk: The Impact of Business upon Human Rights Defenders

Máxima's story highlights several risks for human rights defenders in the context of natural resource exploration and extraction projects. In this particular case, Amnesty International has identified the following risks: (1) a lack of effective grievance mechanisms to resolve disputes between community members and the company responsible for the project (at least at the beginning of the dispute); (2) the unnecessary use of criminal proceedings to settle civil disputes; (3) the use of police forces to protect private interests, leading to the imposition of restrictions on the right to peaceful assembly which go beyond those permissible under international human rights law; and (4) the stigmatization of human rights defenders and the resultant effect on their capacity to defend human rights.

Lack of effective grievance mechanisms at the beginning of the dispute

The dispute between Máxima Acuña and Yanacocha about the rights over Tragadero Grande began around the late months of 2010 and the beginning of 2011. At the beginning of the dispute, Máxima and her family did not have access to effective grievance mechanisms.

According to Máxima and Jaime, after learning about Yanacocha's planned presence in Tragadero Grande, they visited Yanacocha's offices in Cajamarca on two separate occasions, at the end of 2010 and at the beginning of 2011, to ask for an explanation regarding the circumstances of what was happening. On the first occasion, a receptionist told Jaime that nobody was available in the office to talk to him. On the second occasion, Máxima and her eldest daughter, Isidora, had a conversation with two people. These individuals reviewed the documents that Máxima presented, which included the certificate of possession, and referred the two women to a company engineer. According to Máxima, the engineer told them that Jaime's father had sold the land to the company and Tragadero Grande was therefore now Yanacocha's property. He told them he would call them but did not proceed to do so. In October 2016, when Amnesty International asked a Yanacocha representative about Máxima's claim that she had visited their offices to try to solve the dispute, he said that he could not confirm that the family had ever tried to contact Yanacocha representatives prior to 2011, but neither would he deny the family's claim that such attempts had been made.[23] According to Newmont, prior to this date, Yanacocha has no record of any attempt to engage the company, despite the fact that the company maintains records of all complaints and requests for information at its offices.[24]

In May 2011, the company exercised, for the first time, the 'defence of possession' procedure, a legal mechanism contained in Peru's civil code. This mechanism allows those who consider that someone has invaded their property to, within a specified time period, use force to repel the invasion. This can be done without the need to involve state institutions and without a judicial order.[25] Although legal in Peru, the 'defence of possession' procedure is problematic as, on some occasions, it can result in forced evictions.[26] The civil code does not establish any safeguards in line with international human rights standards, particularly with regard to the obligation of the state to protect the right to adequate housing against third-party interference.[27] In August of the same year, the family suffered a further eviction attempt.[28]

Following the company's use of the 'defence of possession' mechanism in May 2011, Jaime filed a criminal complaint for land invasion (*usurpación*)[29] against Yanacocha. This was dismissed several months later by the Office of the Attorney General.[30] This was the first of a series of criminal complaints filed by the Acuña-Chaupe family for land invasion. While Jaime's initial complaint was dismissed, a complaint filed by Yanacocha was admitted and gave rise to a seven-year criminal case against Máxima Acuña and three other members of her family.[31]

On 20 February 2017, the Office of the Attorney General opened an investigation to determine whether another 'defence of possession' action undertaken on 4 October 2016 violated the rights of Máxima Acuña and Jaime Chaupe. On 8 November 2017, Celendín's criminal judge closed this investigation at the petition of the Office of the Attorney General. A subsequent appeal of the decision filed by Máxima Acuña and her family was rejected on 20 November 2017.

The RESOLVE fact-finding mission observed that, according to Yanacocha, the 'defence of possession' actions included eviction attempts and the removal of crops and constructions. It also points out that they occurred 'without an opportunity for the family to enter into dialogue with Yanacocha regarding their ownership claims. The company did not attempt to open dialogue with the family until 2015'.[32] Indeed the mission concluded that as of September 2016, the company had not at any moment sought to identify and understand the root causes of the Tragadero Grande Conflict and that it had not adopted a systematic approach to assessing and mitigating human rights risks.

In an interview with Amnesty International,[33] a Yanacocha representative assured Amnesty that a risk assessment was carried out before every 'defence of possession' action, that the attorney general's office was informed prior to each such event and that security personnel participating in these actions were fully trained in human rights standards and the Voluntary Principles on Security and Human Rights.[34] The representative described to Amnesty International the internal procedures the company has in place to address complaints of human rights abuses allegedly committed by Yanacocha personnel. Regarding land conflicts, the representative affirmed that once the company identifies a conflict, they first send a team to initiate dialogue with those living on the disputed land in order to attempt to resolve the problem.

Additionally, according to RESOLVE, to file complaints relating to land acquisition for the Yanacocha mine and the Conga Project, local communities have used the Compliance Adviser Ombudsman, a non-judicial grievance mechanism, incorporated into the International Finance Corporation's Environmental and Social Performance Standards. Newmont has applied these standards since their publication.[35] RESOLVE also points out that 'Newmont's current standards emphasize the identification of all stakeholders with socio-eco or legal interest, comprehensive record keeping and consultation and negotiation with project affected people'.[36]

Newmont representatives told Amnesty International that since 2010, Newmont and Yanacocha have taken measures in order to improve the complaint and grievance mechanisms they use globally. According to Newmont's April 2017 Guide to Respecting Human Rights, there are three mechanisms by which issues related to human rights can be raised, two of which are available to external stakeholders. These are the 'complaints and grievances (C&G) mechanism and registers (an operational-level mechanism), which are required at all sites, that aim to address external stakeholder concerns in a timely and effective manner to avoid conflict and build trust'. And 'the Ethics Solutions Tool – a confidential channel for workers and external stakeholders to report any concern about compliance with [their] Code of Conduct, including potential human rights issues'.[37]

In addition, the Human Rights Standard of January 2015 provides that 'sites shall develop community complaint and/or grievance mechanisms consistent with the UN Guiding Principles on Business and Human Rights'.[38]

According to RESOLVE, Yanacocha has a mechanism in place to address grievances and human rights complaints that includes four steps (investigation, the suspension of any company activity allegedly involved, a third-party investigation and implementation of action to address the findings). However, in the case of Máxima Acuña, 'the company failed to self-employ this mechanism to systematically record allegations of human rights violations which, according to the procedural requirements of the mechanism, would have triggered an early, internal investigation'.[39]

At the beginning of the dispute, the company does not appear to have effectively applied a grievance mechanism by which the land dispute could be examined and resolved in an amicable manner. This situation and the measures taken by Newmont and Yanacocha, throughout the years, highlight the importance of continuously assessing and improving mechanisms aimed at the resolution of controversies, particularly those aimed at addressing complaints related to human rights.

Use of the criminal justice system as a means of settling land disputes

The struggle between Máxima Acuña and Yanacocha highlights a common attack that human rights defenders face: the misuse of the criminal justice system through baseless criminal proceeding to silence their campaigns on human rights. Yanacocha made the decision to pursue a criminal case against Máxima and her family for land invasion, rather than attempting to resolve the land rights dispute through a civil action. The selection of a criminal prosecution approach presented a risk to Máxima's right to liberty and security, while failing to answer the issue regarding ownership and possession of the land, which negatively impacted the lives of Máxima and her family.

In August 2011, Yanacocha filed a criminal complaint for land invasion (*usurpación*) against Máxima Acuña, her husband Jaime Chaupe, her daughter Isidora and her son-in-law Elías Rodríguez. The public prosecutor filed charges based on allegations that Máxima and her family had used violence and threats to evict the Yanacocha mining company from the parcel of land in Tragadero Grande.

Amnesty International has had access to the court file containing the criminal charges brought against the defender and members of her family and has concluded that the prosecutor presented no evidence to support the charge and allegation that Máxima and her family would have used violence and threats when entering the plot of land.[40]

In 2012, the family was declared guilty but in 2013 a higher court declared void the judicial decision on appeal. In August 2014, a new procedure took place and a judge again declared the family guilty. In December of the same year, however, a higher court acquitted the family. Yanacocha subsequently filed a *casación* before the Supreme Court – a special appeal of the decision. In May 2017, the Supreme Court finally put an end to the case, ruling in favour of the family.

After several years of proceedings, Máxima and her family are exhausted. They consider the criminal proceedings as an attack from authorities to try to silence them by wearing them down. They never understood why the initial complaint for land invasion they filed against Yanacocha was closed at the very beginning of the investigation while the complaint filed against them continued for several years and why even the highest court in Peru, the Supreme Court, had to study the case to declare something that was very clear to them since the beginning – that they are not criminals.

When Amnesty International asked Yanacocha representatives why criminal charges were pursued instead of a civil suit, they answered that it seemed to be the right strategy in response to the criminal complaint filed by the family. They also pointed out that criminal proceedings in Peru are resolved more quickly than civil proceedings, and that offences can be investigated *ex officio*, meaning that once the Public Prosecutor's Office has found evidence of the commission of a criminal offence, investigations can continue regardless of whether or not the complainant wishes to proceed. In Máxima's case, however, company representatives were very active during the criminal proceedings and employed significant legal resources to continue with the case, including during the extraordinary appeal before the Supreme Court of Justice. In 2015, after the family was first acquitted of the criminal offence of *usurpación*, the company initiated two civil cases which sought to define who held rights over two portions of the parcel of land in dispute.[41] One related to the portion over which 'defence of possession' actions had been exercised in 2011. The other related to a portion of land that Yanacocha claimed the family had only begun to use recently, and that had consequently originated a series of 'defence of possession' actions from 2015.

The use of police forces to protect private interests

In 2013 and 2014, Máxima Acuña and her family reported several acts of harassment and intimidation allegedly perpetrated by members of the police.[42] Paradoxically, this is the same institution responsible for providing protection to Máxima and her family under the precautionary measures granted by the Inter-American Commission on Human Rights in 2014. Over this same period, the police were engaged in a specific contract with Yanacocha to provide security services.

While the RESOLVE fact-finding mission did not discover conclusive evidence suggesting that Yanacocha violated the human rights of the Chaupe-Acuña family, it did note that the family's human rights were placed at risk as a result of the company's failure to conduct adequate human rights due diligence and to consider the human rights dimensions of the case. This responsibility was shared with Peruvian authorities. The fact-finding mission identified that the company received more protection from police and private security than that which was afforded to the family.

Between 31 March 2011 and 30 September 2015, Yanacocha and Peru's National Police had in place a security agreement in which the company paid the police for the provision of security services. The agreement aimed to guarantee the normal functioning of Yanacocha's administrative and productive activities and sought to prevent the commission of crimes or other illegal acts perpetrated by people who might seek to harm the personnel, goods or facilities of the Yanacocha mining company. The agreement included prevention measures and patrolling by police in order to detect and neutralize any potential risks that might arise. On 9 October 2017, the Ministry of Interior approved the signing of a new security agreement between Yanacocha and the National Police of Peru.[43]

On 30 January 2013, police allegedly came to Máxima Acuña's home, beat her and her family and damaged their property. On 30 January 2014, she received a telephone call from an unidentified male warning her to 'get out of the property or you'll die'. Shortly after the call, she reported that two police officers approached her and told her to stop farming the land as it did not belong to her. According to Máxima, the police came back to her property on 4 February to intimidate her again. Between 2011 and 2015, Yanacocha did not exercise 'defence of possession' actions, and these alleged incidents of police harassment do not appear to be linked to the company.

In 2015 and 2016, however, Yanacocha security personnel carried out several 'defence of possession' actions against Máxima and her family. As mentioned before, the perception of the different stakeholders involved in the dispute on this 'defence of possession' varies a lot: Newmont sees them as lawful measures while the family considers them attacks which threaten their human rights. Yanacocha uses a private security services provider that is required to implement the Voluntary Principles on Security and Human Rights. According to Newmont, security personnel are equipped with non-lethal equipment and have received training in human rights standards.[44] According to RESOLVE, Yanacocha 'indicates that it has defended possession with the protection of private security and in the presence of police who were individually contracted by the company to provide security services'. In addition, the fact-finding mission raises the concern that in one 'defence of possession' action, private security personnel were photographed using police equipment.[45] This created confusion about the role of state and non-state security providers.

Given the high levels of social tension and opposition to the mine, this type of arrangement between the police and the company has the potential to give rise to an actual or perceived serious conflict of interest. In a context in which those protesting against the company's operations have allegedly been killed as a result of action by the police, human rights defenders and community leaders mistrust the police, who they see as biased and working to protect corporate interests:

> How could the same police that attack me effectively protect me?
>
> –Máxima Acuña, Tragadero Grande, October 2016

Human rights defenders and community leaders interviewed in 2016 and 2017 by Amnesty International reported that they could not trust the police to protect the rights to freedom of expression and peaceful assembly of those who oppose the mining activities of Yanacocha given that the police were engaged in a specific contract with the company to provide security services. These security arrangements often lead to confusion among the general population, and among the police themselves, regarding the role and responsibilities of this state body and to whom the police are accountable. They also lead to mistrust and a perception of bias among local communities.[46]

Representatives of Peru's Ministry of Interior questioned by Amnesty on the matter in October 2016 stated that they would publish in January 2017 all agreements signed with private companies,[47] and that Peru would adhere to the Voluntary Principles on Security and Human Rights.[48] In addition, representatives of the regional police in Cajamarca assured Amnesty International that in the context of public demonstrations against mining projects, security is always provided to both protestors and the company and in the event that protestors damage property, police are required to file a report with the Public Prosecutor's Office.

However, police officers also expressed worrying opinions about the protestors that illustrate the potential for bias when policing demonstrations against private companies to which they are also providing security services.

> If there are 1000 people demonstrating I will be concerned. If there are 80, I can call for support. It is not necessary for 1000 people to come to verify the levels of water. So, what is their real motivation?
>
> –Police officer, Cajamarca, October 2016

Language is not innocuous: The stigmatization of human rights defenders

Yanacocha representatives have regularly accused Máxima of being a 'squatter'[49] despite the fact that the judicial decision relating to ownership of the land is still pending. These statements discredit Máxima, her image and reputation and undermine the legitimacy of her struggle at the national and community level.

Yanacocha representatives have also called into question the legitimacy and credibility of Grufides, the non-governmental organization that has provided legal support to Máxima and her family. On 20 September 2016, a Yanacocha representative declared during a television interview that 'the family systematically enters the other Yanacocha terrain, and we see that the advice of the NGO Grufides is behind that, looking to continuously invade Yanacocha property'. In the same interview, the television host also stated, 'Of course Grufides has claimed that they have been attacked and whatever else. This is a strategy, don't you think?' The Yanacocha representative answered, 'Obviously, a strategy of lies and the fabrication of the situation'.[50] This language was used despite the fact that neither the criminal nor the civil complaints had been resolved at the time. In this context, the use of this language equates to calling Máxima, her family and her lawyers 'criminals'.

Stigmatization has had negative effects on the reputation of Máxima Acuña. This has negatively affected her personal, familial and social lives, and those of her family, in addition to undermining the social fabric that surrounds and supports them. Máxima and other leaders have reported that they have been perceived as responsible for the loss of jobs and infrastructure (roads, health centres, etc.) in the Cajamarca region as a consequence of Yanacocha decision to freeze the Conga project in response to mobilization. They felt this has put them at a greater risk of attacks or retaliations by sectors which support the mining project.

Máxima has also reported that rumours have circulated in nearby communities about her using her struggle to enrich herself and her family. On the basis of these rumours, she has been called a 'crook' by certain people in the community. She has also faced accusations aimed at sowing distrust in the relationship with her husband, centred around her role as a leader, which does not conform to traditional gender roles assigned to women in the Peruvian Andes. For example, people have approached Jaime Chaupe to criticize Máxima, claiming that she is too vocal and travels too much while her husband, a Peruvian male, stays at home. Rumours surrounding Máxima's enrichment as a consequence of her struggle have generated distrust within the communities and even some sectors of the social mobilization against the Conga mining project.

In addition, even if some sectors of society see Máxima as a woman human rights defender, other sectors see her and her family simply as 'trouble makers'. The attribution of the label 'trouble maker' to people who defend human rights is common in Peru and in the Americas. Given Máxima Acuña's high profile, she is regarded as one of the most relevant representatives of those who are seen as 'agitators' and as a result her behaviour is judged to higher standards. Máxima has told Amnesty International that she is readily criticized for each statement she makes, trip she takes or interview she holds.

All these years of struggles and legal battles have affected the family deeply. Máxima, her husband and her children are exhausted. The legal proceedings have required the use of the family's scarce financial resources to attend hearings and prepare evidence, even though legal representation for the family is being provided *pro bono* by the local NGO Grufides.

Both stigmatization and the misuse of the criminal justice system against Máxima Acuña have had an impact on her health. She often suffers from exhaustion. She has told Amnesty International that the best way to protect her would be for things to go back to how they were before the beginning of her struggle with Yanacocha. Unfortunately, after seven years of struggle that now seems impossible. She and her family have suffered deeply and do not want to negotiate with a company which they perceive to be the root cause of their suffering and is unwilling to engage in real dialogue. Still, Máxima has told Amnesty International that she will continue to defend human rights in spite of the struggle with Yanacocha because of '[her] dignity, [her] love of the earth and work. Predominately [her] love for people of humble means, the youth and the future generations'.[51]

The protracted legal battles and the public use of denigrating language against Máxima and her family have pushed the parties further and further apart. Yanacocha representatives have told Amnesty International that they have attempted to approach the family to try and solve the dispute. Since 2015, Yanacocha has sent a number of communications to Máxima, her family and her lawyer to this end. However, Máxima does not consider these to be genuine approaches given that the company repeatedly sent people to negotiate who, in the defender's eyes, had been involved in what she considers to be harassment and who have used offensive language to undermine the legitimacy of her claims. Máxima has publicly declared that she is not in the process of negotiating with Yanacocha. According to Newmont, relations have improved over the last year and a resettlement offer has been made. However, this rapprochement was put to a hold by a recent civil claim in the United States.[52]

The stigmatization and criminalization of human rights defenders negatively impacts in a serious manner the social movements and organizations to which they belong. Such acts project a public image that human rights defenders are 'criminals' and undermine the legitimacy of the important work they do. They also consolidate a hostile environment in terms of the right to promote and defend human rights which, in turn, enables physical assaults against human rights defenders and even murder.

Lessons Learned: Moving towards a Safe and Enabling Environment for Human Rights Defenders

The case of Máxima Acuña, in the light of the UNGPs, presents several lessons for both the state and corporations in Peru to increase security for human rights defenders and create an enabling environment in which they can work. It is worth noting that Newmont formally recognized the UNGPs in its 2014 Sustainability and Stakeholder Engagement Policy and became the first mining company to adopt the UNGP Reporting Framework in 2015.[53] This commitment applies to Yanacocha of which Newmont is the majority shareholder.

Need for effective grievance mechanisms

During its visit to Peru, the UN Working Group on Business and Human Rights noted the high number of social protests surrounding foreign direct investment projects.[54] According to the Group, this suggests a failure of existing strategies to prevent and mitigate adverse human rights impacts. The UNGPs state,

> To enable business enterprises to assess their human rights impacts accurately, they should seek to understand the concerns of potentially affected stakeholders by consulting them directly [...] In situations where such consultation is not possible, business enterprises should consider reasonable alternatives such as consulting [...] human rights defenders and others from civil society.[55]

A first crucial step is the establishment of effective grievance mechanisms by the company. The UNGPs encourage companies to establish operational-level grievance mechanisms for those potentially impacted by their operations.[56] These mechanisms can help to identify and resolve problems early and before they escalate to major disputes. In order for these grievance mechanisms to be effective, the UNGPs state that they should follow certain core criteria.[57] Companies should at least provide information in a complete and comprehensible way to those who are trying to present a complaint.

In Máxima Acuña's case, it is clear that even if Yanacocha had a grievance procedure in place, this was not effective to deal with her claim. Máxima and Jaime claim that their initial first approaches to the company to raise concerns went unanswered. Instead, the company chose to deal with the problem by using the 'defence of possession' action and filing a criminal complaint against Máxima and some members of her family. This marked the beginning of a highly contentious relationship in which the possibility of genuine dialogue became increasingly remote. This case demonstrates the escalation of tension and the risk of causing or contributing to further human rights abuses that can derive from the absence of an effective, on-site grievance procedure capable of detecting and addressing community concerns early and in a human rights-compatible manner.

Newmont and Yanacocha have taken measures to improve their grievance mechanisms since 2010. This is a good practice that can contribute to prevent human right abuses and identify solutions to situations where human rights are at risk in the context of natural resource extraction projects.

Criminal proceedings are not the best way to resolve a dispute

Yanacocha's support for criminal proceedings, despite the existence of civil avenues, increased the lack of trust held by the family towards the company and created a negative image of them as criminals. It is however important to recognize the positive steps taken by Yanacocha's majority shareholder Newmont. The company established an independent fact-finding mission regarding the land dispute in the case of Máxima Acuña.[58] The study concluded that finding a pathway towards a solution had been delayed by a dominant legalistic orientation, a lack of willingness to gather information on the root cause of the situation and a preference for litigation over dialogue.

As part of their responsibility to respect human rights and to contribute towards a safe and enabling environment for human rights defenders, corporations should oppose or refrain from instigating or pursuing criminal proceedings that have the potential to negatively impact on the legitimate work of human rights defenders.

As the UNGPs indicate, states must ensure that the justice system 'is not prevented by corruption of the judicial process, that courts are independent of economic or political pressures from other state agents and from business actors, and that the legitimate and peaceful activities of human rights defenders are not obstructed'.[59]

Companies should avoid resorting to legal action as a means of harassing or intimidating human rights defenders or as a tactic to drain them of their usually scarce resources and should seek the least aggressive forms of dispute settlement to protect their interests. Yanacocha should reassess its decision to pursue criminal charges against Máxima Acuña and her family, with the financial, personal and social implications that the process and a potential jail term could have had on them. Instead, a civil claim or other means of dispute resolution should be considered.

Measures to ensure that police are and seem impartial are crucial

The UN Working group on Business and Human Rights drew attention to the police agreements with corporations that exist in Peru and through which police personnel are allowed to provide extraordinary police services to private and public companies in situations that may affect public order and citizen security.[60] The Working Group expresses that such a scheme creates confusion over the role of the National Police in protecting the population and reinforces a lack of trust in this institution. This was indeed one of the main problems documented by Amnesty International. In the case of Máxima Acuña, this was even more worrying since the police, the very same people who provided security services to the company, were also the main actors responsible for the implementation of the protection measures ordered by the Inter-American Commission.

When police provide security services to a company under a contract, international law provides that police must nevertheless and at all times fulfil their duty to defend the human rights of all people including those of protestors.[61] In view of the confusion and perception of bias expressed by human rights defenders towards police, the state of Peru and the company should take all measures necessary to ensure that the police are impartial, act as such and are perceived as such. In particular, they should ensure that the same individual police officers who are dedicated to providing security to the company do not participate in the surveillance of the protests or the protection of human rights defenders at risk and vice versa.

In addition, Peru should review the regulations that allow agreements between the National Police and private companies, to avoid bringing the impartiality of state bodies into question. The state should not sign these agreements when there are indications that they may put at risk the human rights of communities defending the rights to the territory, the environment and those linked to access to land.

Authorities and businesses must recognize publicly the important role played by human rights defenders

The use of stigmatizing language increased the risk faced by Máxima. Peruvian authorities and the company should refrain from using language that stigmatizes, violates, discredits or discriminates against human rights defenders, including words such as 'delinquent', 'anti-development', 'bullfighting', etc.

Instead, as a crucial step, authorities and the company should publicly recognize the important role that human rights defenders play in order to reverse the negative narratives that have been constructed against Máxima Acuña and other environmental human rights defenders.

Since 2015, Yanacocha has attempted to establish a dialogue with the family and has sent a number of communications to this end to Máxima, her family and her lawyer. However, by then the dispute had already escalated into a conflict. After years of hostile litigation, including criminal prosecution, police intimidation and the use of offensive language in public, it will take significant efforts on the part of the company to generate trust and to demonstrate a genuine intention to engage in dialogue.

States and corporations can learn important lessons from the story of Máxima Acuña and in the light of the UNGPs. At least four simple measures could have prevented the conflict to escalate. First, the company should have implemented effective grievance mechanisms. Second, it should have sought to settle the dispute through a civil claim or a less aggressive mechanism than criminal proceedings. Third, the company and the Peruvian state should have taken all measures necessary to ensure that the police were impartial, acted as such and were perceived as such. And finally, company and state officials should have avoided the use of stigmatizing language when referring to Máxima Acuña, her family and their lawyers.

It is imperative that states and companies protect, respect and create an enabling environment for human rights defenders. Those are the ones who speak out on behalf of entire communities and watch over their collective interest. In the current context of environmental crisis that our planet is facing, these people are often also at the forefront of the defence of the environment. Without their voices, we all lose.

Notes

1 RESOLVE is an organization that uses dispute resolution techniques in policymaking processes. RESOLVE, 'Tragadero Grande: Land, Human Rights, and International Standards in the Conflict between the Chaupe Family and Minera Yanacocha', *Report of the Independent Fact Finding Mission*, 28 September 2016, http://www.resolv.org/site-yiffm/final-report-english/.

2 John Ruggie, Report of the Special Representative of the Secretary-General on the issue of human rights and transnational corporations and other business enterprises, 'Guiding Principles on Business and Human Rights: Implementing the United Nations Protect, Respect and Remedy Framework', A/HRC/17/31, 21 March 2011, http://www.ohchr.org/Documents/Publications/GuidingPrinciplesBusinessHR_EN.pdf.

3 United Nations Working Group on Business and Human Rights, 'Statement at the End of Visit to Peru', July 2017, http://www.ohchr.org/EN/NewsEvents/Pages/DisplayNews.aspx?NewsID=21888&LangID=E.

4 Ibid.

5 Those campaigning for access to the land are working to protect a range of rights including the rights to food (Article 12 of the Additional Protocol to the American Convention on Human Rights in the Area of Economic, Social and Cultural Rights), adequate housing (Article 11 of the International Covenant on Economic, Social and Cultural Rights), health (Article 12 of the International Covenant on Economic, Social and Cultural Rights and Article 10 of the Additional Protocol to the American Convention on Human Rights in the Area of Economic, Social and Cultural Rights) and work (Article 6 of the International Covenant on Economic, Social and Cultural Rights and the Additional Protocol to the American Convention on Human Rights in the Area of Economic, Social and Cultural Rights).

6 The right to territory is based on Article 17 of the Universal Declaration of Human Rights; Article 1 of the International Covenant on Civil and Political Rights and of the International Covenant on Economic, Social and Cultural Rights; Articles 3, 10, 25 and 26 of the UN Declaration on the Rights of Indigenous Peoples; and International Labour (ILO) Convention 169 on Indigenous and Tribal Peoples.

7 The right to a healthy environment is set out in Article 12 of the International Covenant on Economic, Social and Cultural Rights, Article 29 of the UN Declaration on the Rights of Indigenous Peoples and Article 11 of the Additional Protocol to the American Convention on Human Rights in Area of Economic, Social and Cultural Rights.

8 General Law of Campesino Communities, Law n°24656, Peru, April 1987, http://extwprlegs1.fao.org/docs/pdf/per20093.pdf. This law recognizes the *campesino* communities as legal organizations that control defined territories to which they are linked by ancestral, social and cultural ties. The Peruvian constitution also recognizes the existence and authority of native and *campesino* communities. In Peru, the term 'native communities' refers to the indigenous communities in the Amazon. The term 'campesino communities' refers to the peasant farmer communities in the Andes. The *campesino* communities have their own identity and traditions. As such, they defend their recognition as indigenous communities and claim to have the rights stated in the 169 ILO Convention. Indeed, the constitution does not make any difference between the two kinds of communities.

9 The Peruvian Civil Code defines in its article 896 the possession as 'the de facto exercise of one or more powers inherent to property' and in its article 923 the property as 'the legal power to use, enjoy, dispose and claim a good'. 'Codigo Civil: Decreto Legilsativo No. 295', *Ministerio de Justicia y Derechos Humanos*, http://spij.minjus.gob.pe/notificacion/guias/CODIGO-CIVIL.pdf (last accessed 2 November 2018).

10 Amnesty International, 'Peru: Peruvian Authorities Put an End to the Criminalization of Defender Máxima Acuña', 3 May 2017, https://www.amnesty.org/en/latest/news/2017/05/peru-autoridades-peruanas-ponen-punto-final-a-la-criminalizacion-de-la-defensora-Máxima-acuna/.

11 Knight Piésold Consultores S.A., 'Proyecto Conga Estudio de Impacto Ambiental, Informe Final', prepared for Mineral Yanacocha S.R.L., 3–614 to 3–615, February 2013, http://www2.congreso.gob.pe/sicr/cendocbib/con4_uibd.nsf/8945402C7A86188B05257A39005AAFCF/$FILE/ProyectoConga.pdf.

12 Ibid. According to the Knight Piésold report, the project will affect the sources of the following rivers: Alto Chirimayo, Chailhuagón, Toromacho, Alto Jadibamba, Chugurmayo. The report also says that the lakes Chailhuagón, Perol, Azul, Mala and Cortada will be affected. The water of these lakes then goes to the Marañón River (a tributary of the Amazon River that flows into the Atlantic Ocean).

13 Knight Piésold Consultores S.A., 'Proyecto Conga Estudio de Impacto Ambiental, Informe Final', 3–751 to 3–757.

14 Interview with representatives of Minera Yanacocha, Cajamarca, 26 October 2016. See also Knight Piésold Consultores S.A., 'Proyecto Conga Estudio de Impacto Ambiental, Informe Final', prepared for Minera Yanacocha S.R.L., 4–11, 4–24, 4–25, 5–12 and 6–19 to 6–20, February 2010.

15 Ministerio del Ambiente del Perú, 'Comentarios al Estudio de Impacto Ambiental del proyecto CONGA aprobado en octubre 2010', Report n°001-2011, 4, 21 November 2011, http://www.justiciaviva.org.pe/webpanel/doc_int/doc19012012-111232.pdf.

16 IACHR, Res 9/2014, Precautionary Measure n°452-11 ('Lideres y lideresas de Comunidades Campesinas y Rondas Campesinas de Cajamarca respecto de la República de Perú'), 5 May 2014, https://www.oas.org/es/cidh/decisiones/pdf/2014/MC452-11-ES.pdf.

17 On December 2017, the Superior Court of Justice of Cajamarca ruled that Yanacocha should also be included in this case as a third party. See Sala Penal de Apelaciones de Cajamarca, Caso Elmer Eduardo Campos Alvarez y otros, 'Apelación de auto que declara infundada la solicitud de incorporación de la empresa minera Yanacocha SRL como de tercero civil responsable', Exp. 00090-2016-1-0601-SP-PE-01, Res. 23, 7 December 2017.

18 Decreto Supremo 093-2011-PCM, Peru, 4 December 2011, http://www2.congreso.gob.pe/sicr/cendocbib/con4_uibd.nsf/46DF806550A9514205257A3A007DD1FA/$FILE/2.-DS-093-2011.pdf.

19 Decreto Supremo 070-2012-PCM, Peru, 3 July 2012, http://www.pcm.gob.pe/normaslegales/2012/DS-070-2012-PCM.pdf.

20 IACHR, Res 9/2014, Precautionary Measure n°452-1.

21 See Urgent Actions published by Amnesty International between 2013 and 2017, last accessed on 1 February 2018:

- Peru: Family at risk of violence and forced eviction, AMR 46/004/2013, 18 July 2013, https://www.amnesty.org/en/documents/amr46/004/2013/en/.
- Peru: Further Information: Family receives threats and faces eviction: Máxima Acuña, AMR 46/004/2014, 5 February 2014, https://www.amnesty.org/en/documents/amr46/004/2014/en/.
- Peru: Further information: Family continues facing police harassment, AMR 46/0002/2015, 4 February 2015, https://www.amnesty.org/en/documents/amr46/0002/2015/en/.

- Peru: Further information: Family harassed by mining company personnel, AMR 46/3392/2016, 4 February 2016, https://www.amnesty.org/en/documents/amr46/3392/2016/en/.
- Peru: Further information: Family attacked by mining company personnel, AMR 46/4860/2016, 21 September 2016, https://www.amnesty.org/en/documents/amr46/4860/2016/en/.
- Peru: Human rights defender Máxima Acuña criminalized by unsubstantiated criminal prosecution for land invasion, AMR 46/5879/2017, 15 March 2017, https://www.amnesty.org/en/documents/amr46/5879/2017/en/.

22 RESOLVE, 'Tragadero Grande'.

23 Interview with the General Manager of Yanacocha, in Lima, 3 November 2016.

24 Email Exchange with the Vice President of the External Relations and Social Responsibility Department at Newmont, 2 March 2018.

25 Peruvian Civil Code. Art. 920, last accessed 1 February 2018, http://spij.minjus.gob.pe/notificacion/guias/CODIGO-CIVIL.pdf.

26 UN Committee on Economic, Social and Cultural Rights (CESCR), General Comment 7: 'The Right to Adequate Housing (Art. 11.1): Forced Evictions', E/1998/22, last accessed 1 February 2018, http://www.refworld.org/docid/47a70799d.html. The General Comment defines forced evictions as 'the permanent or temporary removal against their will of individuals, families and/or communities from the homes and/or land which they occupy, without the provision of, and access to, appropriate forms of legal or other protection'. Evictions are not prohibited under international law but they must been done in accordance with the following provisions: (1) all other possibilities for eviction have been studied in consultation with the people to be evicted; (2) the people affected have been consulted; (3) all affected persons have been notified in advance, within a reasonable and sufficient time; (4) information has been provided to all interested persons, within a reasonable period of time, about the planned eviction and, when applicable, about the purposes to which the land or housing will be allocated; (5) during the execution of the eviction, state authorities are present, especially when groups of people are evicted; (6) the persons who execute the eviction are duly identified; (7) they are not carried out in bad weather conditions or during the night, unless consent of the affected people; (8) there are effective resources for people evicted; (9) affected persons are offered, whenever possible, legal assistance to seek redress before the courts; (10) alternative housing, resettlement or access to productive land are offered, as appropriate, and; (11) the affected persons can have access to compensation.

27 Even though the Civil Code provides some limits to the defence of possession, these are so vague that they facilitate abuses: (1) defence of possession can be executed within 15 days after the moment in which the person exercising it says she/he is aware of the dispossession of the property. Thus, the definition of the period of time is left to the discretion of who will use it; (2) whoever exercises it must refrain from using 'means not justified by the circumstances'. The law does not define what these expressions means and, therefore, leaves it to the discretion of the person who uses it. It does not prohibit either the use of force and as a result, any individual could use force against another, without any control of the authorities; (3) it does not foresee the participation or compulsory observation of any authority during the exercise of the defence of possession and limits itself to establishing that the intervention of the police and the local authorities must guarantee the fulfilment of the defence of possession within the limits of the norm.

28 After 2011, 'defence of possession' continued. According to Yanacocha, 'defence of possession' actions over Tragadero Grande have been used more than 10 times since 2015 to destroy crops on a portion of land that was not used by Máxima's family back in 2011 and which is not covered by the civil complaint. See Yanacocha Communication Office, Public Statement, 'Yanacocha ejerció una vez más defensa posesoria en predio invadido recientemente por la familia Chaupe', 4 October 2016, http://www.yanacocha.com/yanacocha-ejercio-una-vez-mas-defensa-posesoria-en-predio-invadido-recientemente-por-la-familia-chaupe/.

29 The crime of 'usurpación' in Peru implied that the land invasion was carried out with violence and threats; see Criminal Penal Code, Peru, 1991, Art. 202-2, last accessed 2 February 2018, https://www.oas.org/juridico/mla/sp/per/sp_per_cod_pen.pdf.

30 Primera Fiscal Provincial Penal Corporativa de Celendín, Disposiciones 004-2001-1FPPC-CEL y 464-2011MP-TESP-CAJ, 11 August 2011.

31 Amnesty International, 'Peru: Human Rights Defender Máxima Acuña Criminalized by Unsubstantiated Criminal Prosecution for Land Invasion', AMR 46/5879/2017, 15 March 2017, https://www.amnesty.org/en/documents/amr46/5879/2017/en/.

32 RESOLVE, 'Tragadero Grande', 33.

33 Amnesty International interview with Javier Velarde, representative of Minera Yanacocha, during a joint visit to Tragadero Grande on October 2016.

34 Newmont became a member of the Voluntary Principles in 2002. The company participates in a multi-stakeholder group at the national level that pushes for the implementation of the principles in Peru and reports to conduct trainings sessions with employees and contractors each year as well as an annual workshop with several stakeholders. Established in 2000, the Voluntary Principles on Security and Human Rights are a set of principles designed to guide companies in maintaining the safety and security of their operations within an operating framework that encourages respect for human rights. 'Voluntary Principles on Security and Human Rights', last accessed 1 February 2018, http://www.voluntaryprinciples.org/.

35 The IFC's Environmental and Social Performance Standards are standards developed by the World Bank Group and define their client's responsibilities for managing their environmental and social risks. They include six performance standards, including regarding land resettlement and indigenous peoples. 'Performance Standards', *IFC World Bank Group*, last accessed 1 February 2018, www.ifc.org/performancestandards.

36 RESOLVE, 'Tragadero Grande', 16.

37 Newmont, Guide to Respecting Human Rights April 2017, last accessed 6 March 2018, https://www.newmont.com/sustainability/Human-Rights/default.aspx.

38 Ibid.

39 RESOLVE, 'Tragadero Grande', 35.

40 Ibid., 32.

41 According to Yanacocha representatives, the first procedure was initiated after the failed eviction of August 2011, since exercising another 'defence of possession' action would contravene the time limit allowed by law for such actions – 15 days. A civil suit consequently had to be used.

42 See Urgent Actions published by Amnesty International between 2013 and 2017, last accessed on 1 February 2018; "Peru: Family at Risk of Violence and Forced Eviction', AMR 46/004/2013, 18 July 2013, https://www.amnesty.org/en/documents/amr46/004/2013/en/; 'Peru: Further Information: Family Receives Threats and Faces Eviction: Máxima Acuña', AMR 46/004/2014, 5 February 2014,

https://www.amnesty.org/en/documents/amr46/004/2014/en/; 'Peru: Further Information: Family Continues Facing Police Harassment'.

43 Resolución Ministerial 1003-2017-IN, Peru, 9 October 2017.

44 RESOLVE, 'Tragadero Grande', 15.

45 Ibid., 33, 38.

46 Interviews with human rights defenders from Cajamarca carried out by Amnesty International in October 2016.

47 Indeed, agreements from 2017 have been published on the Internet but previous one can only been accessed through a formal request for access to information.

48 Voluntary Principles on Security and Human Rights, 2000, last accessed 1 February 2018, http://www.voluntaryprinciples.org/.

49 Media and press releases dated 29 April, 22 May, 22 July and 12 August 2015, and 2 February and 12 March 2016. See 'Máxima Acuña', *Speak Out 4 Defenders*, last accessed 30 October 2018, https://speakout4defenders.com/en/single/584612f9de7ed16d3aba187c.

50 'Jaime de Althaus sobre caso Máxima Acuña: "Es una estrategia de mentira" [VIDEO]', *Lamula.Pe*, last accessed 1 February 2018, https://redaccion.lamula.pe/2016/09/20/Máxima-acuna-yanacocha-jaime-de-althaus-canal-n-mentira/jorgepaucar/.

51 Interview with Máxima Acuña, Tragadero Grande, October 2016.

52 'Peruvian Subsistence Farmers Take U.S. Gold Mining Giant to Court', *Earth Rights International*, 19 September 2017, https://earthrights.org/media/peruvian-subsistence-farmers-take-u-s-gold-mining-giant-to-court/.

53 Newmont Sustainability Report, 2017, last accessed 29 October 2018, https://sustainabilityreport.newmont.com/2017/overview/un-guiding-principles-reporting-framework.

54 UN Working Group on Business and Human Rights, 'Statement at the End of Visit to Peru'.

55 Ruggie, 'Guiding Principles on Business and Human Rights', Principle 18

56 Ibid., Principle 22.

57 Ibid., Principle 31. According to the UNGPs, in order to ensure their effectiveness, non-judicial grievance mechanisms should be legitimate, accessible, predictable, equitable, transparent, rights-compatible, a source of continuous learning and based on engagement and dialogue.

58 RESOLVE, 'Tragadero Grande'.

59 UN Working Group on Business and Human Rights, 'Statement at the End of Visit to Peru'.

60 Ibid.

61 Interview with Máxima Acuña, October 2016.

Chapter 7

COMMUNITY INTERRUPTED, 'LIFE PROJECTS' DISRUPTED

CAJAMARCA, IBAGUÉ, AND THE LA COLOSA MINE IN COLOMBIA

Tara L. Van Ho with residents of Cajamarca, Ibague and surrounding areas

Introduction

> First of all, I was born in Cajamarca but I have lived all my life in Ibagué because my family, when I was a child, was forcefully displaced from Cajamarca during the political violence during the '40s and '50s in Colombia. I am a forestry engineer and I used to work for the Ministry of Tolima, and I have dedicated myself full-time for the last 9 years to defend Cajamarca in the case of the mining.[1]

'Jorge Enrique', not his real name,[2] sits across from me in a restaurant of his choosing with maps and newsletters. He is one of two leaders of Eccoterra, a local group opposed to the development of a mine in and around Cajamarca, Tolima Department, Colombia, by AngloGold Ashanti, the South African mining giant. There are several opposition groups in the towns surrounding the Tolima capital of Ibagué but the ones I am introduced to are Eccoterra and Comité Ambiental de Cajamarca.

That Jorge Enrique had been fighting for nine years to preserve a community he was displaced from as a child struck me. It reminded me of something

This research was undertaken while I served as a postdoctoral researcher at INTRALaw Centre, Aarhus University, and complied with Danish ethics standards. Financial support was provided by the Julie von Müllens Fond. Logistical support was provided by the non-governmental organization Dejusticia.

an older man had said to me the day before. A member of the Comité had almost joked when he said, 'It is no longer going to be said that time is gold, but that time is water.' The proposed mine was having a significant effect on the way local environmental and human rights defenders ('E-HRDs' or 'defenders') were spending their lives. The Comité member viewed both water and time as precious, but to protect the water they had to sacrifice their time.

I visited Ibagué in May 2016 to examine the impact of the intended La Colosa mine, whose trailings (mine waste) would reportedly flow from Cajamarca through Ibagué and into another village, Piedres. Literally translating to 'the Colossus mine', it was expected to be the largest gold mine in Latin America. The mine's name was not a pejorative chosen by the opposition; it was a branding choice by AngloGold Ashanti, the South African mining company that was given an exploration license for the area on which the mine was to sit. The name seems to highlight the disconnect between the company and the community over the promise of the mine. In anthropology, the notion of 'equivocation' is sometimes used to refer to an error in cultural translation that comes about when two individuals use the same word to express their own realities without realizing that they are actually discussing two different realities because each understands the word through their own worldview.[3] As Eduardo Viverios de Castro explains, 'An equivocation is not just a "failure to understand" [...] but a failure to understand that understandings are necessarily not the same, and that they are not related to imaginary ways of "seeing the world" but to the real worlds that are being seen.'[4] The name 'La Colosa' seems to be the embodiment of such equivocations: the company did not seem to understand that its approach to, and excitement over, the 'colossal' (gigantic, extraordinary, impressive, profitable) gold reserve would be deemed a threat by those who would be impacted by the 'colossal' (gigantic, encroaching, looming, land-intensive) mine. It is a disconnect that often appears in business and human rights stories: what is desirable for the company and its shareholders is the very thing deemed a threat by rights holders.

Like most cases in business and human rights, the impact of 'La Colosa' on Cajamarca and Ibagué is not a singular story. It is a collection of thousands of smaller stories whose common thread is the promise – or, for the E-HRDs, the threat – of that mine. When I arrived, I expected to learn about the impact the mine would have on land and water, but what struck me was how a community had been transformed by the threat of the mine. One of the more obvious impacts was the transformation of the lives of the E-HRDs. Grass-roots defenders must work to accumulate technical and legal knowledge that the company and state representatives, as well national or international E-HRDs, have gained through formal education and training experiences. 'So much of the information we have gathered up to date is thanks to friends we have and other professionals specializing' in relevant issues, one Comité member explained. 'However, if you talk about it like persons and people who do not have their technical knowledge, we are definitely far behind from actually accessing this information.' Another member added, 'What we actually know, and the real information' has come

> through trainings that have been held by the national university and others, who have actually talked to us in a very honest way about the social problems that these activities can bring into our community. It's been through [...] these trainings that we have actually felt properly empowered and encouraged to say no to this kind of mining activity, to spread this information with the locals and to realize and raise awareness of the fact that what is really valuable for them is the water they have.

For the Cajamarca defenders, there was an investment of time and effort to gain the necessary knowledge to understand and respond to the mine's impact on their lives. They needed to catch up to the knowledge of the company and the state in order to adequately counteract what they felt were false narratives. The timing of my visit perhaps highlighted these issues. In less than a year, Cajamarca would hold a referendum they believed would decide whether mining operations would be allowed in the territory of the village. The E-HRDs were busy trying to educate the local community, meaning they were engaged in the difficult task of 'knowledge transfer', learning what they could to effectively educate and persuade others.

This chapter relies on the narratives of E-HRDs in the Cajamarca-Ibagué area to consider how a state's failure to protect human rights, and a business's failure to respect human rights, transforms the lives of E-HRDs. In doing so, it questions a collective failure within the field of business and human rights – by states, businesses, NGOs and academia – to consider how these transformative impacts should be remedied. Divided into five sections, I first explain how I undertook the research along with ethical concerns raised by the process. Section 2 uses the words of the defenders to explain the lack of a consultation and the impact on human rights in Cajamarca and Ibagué, which leads to an examination in Section 4 of the impact of the mining project on the defenders, and consideration of how this impact should be remedied. Section 5 concludes by offering reflections on what can be learned from the Cajamarca-Ibagué experience.

Methodology, Ethics and the Definition of Human Rights

In the best of circumstances, undertaking field research and interviews raises 'practical, epistemological, ethical and existential 'troubles''[5]: securing informed consent and conducting the interviews requires considerations of power relations between the interviewer and the interviewee;[6] one needs to guard against 'feedback', meaning responses given because the interviewee believes these are the responses that are desired,[7] maintain a 'critical consciousness' that ensures and facilitates the voice of the interviewee is heard and understood,[8] and be conscious of both how the selection of interviewees can privilege certain voices or stories over others[9] and how differences in language and experiences can give rise to equivocations, discussed above.

The situation in Ibagué and the surrounding areas is not the best of circumstances and carries additional dangers. To hear the stories of the E-HRDs organized around the Cajamarca proposal, I used semi-structured individual and group interviews. Simultaneous translations were provided. For the group interviews, translations were confirmed through a second translator. I then engaged in discourse analysis to both compile the interviews into a coherent story and to assess the meaning of these stories for business and human rights.

Informed consent about the purpose of the interview and the use in academic publications was given both orally and in writing. The activists were then asked how they wished to be identified in subsequent publications. All who were interviewed agreed to have their full names used. They were local activists who were known and proud of the work they undertook. They knew of the dangers of speaking publicly; one of their colleagues and friends, Pedro César García Moreno, was killed in 2013. García Moreno's murder was believed to be linked to his anti-mining work.[10] For ethical reasons, I reminded them of the potential for retribution if I named them in this work and detailed the forms of potential retribution. They laughed and nodded their heads before confirming they wanted their names used. In better circumstances, I would have honoured their decision. But, Colombia generally, and Cajarmarca specifically, has been plagued by violence targeting E-HRDs. Following my visit, death threats were reportedly sent to several E-HRDs involved in the La Colosa mine resistance, including some I interviewed. Nationally, 2017 would become the 'deadliest year on record for Colombian human rights defenders'.[11] At a time when 'the general homicide rate has fallen by some 40 percent', violence against E-HRDs rose.[12] According to the United Nations, there were 441 attacks on E-HRDs resulting in 121 people killed in 2017 alone.[13] This represented double the number of E-HRDs killed in Colombia in 2016, 60, and almost three times as many as were killed in 2015, 41.[14] There were also 41 attempted killings of E-HRDs in 2017 as well as other attacks and threats.[15]

There are legitimate concerns that the state is not taking the threat to E-HRDs seriously. The current minister of defence, Luis Carlos Villegas, attributed the attacks to 'problems in their personal lives' rather than their work as E-HRDs.[16] The UN Special Rapporteur on the situation of human rights defenders, Michael Forst, found in December 2018 that 'human rights defenders in Colombia are operating in a coercive and unsafe environment. [...] Not only that, they are depicted by different sectors of society as guerrillas, "the internal enemy", "informants," or as being "anti-development".'[17]

Given the threats, and the ongoing disputes over the mine's future, and over Colombia's future as a mining hub, the ethical standards developed in advance of the project dictated that I independently re-evaluate whether to use the E-HRD's names. Consequently, when quoting individual E-HRD, I primarily refer only to their affiliation. The only exception to this is 'Jorge Enrique', who chose his own pseudonym. I chose to give him a name because of how frequently his narrative appears throughout this piece.

The unique purpose of this book raises other ethical concerns. This book is primarily intended to express the views of individuals and communities whose human rights were impacted by business activities. Given this focus, I have not sought a response from either the company or the state, although some public statements are used here. This carries several risks. First, this chapter only presents a part of the larger story of La Colosa. Second, at times those interviewed presented opinions, stories and disputed data as facts while the company or the state might disagree with these characterizations. This presents a methodological challenge that is not unique to this chapter: how to present first-person narration of perceptions that are disputed or may not be entirely factual. When using qualitative interviews in the social sciences, the subjective belief of facts is a legitimate point of inquiry even where the 'fact' is not objectively true.[18] Yet, as both the United Nations Working Group on Business and Human Rights and the UN Special Rapporteur on the Rights to Freedom of Peaceful Assembly and Association have separately noted, businesses are increasingly using so-called Strategic Lawsuits against Public Participation (SLAPPs), civil lawsuits aimed to silence critics.[19] Some of the Cajamarca E-HRDs had been threatened with such a lawsuit. This raised a second ethical dilemma: how much should I, a legal academic, use disputed assertions when those assertions could place vulnerable people at risk for legal action? I have attempted to address this through the phrasing of the chapter itself, but it has meant at times leaving aside some assertions by the E-HRDs, complicating the narrative further.

Despite the complexity and the potential disputes over some of the assertions, there is both academic and pragmatic value to allowing the words and stories of the affected individuals and communities to stand on their own. Anthropologically and sociologically, allowing individuals and communities to present their own perceptions of truth and knowledge without correction or condemnation can represent a value in and of itself. It allows us to observe why the anti-mining mobilization occurred, its components and its understanding of the situation. Sociolegally, the interviews provide a dataset for assessing the appropriateness and effectiveness of business and human rights standards in this case, so long as it is understood as a single dataset. Legally, the testimonies operate exactly as that: testimony to a factual situation that should be weighed and used to assess the adequacy of the law to address these claims. Pragmatically, accessing the stories of affected communities allows us to better understand the progress of business and human rights and whether current approaches meet the needs of human rights defenders.

In addition to ethical considerations inherent in using qualitative interviews, there are legitimate questions about how one defines human rights. Human rights are inherently interdisciplinary and can be understood morally, socially, politically, philosophically and domestically, internationally or a combination thereof. This chapter places the narrative within the context of Colombia's legal obligations. The state is a party to several international human rights treaties[20] and is bound by customary international human rights law obligations. In the area of business and human rights, Colombia and businesses operating in the state are expected to meet the obligations and responsibilities set out in the UN Guiding Principles on Business and Human Rights ('UNGP').[21] Sometimes, however, activists may consider human rights in other terms, invoking moral or domestic constitutional approaches. For scholars in business and human rights, it is important to both recognize and acknowledge when an individual or community feels their human rights have been violated while also objectively identifying whether this meets the legal criteria for state or business responsibility. In order to achieve this balance, I offer minimal reflections during the narration to clarify where the law sits in relation to an E-HRD's assertions.

The Conflict(s)

Jorge Enrique, the Eccoterra leader, wants me to understand the unique nature of Cajamarca and the threat the mine poses. This is early in the interview and unprompted by me:

> Unlike projects in other areas of Latin America, Cajamarca is a very special area because it is not a desert. It is full of inhabitants and it is dedicated to the agricultural industry. It is close to a capital city like Ibagué, for example. The main road that protects the capital of Bogota and the Pacific Coast goes through Cajamarca. The population is high and there are a lot of people in the farms.

Jorge Enrique is right that the proximity to a major city sets the Cajamarca mine apart from many other extractive projects. 'The property that the farmers get […] are small properties, which is why there are so many people there.' To develop a mine, the company 'needs the soil, so they must get the land from [the farmers'] hands. The farmers, they only know how to make agricultural activities so even if they have a payment for their lands, they don't have any place to go because they don't know how to do anything besides doing the agricultural activities'.

Land conflicts and Cajamarca

The imagery involved in Jorge Enrique's depiction of mining – the notion of taking land from a farmer's hands – is particularly striking in Colombia, where land inequality was a root cause of the state's ongoing armed conflicts.[22] Forced displacements and forced transfers of land were common practices in the Colombian conflict, aimed at benefiting the economic elite at the expense of peasants.[23] The day before I interviewed Jorge Enrique, I was told that there had been violence in the community related to the mine and some forced displacements in the 2000s, sometime around 2006. I have detailed elsewhere why the forceful displacements in the Colombian conflict generally constituted a breach of human rights and/or humanitarian law obligations, one that requires an effective remedy.[24] I asked Jorge Enrique if he could tell me a little more about the violence. AngloGold didn't show up in Cajamarca in 2006. He gives a date. On its website, the company notes that it began 'actively exploring in Colombia in 2002'.[25]

> 'In Cajamarca, there were actually two massacres between 2000 and 2005, with extrajudicial killings, extrajudicial detentions, mass detentions. The government, because of the presence of guerrillas there, declared the zone as a "red zone." It was a very complicated area because of this. I can't say that that happened because of the mine. I couldn't say that because I have no proof about it, but it's publicly known that companies used to "clean" the territories before a project starts.

By 'cleaning', Jorge Enrique means that companies would pay paramilitaries or guerrilla forces to remove peasants from land the company desired in an effort to secure the land for as little money as possible. Jorge Enrique later confirmed that the guerrillas in the region were those of FARC, the Revolutionary Armed Forces of Colombia, who in 2016 struck a controversial peace agreement with the Colombian government.[26] 'Because of the presence of these armed groups in the zone, it wouldn't be strange if [the company] would be involved. But I don't have any evidence about it. I wouldn't say it is because of the mine.'

It is necessary to reflect briefly on Jorge Enrique's language here. It is practiced language. He references the company's reports to support any direct assertions, while couching other potential accusations in language that evades the assignment of any legal responsibility to the company. It also sits in contrast to the more visceral language he used when discussing the more general issue of land transfers and expropriation. Jorge Enrique's response is not what one might expect from a Colombian forestry engineer. This should perhaps be expected. SLAPPs, the lawsuits the UN experts have recognized as a threat to E-HRDs, are intended to ensure critics understand that there is a price for their criticism.[27] Once a US phenomenon, SLAPPs have become a global corporate strategy.[28] Jorge Enrique indicated he was aware of the potential of a SLAPP suit, and it seemingly impacted the way he was speaking to me. SLAPPs represent another means by which an E-HRD's time, energy and resources are affected, and I wondered how much time Jorge Enrique had put into crafting his language so as to avoid such a lawsuit.

A failure to inform or consult

Later in the conversation, Jorge Enrique appears slightly more relaxed as he discusses the first interactions between the mining company and the community. 'The mining company doesn't like the opposition at all. That's why when they started the project, they came to the community with presents. I wonder, if mining would not harm communities […] why are they giving presents? My grandfather, who had liberal ideas, used to say that one shouldn't receive gifts from somebody that one doesn't know. That one should work for the things one has.' I ask about the kinds of presents the company gave. 'They gave, for example, paint to paint the schools, academic materials. They financially support the fiestas in Cajamarca. […] They gave us uniforms, and cups, and hats with the logo of AngloGold on their shoulders or on the cap. But if the mining is so good, why are they doing that? That's the question.' Later, he also explained that AngloGold had given money to the mayor to support infrastructural developments, such as the expansion of gas lines for heating homes. This seems to be an example of another anthropological equivocation: what Jorge Enrique understood as a deceptive practice would likely be, for AngloGold Ashanti, a form of corporate social responsibility and community or public relations.

However, Jorge Enrique might not have been reacting only to AngloGold's actions; he might have been implicitly reacting to the company's inactions as well. Neither the government nor seemingly the mining company disclosed the company's presence until 2007 when the government granted the company an exploration license. The members of the Comité Ambiental learned about the mine in different ways: one from a campus group, another from the Catholic

Church. One when former president Álvaro Uribe's administration sent out press releases in 2007 acknowledging the company had been in the area since 2003. By the time the company and the state were willing to acknowledge the activities in 2007, the community members were already organizing in response. As one member of the Comité Ambiental de Cajamarca explained,

> We came together with another NGO called Eccoterra. We have worked with Eccoterra and also created a collective called La Reversa [the Reverse]. [...] [But] it is important to note that the government has not made an official kind of statement to the local community to make them aware of the mining activity or the project that has been taking place in the region. We only started to witness government intervention [...] in or around 2011 and 2012 and that was a result of what was happening in the region. Before that, there was a public hearing that was held in 2008 in Cajamarca, however, the information shared by the government and the company was just about certain studies that had been done, like considering certain projects. However, the community itself had already received a lot of information about the real reasons behind the projects and the real reasons behind the studies that had been carried out in the region. We were especially aware of the good and the negative impacts that we were going to have in the region. It is actually not until three years ago that the mining company itself started to write and report to the local council in the region. But up until today there's actually not any detailed information about La Colosa.[29]

Much of the information that the community has now had been collected from other areas within Colombia. 'So to conclude, we could say that as a community we have not been informed about the activity properly.'

This position was affirmed by other activists in the area and seemingly by the company itself. AngloGold Ashanti's Felipe Marquez gave an interview in 2014 in which he reflected on a referendum in nearby Piedres, which also was in response to proposals associated with La Colosa. At the time of the interview and through the Cajamarca referendum, Marquez was vice president of sustainability, corporate affairs and general counsel. Following the Cajamarca referendum, Marquez was appointed senior vice president of sustainable development for AngloGold Ashanti globally and now serves as the country manager for Colombia. In that 2014 interview, Marquez argued, 'There were many mistakes from the company but the community hasn't helped in trying to have a more constructive dialogue.'[30] According to Marquez, the company's mistakes included not engaging local leaders early. 'All communities have leaders. Those leaders weren't taken into account' by the company 'and those leaders were the ones that started being a little bit afraid of the process. They are the ones that blocked the process, that pushed the community for a process of legitimate defence. When the process of public consultation started, there wasn't a way of actually having a real, constructive dialogue with the community. [...] That was the biggest problem, we didn't arrive with the correct information through the correct channels with the correct people.'[31]

I asked the Comité Ambiental if they had heard from the government since 2008, following the initial disclosure of the mine. One member explained,

> Most of the information is meant to be uploaded on the website of Ingeominas.[32] The state agency actually collapses most of the time because it is giving away so much land, Colombian land, that they have decided to give some of the duties to the national agency for environmental licenses. However, the problem with the website in this government institution is that the information is not accessible in a very easy way and at the same time it is not completely updated.

Providing information on a website is not sufficient for some of the Comité's members.

> Even though that information is uploaded by Ingeominas, I strongly believe that the government should have public servants [...] specifically to go to their local community and explain this information to [the community], letting them know what is happening and what the effects are and what the future looks like for them.

There is some legal support for this position, in both International Human Rights Law (IHRL) and in Colombia's domestic system. The UN Committee on Economic, Social and Cultural Rights (CESCR), the treaty body responsible for overseeing compliance with the International Covenant on Economic, Social and Cultural Rights, to which Colombia is a party, has found that the rights to health and water both include obligations on the state to provide individuals with accessible information and ensure public participation in decisions that are likely to impact the realization of those rights.[33] CESCR is clear that the obligation is more than simply providing information on a website. Instead, given the potential for mining to impact water use and health conditions in the area, the Colombian government should have provided an opportunity for 'genuine consultation with those affected', which would include 'timely and full disclosure of information' about the project, a means for legal recourse and 'legal assistance for obtaining legal remedies'.[34]

The Colombian Supreme Court has also recognized that, domestically, individuals have a right to genuine participation in decisions affecting them, particularly as a result of mining.[35] The court has found that the legislature has an obligation to ensure, and define the means by which, participation can occur.[36] The government's failure to substantially engage with the local community therefore breaches its international legal obligations and appears to breach the Colombian constitution.

Colombia's domestic mining laws and its international investment commitments suggest any consultation should have occurred before the grant of the exploration licence in 2006. There are generally two main types of licenses for mining; exploration and exploitation. A mining company will first secure a license from the state to explore an area. The exploration license already gives its holder the right to undertake drilling and other activities but only for the purpose of determining the existence of deposits and the environmental feasibility of exploiting those deposits. If a company receives an exploration license, it is expected to receive the exploitation license if deposits are located. The exploitation license gives the holder a right to develop the mine and make use of the minerals discovered there. Under the Colombian Mining Law of 2001, an exploration license contains 'a right of priority or preference' over other non-state actors to an exploitation agreement so long as the license holder meets the legal requirements.[37] It is not intended to convey a guaranteed right to exploit, but under international investment law, the license to explore is an investment with an expectation of a right to exploit, meaning the state must have a legitimate reason to denying the exploitation license. Impacts on the environment may be sufficient,[38] but local opposition, absent an established legal procedure, is unlikely to be an accepted reason to deny a license to exploit or to terminate an exploration or exploitation license once it is given.[39] This means that with the mere granting of an exploration license, the state is beginning to make decisions about the establishment of a mine and it is granting the company the right to undertake activities, including drilling, on the licensed area. The ICESCR obligation to ensure public participation in relevant decisions is therefore triggered with the application for and the processing of this license. At this stage, there may be very little concrete information to provide the community, but there will be information about the application, the company, what is known about potential deposits, the process that will take place, the expectations of the government and the relevant protections in place for the environment, health and the right to water. This information should have begun a dialogue with the community.

Whether informed communication and consultation is also an obligation on the company is still debated within business and human rights. The dominant position, found in the UNGP, is that businesses have a non-binding, social 'responsibility' to 'respect' human rights, meaning companies should refrain from interfering in the realization of the rights. To achieve this, businesses should undertake 'human rights due diligence', a process aimed at identifying actual and potential negative impacts on human rights holders.[40] Due diligence processes, by their nature, should include consultations and communications with affected communities for two reasons. First, a failure to exchange information with a community is likely to mean the business does not have sufficient information to identify actual or potential human rights impacts. Second, the

International Covenant on Civil and Political Rights, which Colombia is also a party to, protects the right to information as part of the right to freedom of expression.[41] For a company to respect the right to information, they must design processes that ensure access to relevant information by affected individuals and communities. The responsibility to respect the right to access is rendered meaningless if a company is the only one likely to know such information exists as the lack of information becomes cyclical: individuals lack information because they do not know such information exists and they do not know such information exists because they lack information. The only meaningful way to respect the right to information is to communicate with the community from the point that the exploration license is sought. This generally does not happen, however, in part because companies fear opposition. As AngloGold Ashanti learned, however, the failure to inform and consult may lead community members to look for that information from someone or somewhere else.

Regardless of the outcome of the consultation, the early communication of information about the mine's potential impact on the rights to health and water is the state's obligation. AngloGold Ashanti's Marquez claims his company's operations would not have harmed either the right to water or the right to health, but that the company was never given the opportunity to discuss the potential impacts because the community shut down the dialogue.[42] Marquez seemed to blame the community, at least in part, for this break down, but it seems the state's failure to meet its human rights obligations led to the disputes.

AngloGold's expectation that a consultation would have resulted in the mine's approval appears to be another example of an anthropological equivocation on the meaning and purpose of the consultation. There is, of course, an open question as to what would have happened had the government and the company engaged in an appropriate consultation with the local community. Marquez's belief that an appropriate dialogue could have occurred – an insistence that extends beyond the short quote above – seems to carry an expectation that the community would have eventually agreed with the company's assessment. For at least some of the members of the Comité Ambiental, the dialogue was largely unnecessary. One member stated that 'the main issue is that mining activity in the region is quite rough and what people in the region are actually looking for is the actual prohibition of mining activity in the region and in the world because it is a very harmful activity. Not dialogue'. In other words, the problem with the mine was not any particular threat but the general threat mining poses to the environment. Comité members who share this view do not seek assurance of the mine's safety because they do not believe such mining can ever be truly safe or good for the community or the world. For these members, the consultation was an opportunity to reject the mining while for AngloGold Ashanti, the consultation was for the purpose of securing their approval.

A threat to the right to a dignified life

For the Comité members, the threat posed is not only to their water and the environment. As one member stated,

> Extractivisim not only affects security and nature's biological cycles, but it also violates fundamental rights, such as the right to a dignified life. The right these communities have to their territory, to decide what effective way of production they may participate in.

For her, the mine represents a threat to the right to life. I do not ask her to define that right to life or to explicate the relationship between the breaches she outlined and the right to life. She sees a connection that is also palpable to others in the room: all rights are universal, interrelated and interdependent.

There is, again, a legal foundation to these assertions. The Inter-American Court of Human Rights has recognized that the right to life includes 'not only the right of every human being not to be deprived of his life arbitrarily, but also the right that he will not be prevented from having access to the conditions that guarantee a dignified existence'.[43] Colombia is also a party to the International Covenant on Civil and Political Rights, and in 2018, the UN Human Rights Committee, the treaty body responsible for monitoring compliance with that treaty, seemed to follow the Inter-American Court's approach to defining the right to life.[44] Recognizing that the right to life included the right to 'enjoy a life with dignity', the committee found that states must protect the right to life by, inter alia, 'address[ing] the general conditions in society that may give rise to direct threats to life or prevent individuals from enjoying their right to life with dignity. These general conditions may include [...] degradation of the environment.'[45] While the Human Rights Committee did not address extractive industries in particular, it did find that 'environmental degradation, climate change and unsustainable development constitute some of the most pressing and serious threats'[46] to the enjoyment of the right to life. What the Comité members understood in 2016 has now seemingly been confirmed by the UN Human Rights Committee in 2018: threats to environmental security can represent a violation of the right to life.

The Impact on Defenders

Organizing in resistance

The underlying threats from the mining project to the rights to education, healthcare, and life have not yet come to fruition. The project has not started, so the E-HRDs can only allege a human rights failure in regards to the right to state's obligation to consult them over the project and to ensure they remain informed about the project's plans. Yet, the impact of the mine was already palpable in 2016, altering how the defenders spent their time, energy and resources. One Comité member explained how communication with the state and the company came about:

> Many of these interactions with the state and society have come through activities organized with the environmental committee, such as the carnival march which seeks to express the opposition and mobilizes the whole society. […] We also use different sessions to raise awareness in the city, and we are now also aiming at utilizing popular consultation to settle the strong opposition to the project. By my personal profession – I am a journalist – I have also written different pieces in relation to the subject to raise awareness and to show the work that has been done. […] The carnival marches have actually been held every year, and some years it's been twice. [2016] is the eighth year in which we have celebrated this massive mobilization of civil society. The theme of the march […] it is just to break the stigma that has been built around any kind of protest in the country and it is also a carnival because it once portrays joy and promotes life as an opposition to what this project encourages, which would be the opposite to life and it would be the opposite to joy.

In explaining the lack of information coming from the state and the company, she explained how much time and energy had been sacrificed as a result of the state and company's failure to inform or consult. For eight years, the community had held annual or biannual marches to protest the mine. In doing so, they also opened up interactions with the state and company, effectively accomplishing what those with the obligation (the state) or the responsibility (the company) had failed to do. The organizational work had affected her professional responsibilities as a journalist, suggesting that the work was, at times, all-encompassing. Finally, she also mentioned 'different sessions', referring to the training and informational sessions, outreach events and organizational meetings the Comité had organized and that were mentioned by other activists. According to another Comité member,

> Interactions made with the state and society have been of different kinds, especially […] the interactions with society have been done through campaigns to raise awareness in local neighbourhoods and schools, companies and others. There has been a campaign through physical, scientific, spiritual and cultural issues as to why not to support this project in the region. In terms of interactions with the state, it's been done through political and social mobilization.

Another added to this list:

> We can observe the fact that, as others have said, there has been different social mobilizations. There have been different public [popular] actions, there have been different petitions and the community itself has been making use of a very diverse bunch of initiatives to show their opposition to the project. And in the meantime, we have also been part of the initiatives with the fifth commission in the Senate, and different public audiences, for example, in local councils. Some of the 11 local MPs say that they are not supportive of La Colosa. But to be honest, the government has not seemed to react accordingly to all these facts.

While one Comité member was able to rely on her professional expertise as a journalist to assist in the opposition work, other members had to develop new areas of expertise. How the defenders spoke and what they chose to speak about pointed to lives now engrained with legal nuance and technical knowledge that takes time and energy to develop. One of my translators, who asked that his name not be used, joked on the way to Ibagué that Colombia is a 'country where everyone is a lawyer'. With some of the defenders, this became more than a joke. Referring to three prominent investment arbitration cases filed or threatened against Colombia, one Comité member explained that 'the companies have chosen to go to arbitration tribunals, where the communities have been at a legal disadvantage because the state no longer seems to represent our interests'. At the time of the Cajamarca referendum, Canadian company Gran Colombia Gold was reportedly seeking US$700 million from the Colombian government as compensation for disruptions to its mining operations caused by local community opposition.[47] Gran Colombia Gold had filed a notice of arbitration under the Canada-Colombia Free Trade Agreement, which entered into force in 2011 and which has a chapter that protects investors from each state when they enter the territory of the other state. Among the common investment protections contained in the Free Trade Agreement are a prohibition on expropriation and a guarantee of fair and equitable treatment.[48] Those provisions have been used in previous investment disputes to hold states responsible when local opposition disrupts a planned investment.[49]

International investment law can be costly for states. Between 2013 and 2016, states spent on average US$5.1 million in costs to defend investment disputes.[50] Excluding the most costly claim, the median amount claimed by investors between 2013 and 2016 was US$196.4 million.[51] The singular case of Cajamarca and AngloGold Ashanti may not have posed a significant problem for Colombia, but the precedent posed a serious threat for the state.

If local opposition disrupted what investment tribunals consider the 'legitimate expectations' of investors to develop and profit from an investment, the state could end up owing investors compensation for the time and energy spent discovering reserves and for investments in infrastructure or equipment. Cajamarca's referendum therefore posed a serious risk to the state's interests, one that clearly arose from the state's failure to meet its human rights obligations and the E-HRDs' efforts to correct that error.

After explaining the investment law implications, the Comité member continued, 'Mining represents a great financial profit for international companies but it leaves damage and lasting environmental consequences to the Earth, to nature in local communities, and to Pachamama', using the indigenous word used throughout Latin America for 'Mother Earth', 'Source of Light' or 'Source of Life'.[52] It is difficult to accurately convey in English or to non-indigenous peoples the identity of Pachamama. For many in the Americas, Pachamama is an actual being – as real as an individual human – but one that inhabits Earth and Nature.[53] Increasingly in the Americas, Pachamama has been used legally and politically to recognize, claim or indicate that the Earth, or Nature, has rights and interests that should be protected.[54]

Investment law does not recognize the rights of Pachamama, or the sacred sense E-HRDs have that they are responsible for defending, and speaking on behalf of, Pachamama. Instead, investment law's focus is solely on the investment and interests of foreigners who enter a territory for the purpose of commercial investment. The investment arbitration tribunals enforce agreements that require the government, in the words of one defender, 'to pay for all the damage that has been done'. Colombians would likely have to compensate foreign companies if the state changed the regulations those companies were subjected to in order to protect human rights the state had previously failed to protect. As the Comité member spoke, it was clear she had developed an understanding of investment law that was stronger than an average lay person. Her language was of someone who had dedicated time to learning about the investment law because she felt a responsibility to do so. The investment regime, while not likely to address the Cajamarca referendum, was still likely to have a profound impact on it. The government had an incentive to oppose the referendum – and eventually to ignore it – because of its investment law commitments. As such, the Comité member – and others within the local E-HRD community – had developed specialized knowledge of an obscure area of international law. This represented an investment of their own time and energy to fight breaches of their human rights.

Then there was Eccoterra's Jorge Enrique, who had mastered the measured language of a lawyer or corporate spokesperson. He had relaxed his language as he discussed the 'presents' the company had given to the community, but he returned to more shrouded language when he considered the impact these presents had on elections.

> In the last two elections, we have heard here an expression that is "political mining strategy." It refers to, supposedly, the money to support campaigns of local authorities during the election from the mining company. We have heard examples from Argentina, Bolivia, and other countries. We don't have evidence about it, properly, here, but it wouldn't be strange if that happened in Cajamarca.

He was able to raise the potential problem without ever asserting that this was objective truth. It was not the natural language of an activist – or seemingly his own natural language – but suggested instead his fear of being quoted in a way that would leave him vulnerable to litigation.

To oppose the mine, Jorge Enrique had learned more than just how to couch an assertion appropriately. As we sat at the table, he rattled off numbers about soil density and water consumption, never relying on the papers in front of him. As a forestry engineer, this was not information that would naturally be included in his specialization. It was information accumulated over nine years of organization, nine years of responding to the threat and to the silence from the state and the corporation. I could not help but wonder what he could have done if he had not needed to spend that energy to protect the human rights of the community members.

Repeatedly, the E-HRDs expressed a toll their resistance and operation had taken on their time, money and energy. Their lives had been transformed because of their concern over the threat the mine posed to human rights and the environment. The opposition to the mine had also altered their relationships. Throughout the interviews, it was clear that tensions had arisen between individuals and groups as a result of differences in their approaches to the resistance. Some E-HRDs believed that opposition leaders should not run for office until the mining issue was settled; others felt that the only way to truly secure a ban on mining was to elect individuals who supported the opposition. While none of the leaders or members were particularly open about the problems, the tensions were revealed multiple times before the discussion changed quickly. Of course, the tensions were not only within the E-HRD community. The death threats made against some E-HRDs, which seemingly originated within the community, suggest broader fractures within the community between those interested in the mine's potential and those opposed to its realization.

The need to remedy the impact on the activists

For the business and human rights field, the experiences of the E-HRDs in Cajamarca and Ibagué raise important questions, which have not yet appeared in scholarship or reports from other stakeholders, about how we ensure adequate and appropriate remedies. The UNGP recognize an obligation on states, and a responsibility on businesses, to ensure remedies when businesses negatively impact human rights.[55] In public international law, a substantive remedy (reparation) should 'as far as possible, wipe out all the consequences of the illegal act and re-establish the situation which would, in all probability, have existed if that act had not been committed'.[56] Reparations should therefore aim to restore the individual to the position she would have enjoyed but for the violation, or to compensate them for losses where restitution is impossible.[57]

The discussion of remedies in business and human rights rarely addresses the substantive remedial obligations, instead focusing on the procedural aspect of remedies.[58] As a consequence, the field is missing sustained analysis of how courts understand and engage with substantive awards. One question raised by the experience in Ibagué and Cajamarca is the following: how do we redress the impact on E-HRDs, whose time, energy, resources and ultimately lives are altered because the state has failed to meet its human rights obligations, and a business operation now threatens individuals' human rights?

Some answers seemingly come from the Inter-American Court of Human Rights, which has recognized that the damage caused to a victim's 'life plan' or 'life project' (proyecto de vida) from an internationally wrongful (unlawful) act should be compensated.[59] According to that court, a life plan

> deals with the full self-actualisation of the person concerned and takes account of her calling in life, her particular circumstances, her potentialities, and her ambitions, thus permitting her to set for herself, in a reasonable manner, specific goals and to attain the goals.
>
> The concept of a 'life plan' is akin to the concept of personal fulfilment, which in turn is based on the options that an individual may have for leading his life and achieving the goal that he sets for himself. […] Those options, in themselves, have an important existential value. Hence, their elimination or curtailment objectively abridges freedom and constitutes the loss of a valuable asset, a loss that this Court cannot disregard.[60]

While recognizing that the disruption of a 'life plan' is a form of damages sustained by the rights holder, the court has not always ordered specific reparations for this damage. In the case of *Loayza-Tamayo v. Peru*, the court only recognized the impact. Antkowiak argues that in doing so, the court may have provided 'some measure of satisfaction for' the victim.[61]

The concept on 'life plans' is primarily raised in cases relating to arbitrary detention, torture and cruel, inhuman or degrading treatment or punishment.[62] There is a notable exception, however. In *Myrna Mack Chang v. Guatemala*, the court recognized that the unlawful detention and killing of a woman disrupted her sister's 'life plan' because it caused the sister to abandon her intended work to seek justice for her sister.[63] According to the court, 'it has been proven that as a consequence of the extra-legal death of her sister, [Helen Mack Chang] undertook the task of searching for justice, for over thirteen years, through her active participation in the' investigation and criminal process, and a general fight against impunity that included the establishment of the Myrna Mack Foundation. She 'gave up her work as a consequence' of her sister's disappearance, 'established the Myrna Mack Foundation, and has spent much of her time struggling against impunity'.[64] The court awarded US$25,000 to the sister for 'consequential damages', which seemingly included the damage to her life plan.

The *Myrna Mack* award would suggest that E-HRDs should be compensated for changes in their lives that arise as a result of the need to fight to protect their human rights. Yet, the jurisprudence on life projects is more complicated. In a 2010 case, the Inter-American Court seemed to move away from the notion that disruptions to a life plan can should be financially compensation. It suggested instead that the damage to a 'life project' should be compensated through forms of satisfaction, the legal term for an acknowledgement of wrongdoing, and guarantees of non-repetition, meaning legal, social and political reforms aimed at securing the rights of the individuals, and society as a whole, in the future.[65] The court seems to recognize a reparation is still required but changes the expected form of reparation.

The court's approach became more complicated in 2012, when disruptions to the life project of a teenager who suffered permanent disability, and his father who rearranged his life to care for the son, were addressed primarily as matters of satisfaction and guarantees of non-recurrence, while compensation was used to address only the loss of income, rather than any moral or emotional damage he sustained.[66] The court did, however, award financial compensation for various 'non-pecuniary damages' while referencing both suffering and anguish and the disruption to the child's life plan.[67] This court based its award on the concept of equity or fairness.[68] In its 2015 decision, *Argüelles y Otros v. Argentina*, the court seemed to adopt a high burden of proof for claiming damage to life plans. While the court found that the state had failed to adjudicate criminal cases in a timely manner, leading to a prolonged detention of the victims, it concluded that the detention in and of itself did not evidence the disruption of a life plan. Without specifying what proof the victims could have offered, the court indicated that the plaintiffs had not met the burden of proving that arbitration detentions lasting between one and seven years disrupted a life project.[69] The court did, however, award damages based 'in equity' for the non-pecuniary damages felt by the claimants.[70]

In 2018, the court seemed to return to the recognition that disruptions to 'life projects' can be compensable. In *Alvarado Espinoza y Otros v. Mexico*, the court indicated that forced displacement by the military had caused community members 'particular losses of opportunities and [personal] development […] that is still repairable'.[71] The court clarified that this damage was distinguishable from other forms of economic or psychological harm.[72] As the state had two ongoing funds to support both the 'children of the victims of the fight against crime' and those who were self-employed in the federal state of Chihuahua, the court ordered Mexico to allow the victims to participate in these programmes or to establish a similar programme for the victims.[73]

The Inter-American Court has consistently recognized that certain breaches of human rights can fundamentally disrupt one's life's purpose, altering its course and its impact. Unfortunately, there remains surprisingly little pertinent scholarship on the issue. To date, most of the literature focuses on the unique nature of the 'life project' jurisprudence as means of fostering full restitution,[74] without interrogating the limits or contours of this category of reparation. The appropriate utility of this reparation needs to be understood. The experience of the Cajamarca E-HRDs offers an important opportunity to address this issue as it has not yet received sufficient scholarly treatment. The court's jurisprudence is progressive, but the Cajamarca experience does not fit neatly within it. The underlying breach in *Myrna Mack* was the enforced disappearance and death of family member, and in *Alvarado Espinoza* the forced displacements that devastated families. The other cases primarily stem from prolonged detentions, enforced disappearances or physical ill treatment. Should each E-HRD harmed by a state's actions be entitled to reparation for the time, energy and focus spent fighting for their rights?

A formalistic approach to reparations building on *Myrna Mack* might suggest that E-HRDs should be compensated for the disruptions to their lives and communities. The very existence of their organizations, and their involvement as E-HRDs, is evidence of both the state's failure to respect human rights and the disruption to the life plans of each individual defender's life. Changes in how the defenders use their time and energy represent identifiable impacts from the breaches. Pulling this together suggests that some form of reparation is needed, and that the reparation should be aimed at redressing the harm to the E-HRDs, not simply the harm of the breach. These compensatory efforts could also be seen as a means of deterring future violations by increasing the cost associated with breaching human rights by fully recognizing the harm suffered by as a consequence of states and businesses breaching their human rights obligations and responsibilities. With investment law arbitrators awarding tens and hundreds of millions in awards, and human rights tribunals responding with hundreds of thousands, international law may be creating an incentive for states like Colombia, and businesses like AngloGold Ashanti, to prioritize investment obligations and business interests over human rights. Greater consideration needs to be given as to how to rebalance this incentive structure. Aaron Marr Page has recently argued that in the context of business and human rights, human rights awards remain undervalued, failing to ensure that the victim is truly made whole. As such, the awards themselves fail to function as an effective deterrent.[75] While greater consideration of this issue is needed, Page's argument suggests that compensation for this disruption of a life project may serve not just the immediate needs of the victims but the longer-term goal of preventing human rights breaches rather than simply remedying them.

Any effort to ensure E-HRDs are compensated for these disruptions raise important questions, concerns and objections for which there may not be any sufficient answers. If a defender is compensated simply because they become passionate about the environment or human rights as a result of a violation, this suggests that the choice to be an E-HRD is in and of itself a type of loss or a damage. If this is treated as a loss, one could argue that a compensation award needs to be offset by any positive developments that arise as a result of the E-HRD's choices: new relationships formed; new passions gained; university or postgraduate admissions and scholarships tied to their new work. Such awards would also raise questions about the appropriate line between compensating those for whom being an E-HRD is a disruption to their life project and those for whom being an E-HRD is, in fact, that project – a passion and purpose they may not have understood before. It would seem inappropriate to provide compensation to professional human rights defenders for each claim they bring as if their time were 'lost'. Doing so could also create a perverse incentive to bring numerous claims, no matter their legal legitimacy, in the hopes that they balance out in a way that provides greater compensation. One could argue, in response, that E-HRDs should be compensated only where they suffer a material or direct impact that gives rise to the changes in their life projects. Yet, in the context of business and human rights, this can be difficult. In Cajamarca, this would perhaps allow for the compensation of E-HRDs who live in Cajarmarca but not a nearby village because the immediate damage and violation – the failure to consult – is a breach of the violation for those in Cajamarca; those in nearby villages might not be harmed by the taking of Cajamarca for the mine but are at risk of any subsequent damage from a mine disaster. E-HRDs who act before the impact is secured, or who act in the interest of the general public rather than their own individual rights, would not receive compensation for the disruptions to their life projects despite the fact that the disruption is caused specifically because of the state's failure to secure human rights. It is not the purpose of this chapter to answer these questions but to raise them because they are the natural consequence of the experience of the E-HRDs in Ibagué and Cajamarca.

Conclusion

The Cajamarca referendum was briefly successful. Of the 19,000 residents in Cajamarca, 6,176 showed up to vote in the referendum. Of those, only 76 people (approximately 1 per cent) voted in favour of mining. The vote was a significant blow to AngloGold Ashanti as well as to the Colombian government.[76] In the immediate aftermath of the vote, Colombia's mining minister German Arce accused the anti-mining activists of misinforming voters.[77] The minister argued that the Cajamarca could not retroactively alter the license given to the company by the federal government. Emphatically, he argued that the rural village 'does not have the capacity to change the Social Rule of Law, that is, to alter the balance of powers between the Executive, the Legislature, and the Courts. […] 6,100 people do not have the capacity to break the State Social Law.'[78] The decision for the future of the La Colosa Mine, according to the minister, would be left to the environmental authority to assess the company's plans for exploitation; the community's vote would not change the mine's future.[79] On 11 October 2018, the Colombian constitutional court seemingly agreed with the government, finding that local municipalities do not have the authority to challenge the federal government's mining licenses through popular votes.[80] While recognizing that there is a right to public consultation that has not been respected during the awarding of mining rights, the court concluded that public referendums were not a constitutionally available tool.[81] The non-governmental organization Dejusticia has submitted an appeal to the constitutional court, asking it to void its earlier order.[82]

Immediately following the vote, AngloGold Ashanti claimed to accept the decision in Cajamarca. Citing 'diverse reasons which range from the institutional, the political and particularly the social', it announced that it would 'stop all project activities and with it all employment and investment, until there's certainty about mining activity in the country and in Tolima'.[83] As this book goes to the publisher, with the constitutional court seemingly paving the way for the company's license, it is unclear if AngloGold Ashanti will continue to respect the referendum. If the company pursues the contract, it is likely that the disruption to the life plan for the E-HRDs will continue.

The Cajamarca experience raises important questions about the impact of violations of business and human rights standards have on E-HRDs. The very existence of the E-HRD organizations in Cajamarca is evidence of the state's failure to respect human rights and of the subsequent changes required in each individual defender's life. Changes in how the defenders use their time and energy represent identifiable impacts from the breaches, disruptions to their life projects. There are outstanding and complex questions about when this compensation is appropriate and how it might be used to encourage more proactive approaches to business and human rights that need to be addressed in further scholarship. The *Myrna Mack* case sets an important precedent allowing for the compensation for disruptions to the 'life plans' of human rights defenders. That lesson should perhaps be more broadly recognized: the assertion of one's rights in the face of a persistent violation by the state often requires a significant allocation of time and energy. While the choice to join the opposition was one each defender made for themselves, the need to make that choice was the result of the state's failure to act in accordance with its international human rights obligations. The alteration to how the Cajamarca E-HRDs spent their time, resources and energy had transformed their lives in clear and measurable ways. It also impacted their relationships with one another, altered their status within the community and opened them up to death threats. To wipe out the consequences of a breach necessarily requires efforts aimed at limiting the long-term effects that arise from fighting that breach. Doing so, however, raises complex questions about how to draw the lines for compensation, and what is communicated by providing such compensation. These questions were outlined in this chapter but the answers fall beyond the scope of this book. The Cajamarca experience highlights the necessity of simply asking the questions and it is hoped that further scholarship will tackle some of these answers.

The Cajamarca and Ibagué organizations are likely to continue to resist the mine, despite knowing the path to victory is limited. The Cajamarca and Ibagué defenders knew the path to victory was limited. They are idealistic. According to one Comité member,

> We are fighting to defend water as a natural resource. Regardless of political affiliation it is necessary to recognize that what we do is political activity. We are raising awareness among people. We ask people whether they believe that fighting for the protection and defence of natural resources is necessary.

The Comité member is not expressing a vapid hope but appears to be signalling the larger purpose of their work within Colombia and beyond. 'Many say that future types of wars will be because of water', he notes, so it is necessary for the state to do a better job protecting that resource. But they are also political and pragmatic and knew the fight would not be an easy one. 'What's been said by the president is that this project is going to be run somehow, regardless of any type of opposition to it', one of the Comité members indicated before the vote. 'And [the President] has definitely not been discussing it with the local community.'

Notes

1 The quotes that form the basis of this chapter come from interviews that I conducted over two days – on 15 May 2016 and 16 May 2016. The interviews with the unnamed members of the Comite´ occurred on 15 May. The interview with 'Jorge' took place the day after.

2 Due to security concerns, I could not use real names. He chose his own pseudonym.

3 Marisol de la Cadena, 'Indigenous Cosmopolitics in the Andes: Conceptual Reflections beyond "Politics" ', *Cultural Anthropology* vol. 25, no. 2 (2010), 334–70.

4 Eduardo Viveiros de Castro, 'Perspectival Anthropology and the Method of Controlled Equivocation', *Tipití: Journal of the Society for the Anthropology of Lowland South America* vol. 2, no. 1 (2012), 3–22, at 11.

5 Sarah M. H. Nouwen, ' "As You Set out for Ithaka": Practical, Epistemological, Ethical, and Existential Questions about Socio-Legal Empirical Research in Conflict', *Leiden Journal of International Law* vol. 27 (2014), 233.

6 Tina Miller and Linda Bell, 'Consenting to What? Issues of Access, Gate-Keeping and "Informed" Consent', in *Ethics in Qualitative Research*, ed. Tina Miller, 2nd ed., 61 (London: Sage Publication, 2012).

7 Sarah M. H. Nouwen, ' "As You Set out for Ithaka": Practical, Epistemological, Ethical, and Existential Questions about Socio-Legal Empirical Research in Conflict', *Leiden Journal of International Law* vol. 27 (2014), 227, 245.

8 Dilmi Aluwihare-Samaranayake, 'Ethics in Qualitative Research: A View of the Participants' and Researchers' World from a Critical Standpoint', *International Journal of Qualitative Methods* vol. 11 (2012), 64, 66–67.

9 Christine Ashby, 'Whose "Voice" Is It Anyway? Giving Voice and Qualitative Research Involving Individuals That Type to Communicate', *Disability Studies Quarterly* vol 31, no. 4 (2011), http://dsq-sds.org/article/view/1723/1771.

10 *Gutierrez-Soler v. Colombia*, Inter-American Court of Human Rights, Judgment of 12 September 2005 (Merits, Reparations and Costs).

11 Karen McVeigh, '2017 Was Deadliest Year on Record for Colombian Human Rights Defenders', *Guardian*, 1 May 2018, https://www.theguardian.com/global-development/2018/may/01/2017-deadliest-year-on-record-colombian-human-rights-defenders.

12 OHCHR, 'Colombia Must Act to Stop Killings and Attacks against Human Rights Defenders – UN Expert', 3 December 2018, https://www.ohchr.org/en/NewsEvents/Pages/DisplayNews.aspx?NewsID=23968&LangID=E.

13 OHCHR, 'Annual Report of the United Nations High Commissioner for Human Rights on the Situation of Human Rights in Colombia', UN Doc. A/HRC/37/3/Add. (2 March 2018) at para 8.

14 Human Rights Watch, 'Colombia: Activists at Risk: Peace Promise Demands Guarantees for Rights Defenders', 2017, https://www.hrw.org/news/2017/04/24/colombia-activists-risk.

15 OHCHR, 'Annual Report of the United Nations High Commissioner' at para 8.

16 'Colombia's Defense Minister Dismisses Killings of Human Rights Defenders', Front-line Defenders Press Release, 19 December 2017, https://www.wola.org/2017/12/colombias-defense-minister-dismisses-killings-human-rights-defenders/.

17 OHCHR, 'Colombia Must Act to Stop Killings and Attacks against Human Rights Defenders – UN expert', 3 December 2018, https://www.ohchr.org/en/NewsEvents/Pages/DisplayNews.aspx?NewsID=23968&LangID=E (last accessed 20 November 2019).

18 Nigel King and Christine Horrocks, *Interviews in Qualitative Research* (London: Sage Publication, 2012), 37.

19 Working Group on Business and Human Rights, 'Protecting and Respecting Those Who Speak Up against Business Impacts on Human Rights – Takeaways from the UN Forum and the Way Forward', *Business and Human Rights Journal Blog*, 25 January 2018, http://blog.journals.cambridge.org/2018/01/25/protecting-and-respecting-those-who-speak-up-against-business-impacts-on-human-rights-takeaways-from-the-un-forum-and-the-way-forward/; Annalisa Ciampi, 'InfoNote: SLAPPs and FoAA Rights', 2017, 1–2, http://www.ohchr.org/Documents/Issues/FAssociation/InfoNoteSLAPPsFoAA.docx.

20 Of relevance to this case, Colombia has been a party to both the International Covenant on Civil and Political Rights (ICCPR) and the International Covenant on Economic, Social and Cultural Rights (ICESCR) since 1969.

21 United Nations Guiding Principles on Business and Human Rights (UNGP), UN Doc. A/HRC/17/31 (2011).

22 Tara Van Ho, 'Is It Already Too Late for Colombia's Land Restitution Process?: The Impact of International Investment Law on Transitional Justice Initiatives', *International Human Rights Law Review* vol. 5, no. 1 (2016), 60–85, https://ssrn.com/abstract=2893733 (accessed 1 July 2016).

23 Lisa J. Laplate and Kimberly Thieson, 'Transitional Justice in Times of Conflict: Colombia's Ley de Justicia y Paz', *Michigan Journal of International Law* vol 28 (2006), 49, 54–55.

24 Tara Van Ho, 'Is It Already Too Late for Colombia's Land Restitution Process?', 60–62.

25 Anglogold Ashanti, 'Americas', https://www.anglogoldashanti.com/americas/ (last accessed 30 December 2018).

26 Presidencia de la República and Todos por un Nuevo País, 'Summary of Colombia's Agreement to End Conflict and Build Peace', 2016, http://www.altocomisionadoparalapaz.gov.co/herramientas/Documents/summary-of-colombias-peace-agreement.pdf.

27 George W. Pring, 'SLAPPs: Strategic Lawsuits against Public Participation', *Pace Environmental Law Review* vol. 7 (1989), 3, 6.

28 See note 16.

29 Personal Interview with Van Ho, Tara, 15 May 2016.

30 La Silla Vacia, 'Entrevista Felipe Marquez, Anglogold Ashanti', 25 July 2014, https://www.youtube.com/watch?v=dujfcpuTf8w.

31 Ibid.

32 Ingeominas is an acronym derived from the formal title 'Instituto de Investicion e Informacion Geocientifica, Minero-Ambiental y Nuclear', which refers to the government's geological and mining institute. In 2011, the agency's name was changed to 'Servicio Geologico Colombiano', the Geological Colombian Service,

but the individuals I interviewed consistently referred to it as Ingeominas, and that is replicated here.

33 Committee on Economic, Social and Cultural Rights, 'General Comment No. 14: The Right to the Highest Attainable Standard of Health (Art. 12)', UN Doc. E/C.12/2000/4, 2000, paras 3, 11, 12(b), 23, 35, 37, 43(f), 50, 54; CESCR, 2003, paras 12(c)(4), 24, 37(f), 48, 56.

34 Committee on Economic, Social and Cultural Rights, 'General Comment No. 15: The Right to Water (Arts. 11 and 12 of the Covenant)', UN Doc. E/C.12/2002/11 2003, para 56.

35 *Mansarovar Energy Company Ltda v. Tribunal Contencioso Administrativo del Meta*, Colombian Constitutional Court, Reference Expediente T-6.298.958, 11 October 2018, http://www.corteconstitucional.gov.co/relatoria/2018/SU095-18.htm.

36 Ibid.

37 Ley 685 de 2001, el Código de Minas [Law 685 of 2001, the Mining Code], Diario Oficial 44.545, Article 16, 15 August 2001.

38 M. Sornarajah, *The International Law on Foreign Investment*, 3rd ed. (Cambridge: Cambridge University Press, 2010), 403.

39 Gus Van Harten, *Sovereign Choices and Sovereign Constraints: Judicial Restraint in Investment Treaty Arbitration* (Oxford: Oxford University Press, 2013), 72–76.

40 United Nations Guiding Principles on Business and Human Rights (UNGP), UN Doc. A/HRC/17/31 (2011), Principles 11, 15.

41 Article 19; Human Rights Committee, General Comment 34.

42 La Silla Vacia, 'Entrevista Felipe Marquez, Anglogold Ashanti', 25 July 2014, https://www.youtube.com/watch?v=dujfcpuTf8w.

43 *Case of the 'Street Children' (Villagra-Morales et al.) v Guatemala*, Inter-American Court of Human Rights, Judgement of 19 November 1999 (Merits), para 144.

44 Human Rights Committee, 2018, paras 3, 26.

45 Ibid. at para 26.

46 Ibid.

47 Gideon Long, 'Mining Groups in Colombia Fear Popular Backlash', *Financial Times*, 17 May 2017, https://www.ft.com/content/80bba74c-38ef-11e7-ac89-b01cc67cfeec; *Gran Colombia Gold v. Colombia*, 'Notice of Arbitration' dated 27 February 2017, available via italaw.com.

48 Canada-Colombia Free Trade Agreement (2008), *entered into force* 2011, at Articles 805, 811.

49 *Tecnicas Medioambientales Tecmed S.A. v. Mexico* (Tecmed v Mexico), ICSID Case No. ARB (AF)/00/2, 29 May 2003, paras 151, 165–74.

50 GAR: The International Journal of Commercial and Treaty Arbitration, 'Damages and Costs in Investment Treaty Arbitration Revisited', *News*, 2, December 2017, http://www.allenovery.com/SiteCollectionDocuments/14-12-17_Damages_and_costs_in_investment_treaty_arbitration_revisited_.pdf.

51 Ibid. at 3.

52 Joni Adamson, 'Indigenous Literatures, Multinaturalism and Avatar: The Emergence of Indigenous cosmopolitics', *American Literary History Review* vol. 24, no. 1, 143–62 at 144.

53 Marisol de la Cadena, 'Indigenous Cosmopolitics in the Andes: Conceptual Reflections beyond "Politics"', *Cultural Anthropology* vol. 25, no. 2 (2010), 334, 350–52.

54 Ibid., 334, 335–36. Republic of Ecuador. Constitution of 2008, Article 71.

55 United Nations Guiding Principles on Business and Human Rights (UNGP), UN Doc. A/HRC/17/31 (2011), Principles 25–29.

56 The Factory at Chorzów (Germany v. Poland), 1928 PCIJ (ser. A) No. 17, 13 September, 47–48; Gabčikovo-Nagymaros Project (Hungary/Slovakia), Judgment, 1997 ICJ Reports 7, 80; Genocide Convention (*Bosnia v. Serbia*), Judgment, 2007 ICJ Reports 43, 232.

57 Dinah Shelton, *Remedies in International Human Rights Law*, 3rd ed. (Oxford: Oxford University Press, 2015), 19.

58 United Nations Guiding Principles on Business and Human Rights (UNGP), UN Doc. A/HRC/17/31, 2011, 22, 25–31; Kristen Genovese, 'Access to Remedy: Non-Judicial Grievance Mechanisms', in *Business and Human Rights: From Principles to Practice*, ed. Dorothée Baumann-Pauly and Justine Nolan (London: Routledge, 2016), 266, 239–98; Jonathan Drimmer and Lisa J. Laplante, 'The Third Pillar: Remedies, Reparations, and the Ruggie Principles', in *The Business and Human Rights Landscape: Moving Forward, Looking Back*, ed. Jena Martin and Karen Bravo (Cambridge: Cambridge University Press, 2016), 316, 316–47; Linda C. Reif, 'The UN Guiding Principles on Business and Human Rights and the Networked Governance: Improving the Role of Human Rights Ombudsman Institutions as National Remedies, *Human Rights Law Review* vol. 17 (2017), 603–32.

59 *Loayza Tamayo v Peru (Reparations and Costs)*, Inter-American Court of Human Rights, 27 November 1998, paras 117, 144–54 (internal quotations omitted).

60 Ibid. at para 148.

61 Thomas M. Antkowiak, 'Remedial Approaches to Human Rights Violations: The Inter-American Court of Human Rights and Beyond', *Columbia Journal of Transnational Law* vol 46 (2008), 351, 370.

62 Ibid.; *Suárez-Rosero v. Ecuador*, Inter-American Court of Human Rights, Judgment of 20 January 1999 (Reparations and Costs); *Cantoral-Benavides v. Peru*, Inter-American Court of Human Rights, Judgment of 3 December 2001 (Reparations and Costs); *Gutierrez-Soler v. Colombia*, Inter-American Court of Human Rights, Judgment of 12 September 2005 (Merits, Reparations and Costs).

63 *Myrna Mack Chang v. Guatemala*, Inter-American Court of Human Rights, Judgment of 25 November 2003 (Merits, Reparations and Costs), para 248(e), 253(1).

64 Ibid. at para 253 (1).

65 *Ibsen Cárdenas and Ibsen Peña v. Bolivia*, Inter-American Court of Human Rights, Judgment of 1 September 2010 (Merits, Reparation and Costs), para 277.

66 *Furlan and Family v. Argentina*, Inter-American Court of Human Rights, Judgment of 31 August 2012 (Preliminary Objections, Merits, Reparations and Costs), para 285–316.

67 Ibid. at para 317–21.

68 Ibid.

69 *Alvarado Espinoza y Otros v. Mexico*, Inter-American Court of Human Rights, Sentencia de 28 de Noviembre de 2018 (Fondo, Reparaciones y Costas) [Judgment of 28 November 2018 (Merits, Reparations and Costs)], para 289.

70 Ibid.

71 Ibid. at para 315.

72 Ibid.

73 Ibid.

74 See Victor Madrigal-Borloz, 'Damage and Redress in the Jurisprudence of the Inter-American Court of Human Rights' (1979–2001), 2001 *Hum Rts Dev. Y.B.* 211, 233–35,

357, 266–67; Tara J. Melish, 'The Inter-American Court of Human Rights', in *Social Rights Jurisprudence: Emerging Trends in Comparative and International Law*, ed. M. Langford (Cambridge: Cambridge University Press, 2008), 30–31, https://papers.ssrn.com/sol3/papers.cfm?abstract_id=1810897; Cañaveral Londoño and Diana Carolina, 'Narrating the History: The Reinterpretation of Symbolic Reparation for the Reconciliation and Redemption of Child Victims of Conflict', *European Journal of Interdisciplinary Studies* vol. 3, no. 4 (2017), 98, 102.

75 Ibid. at 441–43.

76 Carolina Rojas, 'Mining Sector in Colombia – Moving Forward –', Agencia Nacional de Mineria [National Mining Agency of Colombia], last accessed 23 January 2018, https://www.anm.gov.co/sites/default/files/DocumentosAnm/anm_ladu_final.pdf.

77 *El Espectador*, 'Consulta minera en Cajamarca no tiene la Capacidad de Cambiar la ley', 27 March 2017, https://www.elespectador.com/noticias/nacional/consulta-minera-en-cajamarca-no-tiene-la-capacidad-de-cambiar-la-ley-gobierno-articulo-686515.

78 Ibid.

79 Ibid.

80 *Mansarovar Energy Company Ltda v. Tribunal Contencioso Administrativo del Meta*, Colombian Constitutional Court, Reference Expediente T-6.298.958, 11 October 2018, http://www.corteconstitucional.gov.co/relatoria/2018/SU095-18.htm.

81 Ibid.

82 Dejusticia, 'Solicitamos la anulación de la Setencia que le pone Límites a las Consultas Populares', 5 December 2018, https://www.dejusticia.org/solicitamos-la-anulacion-de-la-sentencia-que-le-pone-limites-a-las-consultas-populares/.

83 Reuters, 'AngloGold Suspends Colombia Project after Anti-Mining Vote', 27 April 2017, https://www.reuters.com/article/us-colombia-mining/anglogold-suspends-colombia-project-after-anti-mining-vote-idUSKBN17T3BH.

Chapter 8

OCCUPATIONAL HEALTH AS A HUMAN RIGHT: A CASE STUDY IN A TURKISH FREE TRADE ZONE

Cigdem Cimrin and Yucel Demiral

Introduction

The globalization of the world towards a single market over the last few decades generated an understanding among developed and developing countries that the more private capital flows between countries in the form of foreign direct investment (FDI), the more competing power that the countries can hold in the globalized market's raising competition. Accordingly, to attract more FDI, the world economy has witnessed an unparalleled opening and modernization of the economies of all regions, encompassing deregularization, outsourcing, privatization and private participation in the provision of infrastructures, and the reduction and simplification of tariffs.[1] Thus, the role of FDI in generating technology transfers and beneficial spillovers to local markets has motivated policymakers to adopt policies for attracting more FDI.[2]

Turkey, a country sitting at the crossroads of three continents, has been a salient example of a developing country which directly relies on FDIs brought by transnational corporations (TNCs) in stimulating its economy since it opened its market in the early 1980s. Indeed, in less than 30 years, Turkey has become one of the largest FDI recipient countries with a flow of foreign capital reaching to US$18 billion in 2015 according to the World Investment Report of UNCTAD.[3]

As noted above, for a country to benefit from FDI, regulations (or, as appropriate, deregulation) creating favourable commercial, legal and social conditions that attract FDI should be put in place. This regulatory exercise is usually performed by considering the fact that FDI 'is driven by the availability of cheap labour and the prevalence of weak environmental and labour regulations'.[4]

FDI's economic stimulus for countries is accompanied by huge costs, which one cannot underestimate and must not overlook. Indeed, FDI is 'accompanied by transfer of obsolete and hazardous technologies, chemicals, processes and waste [and] associated with an increase in assembly line, workers' shift, low-quality jobs, with minimal options for advancement and a growth of insecure, precarious employment [particularly] for the less-industrialized countries [like Turkey]'.[5]

Workers in free trade zones (FTZs) have been particularly affected by these subdued employment standards. For instance, FTZs have been associated with high levels of machine-related accidents, dust, noise, poor ventilation and exposure to toxic chemicals.[6] It has been reported that accidents, stress and intense exposure to common hazards arise from unrealistic production quotas, productivity incentives and inadequate controls on overtime.[7] These hazards (particularly those related to productivity quotas) can even give rise to a large spectrum of reactions, ranging from cardiovascular and psychological disorders to impairment of reproduction function in women.[8]

While states are adopting more business-friendly policies to attract foreign capital, this often lies in tension with their human rights obligations. For instance, the right to occupational health, which is 'an integral component of the right to health'[9] is addressed in a number of international human rights instruments. Specifically, Article 23 of the Universal Declaration of Human Rights provides for 'the right of everyone to just and favourable working conditions'.[10] In addition, Article 12.2(b) and (c) of the International Covenant on Economic, Social and Cultural Rights establish that 'states must take steps towards the full realization of the right to health, including the improvement of all aspects of industrial hygiene and the prevention, treatment and control of occupational and other diseases that do still exist'.[11] These obligations, in turn, are enforceable and require states to perform their duties emanating from international human rights law.

The International Labour Organization (ILO) also 'recognizes both the right to a safe and healthy working environment and the protection of the worker against sickness, disease and injury arising out of her employment as fundamental human rights'.[12] ILO has adopted numerous instruments ratified by various states that directly address occupational health. These include the Convention on Occupational Safety and Health, the Occupational Health Services Convention, the Working Environment (Air Pollution, Noise and Vibration) Convention as well as the Protection of Workers' Health Recommendations.

Turkey has ratified the International Bill of Rights (consisting of the Universal Declaration of Human Rights, the International Covenant on Civil and Political Rights and the International Covenant on Economic, Social and Cultural Rights), the eight ILO core conventions (as set out in the Declaration on Fundamental Principles and Rights at Work) and a majority of other international occupational health instruments.

In keeping with other states' practices (and by following international financial organizations' guidance), Turkey has also (1) restructured its legal framework regulating investments (Law on Incentivizing of Investment and Employment 2004, Law on Foreign Direct Investment 2003, Implementation Regulation on Foreign Direct Investment Law 2003); (2) entered into various multilateral and bilateral arrangements; (3) adopted new laws and regulations facilitating the inflow of foreign investment and sectoral investment incentives (i.e. Commercial Code and Code of Obligations); and (4) allowed international arbitration for disputes.[13] This favourable framework has enabled Turkey to host a number of companies that either hold or bring in foreign investments; however, the authors doubt that this favourable framework presented to business has provided similar advantages for workers employed in the factories of these companies; in fact, they believe that, at present, the reality is quite the opposite for workers and their well-being.

Nevertheless, the Turkish Social Security Institution (SSI) data for 2012, 2013, 2014, 2015 and 2016 indicate that there had been no reports of any deaths of workers due to occupational diseases and official statistics show the number of people diagnosed with occupational diseases as 395 in 2012, 371 in 2013, 494 in 2014, 510 in 2015 and 597 in 2016.[14] Despite the fact that the official statistics regarding reported and compensated occupational diseases are extremely low in Turkey,[15] the authors also argue that these official numbers do not actually match the realities of the Turkish job market which offers mostly informal and precarious work and workplaces, weak monitoring and inspection services for occupational safety and health (OSH) by public authorities and both judicial and administrative barriers against workers accessing some sort of remedy.

This chapter seeks to answer two questions at the intersection of medicine and law: (1) Despite the legal framework and companies' various ethical undertakings, how do the organizational factors and working conditions that employees are subject to in some very reputable TNCs' Turkish subsidiaries lead to the deterioration of workers' health? and (2) What kind of sociolegal difficulties do workers diagnosed with occupational disease need to tackle after they lose their health at a very early age? In order to answer these questions, the authors have turned their attention to and echoed what they heard from workers themselves.

The Study

Methods

This qualitative study was done in an FTZ located in Turkey. From the 474 workers, a total of 105 were diagnosed with occupational diseases by occupational health physicians in Dokuz Eylul University Medical Faculty Occupational Medicine Clinic (DEUOC) as of 31 December 2016. A total of 69 of the 105 applicants either had worked or are still working in workplaces which are wholly or partly owned by 20 different TNCs operating in the FTZ. Of the 69, a total of 16 subjects were selected to complete a questionnaire – half female, half male. Out of 16 selected subjects, 10 (5 females, 5 males) responded positively and agreed to participate in the study (the Sample Group). Many workers who declined to participate told the authors that they feared losing their jobs. The ages of the participants varied between 29 and 44 at the time of interviews.[16] The Sample Group consists of either former or current employees of four of these TNCs, which are operating in textile, automotive and energy industries.

The interviews were designed in a semi-structured fashion and consisted of open-ended questions to test: (a) the companies' care for complying with occupational health and safety (OHS) standards as provided under Turkish law as well as standards referred to in their codes of conduct; (b) whether the state performs its duties (i.e. through monitoring, inspection and remedy) regarding the right to health and (c) whether stakeholders – particularly trade unions – function properly or whether trade unions have the capacity or the will to perform their basic duties at all (i.e. supporting workers against the employer).

Occupational health terminology relevant to the study

Occupational diseases are diseases emanated primarily as a result of an exposure to risk factors arising from work activity. According to the Protocol of 2002 to the Occupational Safety and Health Convention dated 1981, the term 'occupational disease' covers any disease contracted as a result of an exposure to risk factors arising from work activity.

> Two main elements are present in the definition of an occupational disease: (1) the causal relationship between exposure in a specific working environment or work activity and a specific disease; and (2) the fact that the disease occurs among a group of exposed persons with a frequency above the average morbidity of the rest of the population.[17]

The clinical features of occupational diseases must fit with what is known about the health effects following exposure to the respective agent or factor and there must be an indication of sufficient occupational exposure. In contrast, work-related diseases have multiple causes. Factors in the work environment may play a role in the development of such diseases.

It has been estimated that the main causes of death globally from all work-related diseases were circulatory diseases (31 per cent), work-related cancers (26 per cent) and respiratory diseases (17 per cent).[18] Yet, in Turkey, the most common type of work-related disease is pneumoconiosis, a respiratory disease, due to the frequent dust exposure of workers in the mining and manufacturing sector.

Occupational diseases are mostly seen among males. For example, in Turkey, 470 out of 494 occupational disease cases were among males and only 24 were among females during 2014.[19]

In the case study, the three main diagnoses by DEUOC medical experts were pneumoconiosis,[20] bronchial asthma[21] and musculoskeletal diseases (i.e. hernia)[22] for the Sample Group.

Female				**Male**			
Subject	**Company and Sector**	**Diagnosis**	**Year of Birth**	**Subject**	**Company and Sector**	**Diagnosis**	**Year of Birth**
W-1	B.Co – Automotive	Disc hernia	1985	M-1	A.Co – Automotive	Asthma	1981
W-2	B.Co – Automotive	Disc hernia	1988	M-2	B.Co – Automotive	Disc hernia	1981
W-3	C.Co – Textile	Asthma	1975	M-3	A.Co – Automotive	Pneumoconiosis	1973
W-4	D.Co – Energy	Asthma	1987	M-4	A.Co – Automotive	Disc hernia	1985
W-5	B.Co – Automotive	Disc hernia	1980	M-5	B.Co – Automotive	Disc hernia	1982

Findings

Since the 1980s, Turkish industry has become more capital-intensive through automation. One of the positive effects of automation has been the removal of people from some of the more hazardous occupational risks; however, there is a downside of more capital-intensive factories and that is the requirement for greater rates of production and equipment utilization.[23] These higher speeds are stressful mentally and apt to induce physical disorders.[24]

Thus, major complaints from the Sample Group were related to the excessive working hours, which cause constant physical fatigue and stress, continuous incidence of diseases from vibration,[25] noise[26] and airborne dusts[27] and occurrence of musculoskeletal complaints caused by repeating the same task for months (if not years), affecting workers' health. Nevertheless, we must note that through a proper design of processes and workspaces by engineers and occupational health specialists, employers can always accommodate their workers' needs and provide better working conditions.

It was disappointing to hear from the Sample Group how their employers ignored the organizational factors in workplaces that led to their health problems:

1. 'I feel as if my lungs are rusting, because of the iron powder that I inhaled for the past 10 years. After my diagnosis, they made me a cleaner in the office section of the factory. Now, the smell of cleaning products is making me very sick. I don't how long I can endure to this torture.' (M#3 – A.Co)
2. 'In every 1,5 minutes, I lift 8–10 kg cable and carried it to a palette that is 5–6 feet away every day for 4 years. After waiting for 3 months, they put me to a more arduous work station. This time I needed to carry 18 kg cables to other stations. I conveyed the same complaint; but I worked for 8 more months until my rotation.' (M#2 – B.Co)
3. 'The workplace doctor prescribed everyone the same muscle relaxant but it wasn't effective at all.' (M#4 – A.Co)
4. 'They rotated me to another station in order to let me get better. But this time, I got cervical disc hernia on top of my lumbar disc hernia. I wasn't even 30 years old at that time.' (M#4 – A.Co)
5. 'I tried to work with a neck brace for one year, but it was almost impossible to work like that. By the way, working with a neck brace or with a bandaged hand is a usual practice in the factory, almost half of the employees are working with a neck brace.' (W#1 – B.Co)
6. 'There was unstoppable and unavoidable noise, which we had to listen to all day, all week, all month, all year […] It was driving me crazy but after some time I got used to it because I had to, because I needed to make my living there.' (W#5, B.Co)
7. 'At the moment, someone else is working in the silicon mounting unit and s/he faces the same danger.' (W#4 – D.Co)
8. 'My psychological health got even worse as my physical conditions deteriorated. My three children and my wife are very upset because my mental and physical problems.' (M#3 (1973) – A.Co)
9. 'Due to my asthma, the doctor strictly forbids me to use tools such as welding and monsters but I have to! Otherwise, I would lose my job and I can't because I have a child.' (M#1– A.Co)

The Sample Group indicated that, most of the time, local management did not report work-related injuries and illnesses nor keep accurate records relating to these issues as they did not want to be seen as the weakest and least successful links by their headquarters. The Sample Group also stated that if all injuries and illnesses would have been reported to headquarters and public authorities, their parent companies and the Ministry of Labour would have no choice but to shut down these workplaces.

Apparently, employers also failed to provide the most basic protective equipment for a long time. Some also complained about lack of sufficient ventilation in workplaces and adequate and effective trainings about health risks attached to their daily operations. It should be noted that training means helping workers to learn how to do something and telling them what they should or should not do. In other words, training is not just about a ticking-box exercise to meet legal duty envisaged under the law. In fact, it should be effective enough in order to contribute towards making workers competent in health and safety issues and ensure that all workers are thoroughly trained and up to date about legal requirements and industry standards.

- 'We have had OHS training once every two years.'[28] (M#1 – A.Co)
- 'I have been working for twelve years; glasses, gloves and steel-nosed shoes have become mandatory in the workplace only in the last three years; we just started wearing helmets this year.' (M#1 – A.Co)
- 'The smell of textile dye had been killing me. There was no air-conditioning in the factory. Summers were the worst.' (W#3 – C.Co)

Meanwhile, the annual revenues of these four TNCs have risen steadily, ranging between US$300 million and US$4.8 billion in 2017 alone. However, the revenue seems to have been achieved at the cost of worker health and safety. Specifically, workers often had to put up with excessive working hours, tight delivery schedules and overtime[29] and were being paid at a minimum wage (net amount was around US$260/month in 2017). High production quotas were common during the course of their employment in those companies and frankly, with normal working hours, it would have been almost impossible to meet the high demand of their parent companies during peak production seasons and generate these revenue figures.

- 'We were working like a robot, there was no opportunity to drink water.' (W#2 – B.Co)
- 'They were racing three shifts against each other in reaching production goals. Sometimes our managers walk around us and keep time in order to

test our performances. They would even question why there is a 10 second delay during our shift.' (M#2 – B.Co)
- 'The factory always wanted us to be altruistic and deliver the orders at any cost. This had caused irreversible physical defects on workers. Human life has never been valued by the management.' (M#4 – A.Co)
- 'We had 8 hours as a normal working time and an additional 8 hours as an overtime.' (M#2 – B.Co)
- 'When a pallet on one station was broken, the pressure on the other stations were increased because the production targets had to be met. During those times you have to perform over human capacity.' (M#2 – B.Co)
- 'I have begun not to endure the workload pressure not only physically but mentally as well.' (W#2 – B.Co)
- 'There are a lot of people working there under these terrible conditions. Every day they have to work under the production pressure and try to survive in order to support their families.' (M#4 – A.Co)

Once these organizational factors became detrimental to workers' health, they first sought help from infirmaries located in production facilities. After their conditions worsened, they went to see doctors outside of their workplaces and those doctors referred them to DEUOC, where they were diagnosed with occupational diseases and began treatment. When they informed their employers about their health conditions and diagnosis, most of them were either forced to resign or directly dismissed. In addition, workers strongly criticized trade unions' passive attitudes and held the unions responsible for contributing to the victimization of workers both before and after their dismissals.

- 'I did not want to make any complaints and/or requests regarding the health problems because I was afraid that I would be fired.' (W#2 – B.Co)
- 'There are more people suffering from musculoskeletal diseases than people with pneumoconiosis. They usually fire people with musculoskeletal diseases.' (M#1 – A.Co)
- 'When you submit your medical report from the state hospital to the company doctor, as soon as the management hears about your condition first they give you leave of absence for 10 days and then they fire you.' (M#1 – A.Co)
- 'One month after I told them that I am diagnosed with occupational disease, they sent a notice via Notary Public stating that they will transfer me to another factory as an assembly operator. And essentially that position is the reason why I started suffering from health problems. I did not accept such transfer and then they fired me because I didn't agree to go and start

working as an assembly operator. They did not give me any compensation. I was working there for more than five years.' (M#4 – A.Co)

- 'They forced us to resign but we chose not to. They sent us back home for four months and then they sent a termination via Notary Public stating that due to economic reasons the company has decided to downsize. While they were claiming to downsize, we heard that they employed new workers.' (M#5 – B.Co)
- 'I was one of the favourite employees as I did not complain about almost anything. When I took my medical report to the company doctor, she warned me that if she was to notify the management about my health status, the management would fire me.' (M#1 – B.Co)
- 'Once you got sick, you become a burden for the company. They would do anything to get rid of you and low performance is the best reason that they can come up. You would be fired within a year.' (W#3 – C.Co)
- 'I lost my health at this very young age in that factory and I put my heart and soul in that job. Thus, I have worked on holidays, on my engagement day and have constantly stayed overtime. When I was leaving there, they even made a big deal out of insignificant sums of money on my compensation. Do I deserve this condescending attitude after permanently losing my health in that factory?' (M#4 – A.Co)
- 'I was refraining from going to the company doctor because otherwise you would be selected as the first person to let go.' (M#2 – B.Co)
- 'HR manager presented me a resignation letter and asked me to sign it. Thank God, I spoke with the lawyer before and I refused to sign it. He told me that if I insist on not to resign by my own and they will terminate my contract and then no company would recruit me.' (W#1 – B.Co)
- 'After the HR forced me to resign, I ran into the union representative on the way. I told him the story while I was crying. He told me not to worry as the union would handle it for me. After waiting for 2 weeks, the HR called me again. This time the union representative was sitting across the table with the management. The union representative started to talk and told me that it was the best solution to resign for my health, and that they jointly came to this verdict. I was very surprised and realized that union has never intended to defend the workers.' (W#1 – B.Co)
- 'The union does not protect and defend our rights, they are on the side of the employer.' (W#5 – B.Co)
- 'No one from the union side approached me after my dismissal due to my occupational diseases diagnosis. One union representative helped me out in the name of our friendship and his help made no difference at all.' (M#3 – A.Co)

- 'After they terminated my contract, I cannot find any jobs due to my health problems.' (M#2 – B.Co)
- 'I am 30 years old now but this disease caught me at the age of 26. I may be suffering from COPD in the future and I have two children and I have to work and look after them. Who else would hire me with these conditions of mine?' (W#4 – D.Co)

It should be noted that these companies do possess publicized comprehensive codes of conduct, which were put in place to serve as constitutions or higher ethical undertakings of their organizations including their subsidiaries abroad. Accordingly, these codes of conduct set mechanisms (i.e. audits, grievance mechanisms) to test each and every unit within the organization's compliance with standards and requirements provided under them. Unfortunately, the Sample Group's response to the question of whether they heard of or were provided with any trainings with respect to the company's code of conduct was negative.

However, the Sample Group was fully aware of audits conducted by headquarters as well as third parties to whom these four TNCs do produce for as their suppliers. The authors also questioned whether they witnessed any labour inspections in their workplaces during the course of their employment and if yes, whether these inspections were effective and gave rise to any improvements in working conditions. For audits and inspections, they told the authors that they were scared to speak out and convey their complaints to auditors or inspectors due to potential repercussions from the local management. The Sample Group also addressed the rareness or inexistence of labour inspections and they said when inspections do take place, the results have never triggered or facilitated an improvement and was often shaped or managed by their employers' skilful tactics.

- 'When the team leader warned us that the factory will be inspected, we immediately started cleaning the work space. We tidied up all cables, made ourselves presentable and the speed of production moved down to a normal level.' (W#2 – B.Co)
- 'Our supervisors were informed about the questions that were going to come up in an audit and directed us on how to answer them. We had no choice except listening to them.' (M#2 – B.Co)
- 'Before Social Security Institute made its decision, the Ministry of Labour inspectors called me. I told them everything. I told them that there is a worker who has been working for 14 years on the same station, and he is holding on just to not lose this severance. If you do not believe me, go check and find him. They said they had already planned to do an inspection.

A week later, I heard that the company rotated that guy who had been working in the same station for 14 years. Their reasoning was "you are so tired, it is time for you to get some rest with less labour-intensive work."' (M#2 – B.Co)

- 'When they hear about an upcoming audit, they would start making arrangements. For example, they slow down the production by 80%. A work that would usually take 1 minute, would start to last 5 minutes during the audit period.' (M#4 – A.Co)
- 'First of all, the State does not fulfil its duty to investigate! Everything wrong is corrected right before labour inspectors arrive to the factory. None of inspectors ever asked us how we were doing. They did not even take a complete tour of the factory.' (M#4 – A.Co)
- 'The primary responsibility is on the employer. The State has to inspect employers and keep them under its surveillance. Unfortunately, those inspections are never performed as they are supposed be.' (M#2 – B.Co)

Last, when the authors questioned whether workers employed any company-level grievance mechanisms provided under codes of conduct to seek remedies for their cases, the Sample Group's responses were negative as they have never heard of nor would they use such mechanisms in their workplaces due to a lack of trust.

Analysis of Findings

Adopting a human rights-based approach to occupational health is crucial in order to assert the fact that occurrences of occupational diseases is not only a medical issue but also a violation of an individual's human rights. Accordingly, the advantages of this approach are that we can hold states responsible for protecting workers under their jurisdictions from any health risks by formulating, enforcing and monitoring laws and policies that are aimed at or have the effect of requiring business to take necessary measures to prevent occupational accidents and diseases in the workplace[30] by ensuring that 'workers are afforded access to adequate reparation, including restitution, compensation, satisfaction or guarantees of non-repetition and that statutes of limitations do not interfere with access to remedies'[31] and by conducting 'regular inspections of workplaces to assess whether [the] employer complies with occupational health laws [...], human rights, health impact assessments and risk surveillance to assess the impact [and effectiveness] of occupational health laws and policies prior to [and during] their implementation [and] collect disaggregated data in order to understand workers' health risks in all sectors'.[32] Also by using a rights-based approach, we can hold states accountable if they fail to meet their duties under the right to health.

With the ratification of the International Bill of Rights and ILO's instruments, Turkey has undertaken to protect the right to health along with other fundamental rights such as the right to life, etc., which are relevant to OHS. Turkey has also incorporated its human rights obligations emanating from these binding international law instruments into its domestic law. For example, Article 50 of the Turkish Constitution states, 'No one shall be required to perform work unsuited to his/her age, sex, and capacity' and Article 56 states, 'Everyone has the right to live in a healthy and balanced environment.' The Law on Occupational Health and Safety enacted in 2012 (Turkish OHS Law) includes regulations for all businesses from public and private sectors regardless of the field of their activity or the number of their employees. According to the Turkish OHS Law, the employer must carry out a risk assessment and is responsible for taking all necessary precautions to establish occupational health services in the workplace and for providing appropriate training and instruction to employees. The state has the authority and obligation to make OHS inspections at workplaces and to implement sanctions. The Ministry of Labour is the agency with the primary responsibility in this field, in collaboration with other ministries and stakeholders. As such, the Ministry of Labour is responsible for developing, implementing and enforcing legislation.[33]

Theoretically, Turkey has put in place (despite some shortcomings) all necessary laws and policies to provide OHS to workers. However, the implementation of the OHS legislation (including social security legislation) in practice is both discouraging and alarming.

For example, 'in 2014, a total of 1,005 inspectors were working at the Labour Inspector Board'.[34] As a result, only one inspector can be made available for every 15,000 workers.[35] This makes the effective enforcement of laws almost impossible as labour inspectors also have a complementary function for securing compliance with national laws. Ultimately, they are unable to support or fulfil their obligations as required by international labour protection system.

Moreover, occupational risks emerge due to failures to take the necessary precautions in the area of OHS and thus 'work accidents' and 'occupational diseases' occur. When they break out, social security mechanism must immediately kick-in. The Social Insurance and General Health Insurance Law No. 5510 (SSI law) defined occupational disease as a physical or mental disability, which a social security beneficiary (or registered worker) may develop. Informal or unregistered workers are outside of this scope even if their conditions would match with the 'occupational disease' definition under the SSI law.

Therefore, unregistered workers who suffer from occupational diseases are unable to benefit from the compensation scheme envisaged under the SSI law. This is also problematic because the Turkish labour market, like many developing economies, is characterized by a widespread informal economy.[36] According to the World Bank, Turkey's informality rate is 33.5 per cent (44.3 per cent for women).[37] The influx of refugees since 2011 has also created another socially disadvantaged group as these people are also employed as unregistered workers. We should underline the importance of the role and effectiveness of labour inspectors in struggling with informal employment problem here as well.

Qualification for occupational disease compensation is also problematic in Turkey. The SSI law defines an occupational accident and an occupational disease in a rather different way than the OHS Law; the scope of the SSI law is compensation-oriented only. According to the SSI law, the final diagnosis and conclusive decision regarding occupational disease and compensation issues are the sole right and responsibility of the SSI. In other words, it does not make any difference whether the worker received a clinical diagnosis for occupational diseases from a hospital (including the state university hospitals and the teaching hospitals of the Ministry of Health) formally authorized to carry out the clinical diagnosis of an occupational disease; the SSI has the ultimate say whether a worker has an occupational disease or not, at least from a compensation determination. This situation hinders workers' access to compensation through judicial and administrative means. The existing practice is doubtful in terms of the state duty to ensure available remedies and provide necessary access, as discussed in the UN Guiding Principles on Business and Human Rights (UNGPs).

Similarly, the current system for registered workers does not allow an accurate measure of the number of occupational diseases in Turkey as it only covers cases found qualified for occupational disease compensation by SSI. As noted above, annual official number of occupational diseases is around several hundred cases only. The rates of occupational diseases were between 15 and 22 per 100,000 workers before 2008 and then decreased to less than 5 per 100,000 whereas considering first, the global rate of occupational diseases (4–12 per thousand workers) the expected number of occupational diseases should have been 50–140 thousand annually[38] and second, for almost a decade an economic and financial crisis has been brewing in the country[39] creating serious implications for labour market and working conditions.

Because Turkey does not have relevant and accurate statistics on occupational accidents and occupational diseases, it is not possible to make an accurate assessment regarding the OHS environment or the current health status of Turkey's labour force. In addition, it is evident that trade unions, which exist for workers' representation, are neither eager nor resourceful in filling the gaps or providing the necessary support to their members. Their inability to react and close relationships with management creates a lack of confidence among workers that further reduces trade unions' leverage in labour relations which, in turn, makes workers even more vulnerable.

Conclusion

This case study presented here is a part of an ongoing research project. Publication of workers' voices will hopefully contribute in raising awareness of health risks to workers in the supply chains of TNCs and point out complementary duties that both business and states can undertake in fulfilling requirements of an individual's right to health.

The results of our case study reveal that at the moment, in Turkey, workers are stuck in a vacuum in which both public and private actors are getting away with egregious behaviour while workers are losing their health as well as their hope for a better future.

The level of health and safety at work, the sustainable economic development and quality of life of the people and the well-being of the working population are all linked to each other. Therefore, when developing countries start to develop and effectively apply comprehensive national health policies with a special focus on occupational health, the continuity of the productivity of the workers will be preserved and improved. In addition, socioeconomic development is boosted and competitiveness maintained. This is in accordance with the obligation of states to respect, protect and fulfil the human rights of individuals in the context of international human rights law.

Also, in practice a primary focus should be always on the workplace in order to understand the health status of a country's labour force. In this respect, companies are responsible for planning and regulating safe and healthy work, workplaces and work organizations and for providing and constantly improving worker health and safety.

Due to the universality of human rights, business actors have a responsibility to respect human rights wherever they operate. This responsibility to respect human rights is independent from the ability or desire of the state in which they operate in. Indeed, the UNGPs iterate that the responsibility to respect human rights exists over and above compliance with national laws and regulations protecting human rights.[40]

The stories discussed in this chapter show that, regardless of state's action or inaction, headquarters of companies sourcing from developing countries like Turkey should be implementing ongoing and comprehensive human rights due diligence processes throughout their supply chains to prevent the risk of occupational accidents and diseases, as well as to stop the exploitations and indecent treatment of workers. During the process, they should be regularly consulting with experts in occupational medicine hospitals or clinics who can collaborate with engineers in designing a better and more humane working environment.

Notes

1 Joong-Wan Cho, 'Foreign Direct Investment: Determinants, Trends in Flows, and Promotional Policies', *Investment Promotion and Enterprise Development Bulletin for Asia and Pacific* vol. 4 (2015), 99–112.

2 Laura Alfaro et al., 'FDI and Economic Growth: The Role of Local Financial Markets', *Journal of International Economics* vol. 64 (2004), 89–112; Joel Deichmann et al., 'Foreign Direct Investment in Turkey: Regional Determinants', *Applied Economics* vol. 35, no. 16) (2003), 1767–78.

3 UN Conference on Trade and Development, *World Investment Report 2018 – Investment and New Industrial Policies*, Geneva, 2018, https://unctad.org/en/PublicationsLibrary/wir2018_en.pdf.

4 A/HRC/20/15 Report.

5 Rene Loewenson, 'Globalization and Occupational Health: A Perspective from Southern Africa', *Bulletin of the World Health Organization* vol. 79, no. 9 (2001), 863–64.

6 Ibid.

7 Ibid.

8 Cigdem Cimrin and Arif Cimrin, 'Globalisation, Occupational Disease and Workers' Abuse in Turkey: A Case Cluster Study Analysis', *Journal of Developing Country Studies* vol. 8, no. 3 (2018), 53.

9 A/HRC/20/15 Report.

10 UN General Assembly, *Universal Declaration of Human Rights*, 217 A (III), 10 December 1948, https://www.refworld.org/docid/3ae6b3712c.html.

11 UN General Assembly, *International Covenant on Economic, Social and Cultural Rights*, United Nations, Treaty Series, vol. 993, p. 3, 16 December 1966, https://www.refworld.org/docid/3ae6b36c0.html.

12 ILO, *Health and Life at Work: A Basic Human Right*, World Day for Safety and Health at Work, 5, 28 April 2009.

13 UN General Assembly, *International Covenant on Economic, Social and Cultural* Rights, 54.

14 TMMOB Makine Mühendisleri Odası, *İş Sağlığı ve İş Güvenliği Oda Raporu*, MMO/689, Ankara, 2018.

15 ILO, *Occupational Safety and Health Profile: Turkey*, Ankara, 78, 2016.

16 All interviews were conducted in Turkish in August 2017. All interview notes were translated in English. Authors refrained from doing any alterations on the English translations of their interview notes in order to retain the genuineness of what they heard from the Sample Group.

17 ILO, *Identification and Recognition of Occupational Diseases: Criteria for Incorporating Diseases in the ILO List of Occupational Diseases*, Meeting of Experts on the Revision of the List of Occupational Diseases (Recommendation No. 194), MERLOD/2009/4, Geneva,

2009, https://www.ilo.org/wcmsp5/groups/public/@ed_protect/@protrav/@safework/documents/meetingdocument/wcms_116820.pdf.

18 Päivi Hämäläinen et al., 'Global Estimates of Occupational Accidents and Work-Related Illnesses 2017', Workplace Safety and Health Institute, 2017, http://www.icohweb.org/site/images/news/pdf/Report%20Global%20Estimates%20of%20Occupational%20Accidents%20and%20Work-related%20Illnesses%202017%20rev1.pdf.

19 Ibid., 79.

20 Pneumoconiosis is a disease of the lungs due to constant inhalation of dust. It is considered an occupational lung disease. Symptoms may include coughing, tightness in the chest and shortness of breath. Pneumoconiosis is a permanent sickness; there is no cure.

21 Bronchial asthma is a chronic inflammatory disease of the lung that is characterized by hyperreactivity and airway obstruction.

22 Work-related musculoskeletal diseases are mostly caused by repetitive motions, awkward work position or heavy lifting.

23 Mark R. Lehto and James R. Buck, 'Introduction to Human Factors and Ergonomics for Engineers', *Lawrence Erlbaum Associates – Taylor & Francis Group*, New York, 606, 2008.

24 Ibid.

25 'It is known that whole body vibration can increase heart rate, oxygen uptake and respiratory rate. In addition, whole body vibration can produce fatigue, insomnia, headache, and shakiness during or shortly after exposure. In the case of hand and arm vibrations, there tends to be a vasospastic syndrome that is known as dead fingers. This circulatory disorder is usually permanent.' Lehto and Buck, 'Introduction to Human Factors and Ergonomics for Engineers', 616.

26 'Excessive noise is a potential safety problem in vehicles and many work environments. Even at low levels, noise can annoy or distract workers […] The effects of long-term exposure to noise are cumulative and non-reversible.' Lehto and Buck, 'Introduction to Human Factors and Ergonomics for Engineers', 616–17.

27 'Airborne dusts are associated with classical widespread occupational lung diseases such as the pneumoconiosis, as well as with systemic intoxications such as lead poisoning, especially at higher levels of exposure. There is also increasing interest in other dust-related diseases, such as cancer, asthma, allergic alveolitis and irritation. Overexposure to dusts causes disease, temporary and permanent disabilities and deaths.' 'Hazard Prevention and Control in the Work Environment: Airborne Dust (WHO, 1999)', *World Health Organization*, 1999, http://www.who.int/occupational_health/publications/airdust/en/.

28 According to Article 17/1 of the Turkish Law on Occupational Health and Safety dated 30 June 2012, 'The employer ensures that employees receive adequate occupational health and safety training. In particular, this training shall be provided prior to employee's commencement of work, change of work place or task, change of work equipment or implementation of new technology. The trainings shall be updated in line with the new and changing risks and repeated as necessary and regularly.' Also, according to the Decree on Workplace Hazard Groups dated 26 December 2012, at least one OHS training (lasting for at least 12 hours) in every two years must be provided to employees in workplaces listed in ordinary hazard group (i.e. manufacturing industries) and at least one OHS training (lasting for at least 16 hours) in every year must be provided to employees in workplaces listed in extra hazard group (i.e. mining,

construction, oil drilling industries). Even though employers may seem to be following local regulations, the general industry practice in OHS trainings is to do them at least once every year to ensure that workers are trained on the most up-to-date regulations and industry requirements.

29 It should be noted that overtime is not legally compulsory; however, in practice employers usually coerce their workers to work overtime by threatening them that they would lose their jobs otherwise and overtime rates are usually very low.

30 See also UN Human Rights Council, 'Guiding Principles on Business and Human Rights: Implementing the United Nations "Protect, Respect and Remedy" Framework', A/HRC/17/31, 21 March 2011, Principle No. 3.

31 A/HRC/20/15 Report, para. 57:

> Restitution requires that States restore the situation that existed prior to the violation. For example, if a statute regulating the use of hazardous materials in the workplace is repealed, resulting in workers falling ill, a remedy of restitution would require States to reinstate the law or draft a new law to address the lacunae. Monetary compensation should cover the cost of medical care, including rehabilitation, and any lost income arising from inability to work due to injury. Satisfaction includes a formal commitment by States, such as legislation or an executive order, to fulfil its obligation to realize the right to health of an individual or a specific population.

32 Ibid. at para. 30.

33 Hämäläinen et al., 'Global Estimates of Occupational Accidents and Work-Related Illnesses 2017', 10.

34 Ibid., 33.

35 Ibid., 99.

36 Melika Ben Salem et al., 'Informal Employment in Turkey: An Overview', *Centre D'Etudes De L'Emploi* vol. 138-2 (2011), 5.

37 The World Bank – International Bank for Reconstruction and Development, *Program Document for a Proposed Loan in the Amount of EUR 350.9 Million to the Republic of Turkey for the Resilience, Inclusion and Growth Development Policy Financing*, Report No. 115772-TR, 25 July 2017.

38 Hämäläinen et al., 'Global Estimates of Occupational Accidents and Work-Related Illnesses 2017',, 10.

39 Larry Elliot, 'How Serious Is Turkey's Lira Crisis and What Are Implications?' *Guardian*, 13 August 2018, https://www.theguardian.com/world/2018/aug/13/how-serious-is-turkeys-lira-crisis-and-what-are-the-implications.

40 UN Human Rights Council, 'Guiding Principles on Business and Human Rights, UNGPs Principle No. 11 Commentary.

Chapter 9

THE PRICE OF THE 'BLACK DOLLAR': VETERAN COAL MINERS AND THE RIGHT TO HEALTH

Jennifer D. Oliva with contributions from Jena Martin

Introduction

Natural resource extraction has played a diminishing role in the economies of affluent nations in the post-industrial economy. Although the United States, like much of the Global North, continues 'to consume vast quantities of natural resources, the contribution of extractive industries to total employment and to total national economic production – as typically measured by gross domestic product – has been declining for decades'.[1] Scholars have attributed this decline to everything from mechanization[2] to coal's failure to achieve cost-competitiveness with other energy-generating natural resources to consumer demand for clean energy.[3] This national-level pattern has manifested itself across the United States in a variety of regions, including Appalachia, whose economies have been historically dominated by the extractive industries, including coal mining, since the mid-1800s.[4] Indeed, Appalachia's identity as a region is inextricably intertwined with coal mining, notwithstanding that relatively few Appalachians are employed in the mining industry today.[5]

> This tendency for many in a community to identify with an industry that was historically important in the local economy, but that may not be any longer, is regularly exploited by extractive industries to maintain their political influence, which is often used to avoid government regulations aimed at ensuring the protection of the environment and public health.[6]

West Virginia is also home to one of the highest per capita veteran populations in the United States.[7] In fact, West Virginia had the highest per capita service and sacrifice rates in the country during the Vietnam War.[8] Military service is similar to coal mining insofar as: (1) enlistees are predominantly young, resource deprived and have little to no higher education beyond high school and (2) the work is extremely dangerous. Moreover, and much like mining, military service exacts a significant toll on the human body and mind. A recent literature review assessing the mental health consequences of the Iraq and Afghanistan wars found 'clear evidence of higher rates of homelessness, alcohol abuse, domestic violence, relationship breakdown, and criminality' among veterans of those conflicts with untreated mental health conditions.[9] Reports further indicate that veterans are more likely to be unemployed than non-veterans, account for 20 per cent of US suicides, and comprise nearly 20 per cent of the American homeless population.[10] In fact, the US Department of Veterans Affairs (VA) confirms 'that veterans face a variety of difficulties related to readjusting to civilian life, including financial and employment, relationships, legal difficulties, homelessness and substance abuse'.[11]

This chapter explores the significant health and environmental impacts military service and the coal industry have wrought on West Virginia veteran coal miners and their communities through first-person narratives. The author's interviews with veteran miners throughout the state illuminate several themes. First, many veteran miners candidly characterized coal mining companies as exclusively profit-driven entities, which frequently prioritized the bottom line at the expense of the health, well-being and safety of miners. Second, while veteran miners acknowledge mining's negative impacts on the natural environment and local community, they generally described such harms as necessary evils where, as in many rural West Virginia communities, mining coal is the only way to make a decent living without a college education. Third and finally, most of the veterans who returned from service to work the mines did so because their significant personal and family financial obligations precluded them from taking advantage of the G.I. Bill and attending college. Unfortunately, it appears that these veterans' inability to attain higher education operated to narrow their employment options in an economy dominated by a single industry to which they became captive.

Veteran Coal Miner Safety, Health and Well-Being

On 5 April 2010, 29 coal miners died in a violent yet entirely preventable[12] explosion at Massey Energy Company's Upper Big Branch (UBB) mine in Montcoal, West Virginia.[13] The United Mine Workers of America (UMWA) conducted an extensive investigation into the UBB explosion, which it characterized as 'the nation's worst mining disaster in 40 years'.[14] At the close of its investigation, the UMWA explained that

> the dangerous conditions that contributed to the explosion existed at the mine on a daily basis. These conditions represented gross violations of mandatory health

and safety standards [and] were not accidental. They were permitted to exist by a corporate management at Massey that created a culture that demanded production at any cost and tolerated a callous disregard for the health and safety of the miners employed at the operation.[15]

The UMWA concluded 'that Massey Energy and its management were on notice of and recklessly tolerated mining conditions that were so egregious that the resulting disaster constituted *a massive slaughter in the nature of an industrial homicide*'.[16]

The US Mine Safety and Health Administration (MSHA) concurred with the UMWA subsequent to its own exhaustive investigation, reporting that 'the unlawful policies and practices implemented by [...] Massey were the root cause of the tragedy' and 'Massey promoted and enforced a workplace culture that valued production over safety'.[17] MSHA's investigation also 'revealed that miners were intimidated by UBB management and were told that raising safety concerns would jeopardize their jobs'.[18] As a result and despite the government's extensive record of UBB safely and health violations throughout the four years preceding the deadly disaster, not once did any UBB miner report a single safety or health complaint or any whistle-blower disclosure to MSHA during that time.[19]

The author recently was privileged to speak with several West Virginia veteran miners, each of whom had either been injured while mining or had witnessed colleagues either badly wounded or, worse, killed on the job. Consistent with the government and union's findings regarding the UBB disaster, a common theme that emerged from the interviews was that the mining companies prioritized profit-making over miner safety, health and well-being. Moreover, none of the veteran coal miners harboured any desire that their children ever work in the local mines.

Daniel Carter was born and raised in Campbell's Creek, West Virginia. At 17, he enlisted in the US Army. He served as an army truck driver from 2000 until 2003 at Ft. Campbell, Kentucky, where he earned several Army Achievement Medals. He then served in the West Virginia Army National Guard (WVARNG) 151st Military Police Battalion from 2006 to 2008. He began working in the West Virginia coal mines in 2007, while still serving in the WVARNG. He worked as an equipment operator at Mammoth Coal in Mammoth, West Virginia, from 2007 to 2010, as a boss at Dana Mining Company in Mt Morris, Pennsylvania, from 2010 to 2013, and as a boss at Murray Energy in Blackville, West Virginia, from 2014 to 2015. He currently works as a kitchen supervisor at the Louis A. Johnson VA Medical Centre (VAMC) in Clarksburg, West Virginia. He was interviewed at his home in Clarksburg, West Virginia, during the summer of 2017.

Carter: Honestly [...] [coal mining is] a dangerous job, and sometimes there just ain't no way around it. A lot of situations, I didn't agree with in the coal mines, seeing my buddies get hurt. I've been hurt [...] you know what you're getting into before you go down there, so, bottom line is, don't get down there and cry about it. Companies use the wage […] to coerce you? Of course they do! But […] you're a grown man, you make that decision for yourself, walk out of there anytime you want to, you're not forced to be there.

…

[Coal mining operators] use proper safety equipment, but, you know, everybody wants that extra coal, makes your paycheck a little bit fatter, and sometimes you're kinda coerced to maybe not obey the law one hundred percent, just so you can get a little more on your bonus check. Sometimes you're coerced by saying […] 'if you don't do it, somebody else will. You get your dinner bucket and go home.'

…

That creates an environment where […] you're competing with everybody. You're competing with people who are laid off now, you're competing with people that are beside you and […] now, when I say competing with the people beside you, one thing you do have to understand is – we are a brotherhood underground. We do watch each other's backs and […] we do care about each other, we go to birthday parties for our kids together. I mean, we're brothers down there, we […] look out for each other. We take pride in that […] but […] the money probably got a little out of hand at some point […] and […] when you give 19, 20, 21-year-old kids, starting out, 60-70-80 grand a year, […] when they come from a little small coal town in southern West Virginia, […] they're not used to that, and […] they're willing to work hard for it. They'll give their lives, literally, as we've all seen now.

…

When you were part of production crew, you knew you had to be there so […] many of us went to work hurt, sick […] some of us went to work so sick sometimes we probably should have been in the hospital […] stopping every five minutes to run somewhere to use the bathroom, you know[…] a bandage full of blood, just so we can keep our job and provide for our families and show how tough, big men we were […] which was stupid! […] I'll be thirty-six years old on Sunday. Some of that stuff I did was plum ignorant […] but we were coerced. 'You wanna keep your job boy? Then get your butt to work!' [If you] tr[ied] to call off sometimes, that's when you got '[it] ain't gonna be an everyday thing is it, you wanna keep your job?' Smart comments like that.

How did your family feel about your decision to work in the coal mines?

Carter: I don't think my pawpaw liked it too much, but he knew I was trying to do what I had to do to be a man, you know […] take care of my family, kids.

...
My grandad actually received black lung benefits. There were stories about him being covered up several times in coal mines and him having his jaws wired shut and his ribs broken. […] You're pretty much guaranteed you're gonna sustain some kind of injury at some point in your career.

You mentioned earlier that the 'same outlaw coal mining went on in the union mines that went on in non-union mines'. Can you give me an example of 'outlaw coal mining'?

Carter: I'll give you a good example […] number one is big, deep cuts like […] when you take a cut with a continuous miner, […] you submit a cut plan[20] which means, with your roof conditions and […] the [other mining] conditions […], you can take a cut of coal twenty feet deep or thirty feet deep and then go in and take the bolt machine and bolt it. Well, what a lot [of miners] say, pretty much, every miner man that I ever ran behind or bossed to, 'you wanna get a little extra coal.' So, if you know there's not any inspectors around or big bosses around from outside [and] you're on a twenty foot cut plan, you might cut thirty feet, and you'll put that in the bank, and next time you go in there […] if you're on a twenty foot cut plan, […] you'll take another thirty foot cut instead of a twenty foot cut and bolt it. […] After you've done that twice […] you have three twenty foot cuts out of there [but] you've only had to move your miner over two times, so that saved you time. [You] got you an extra cut of coal outta there, so now at the end of the shift you got twenty extra feet [that] you can write down on your production report […] if you're cutting out [the extra] time [required to move the miner] back and forth […] and getting that extra cut of coal outta there, […] you're making money. So, that's just one example [of outlaw coal mining] that every coal mine I've been to does.

Isn't it risky to violate cut plans?

Carter: Yeah, it would be very risky because that cut plan is there for a reason. [It] is there because of the conditions of the roof in the coal mine at that time and, [it] also has to do with [whether] […] the top is cracked and busted and not solid and you can only cut twenty feet instead of thirty feet. Let's say you cut that thirty feet, which [isn't] bolted […] you gotta take your bolt machine in there and start bolting. That whole cut can fall in [on you while you are bolting] because [you took that] extra ten feet, then you got your buddies in there in a bad situation. You feel bad about yourself.

Are mining operators ever penalized for violating cut plans?

Carter: [W]hen we were underground and federal and state inspectors would show up on the property […] we always […] found out before they got there […] before they got to us, so we had time to fix things.

Were you ever worried that you might get injured so badly that you would not be able to continue mining?

Carter: Yeah […] there was several times [my wife] begged me not to go to work because I was hurt. Injuries that I had in the coal mine […] there was one time I hurt my back pretty bad in the coal mines and […] I was scared to death to let anybody know about it. Thought for sure I'd lose my damn job if I couldn't perform my job! Which I probably would of.

So […] for about two weeks, she got up every morning, […] she had to help me get out of bed, help me get dressed, […] put my boots on for me, literally […] put my dinner bucket in my arm, helped me down the steps, got to our car, helped me get into my car, then I'd drive an hour and a half to work, and I'd work all day like that, back all wrapped up and dang […] I mean […] we'd wrap ACE bandages around my back to keep the support on there and I'd come home, I wouldn't shower at work. Most of the time you shower at work in the bath house […] but […] I couldn't let anyone know I was hurt. I drove all the way back home, an hour and a half. She would help me get undressed and get in the bath tub and that's how we lived for a little while. She begged me to go to the hospital. That was the kinda life you lived.

Mr. Carter also discussed another mining accident, which almost caused him to lose a finger:

Carter:I was down in the coal mine […] running the [supply] motor […] at the time and I broke, took a load in with my buddy, [and] dropped it off at the end of the track. […] Coming on back out, I had to get out and throw a rail switch to turn left on the railway underground and, when I threw the switch, it got stuck […] so I knelt down to fix it. [W]hen I knelt down, it closed shut on my finger. […] I [was] probably [about] twenty to thirty blocks from my buddy and […] in between two airlock doors when it happened, so […] I'm in there by myself [with] my finger stuck in between two pieces of rail […] and, I could just feel it man, it's crushed. I can feel it and […] to throw the rail the other way to open my finger up is [on the other] side of the rig so I had to yank my finger outta that thing. Of course, I could feel the blood just pouring and I knew it was bad so […] I grabbed it, I got back to my [motor and] drove down there to where my buddy was and I said, 'hey, uh, better go up there and get a first aid kit.' I said, 'I jacked my finger up pretty good.' 'I wouldn't be surprised if it's cut off.' […] We probably only had an hour and a half left in our shift, and then we could go outside and go home. [My buddy] said, 'well, you wanna make our way to the outside?' and I said, 'let's get this thing bandaged up first and then we'll go up there and pick up this load and then we'll head outside […] cause the job still had to be done.'

How are you feeling these days?

Carter: I got problems with my back every day I wake up. When I worked in southern West Virginia, it's not what they consider low coal but, you couldn't stand up in most places. You had to bend down, walk through there, and you're beating your back off the top, and roof bolts hitting you in the back […] I said, I'll be 36 years old Sunday, but, if I had to do that for twenty more years and retire, man, I'd be plum beat to death, would I.

Would you encourage your children to become miners?

Carter: [I] don't ever want my kids to step a foot in a coal mine […] because coal mines will always be coal mines. It will always be about that black dollar. Getting that coal outside on the ground. That is what it will always be about. I want my little boy to go and get an education. I didn't have that opportunity. That's what I want that boy to do.

Would you be worried about your children's safety should they decide to go to work in the mines?

Carter: Yes, ma'am I would […] I'd be very worried. I'd be very, very worried.

Did going to work in the mines seems like an obligation for the men in your community?

Carter: It is a macho thing I guess […] Yes, [it] is a very macho thing.

Frank Andrew 'Andy' Dennison, Jr, was born and raised in Bristol, West Virginia. At 17, he enlisted in the US Army National Guard. Two years later, he enlisted in the US Navy as a boiler technician and, from 1987 to 1991, he served aboard the USS La Salle, USS New Jersey, USS Prairie and USS Knox. After receiving his honourable discharge from the navy in 1991, Mr Dennison relocated to Louisiana. He thereafter returned home to work in the West Virginia coal mines. He served as a supply man, bolter and crew leader at Dana

Mining Company near Morgantown, West Virginia, from 2004 to 2006 and then as a bolter, supply man, pumper, boiler mechanic and electrical mechanic for CONSOL Energy (later Murray Energy) in Blacksville, West Virginia, from 2006 to 2015. He currently works maintenance at the VAMC in Clarksburg, West Virginia . He was interviewed at his home in Fairview, West Virginia, during the summer of 2017.

Have you ever witnessed the death of a fellow miner?

Dennison:I've dug out a friend of mine […] We called him the Marlboro Man […] Johnny Elliot was his name. He got buried […] not even an hour after I came out [of the mine] […] he was going in and […] the whole top just come down […] and he was young, he [had] a little boy, was nine, and [a] little girl. He was a good guy. He just bought his first house.

Yes […] and […] it took us a while to get him dug out […] and […] I've had other guys […] lose fingers and stuff like that. He was the worst that ever happened to me, that I ever witnessed […] and the bad part […] for like two, three weeks, we had to drive by [the place where Johnny was crushed to death] every day. You could see the blood. They wouldn't put a wall up for nothing.

Why do you think the mining operator refused to put up a wall or clean up the scene of Mr Elliot's death?

Dennison: I dunno, they just don't care. They don't care. It's all about money. Jimmy Laurita, the old man, was the one in charge then. He was a […] mother. […] He was hardcore. He was like Bob Murray,[21] you know, greedy, used everything, they didn't care if stuff wasn't working right. […] [Laurita] don't give a crap, he don't. We had a meeting over there one time and he was talking about, this, this and this, and we said, 'well, we need this new equipment, we need this, we need that.' He said, 'you'll work with what you got or you won't work.' That sounds safe! And then I lost a friend of mine at Consol […] top come down on him […] improperly bolted top[22] […] in an old area that […] they didn't take care of […] like they should of. He was down there bolting it up […] and it could fall at any time. They tried to make it out like it was his fault, but I was there, where he got crushed, and it […] was just a piece about the size of this table […] just fell. But the way it hit him, it put him into the bolter and it just crushed him. I mean, completely smashed. He died quick. He died quick. The kid that was with him, they tried to fire him […] blamed [him] […] he was a spotter,[23] saying he wasn't doing his job, and this kid was like 19 years old […] just got his black hat. You can't blame somebody, you know, that's wrong to do that, what they did to that boy, […] he never come back.

Is there anything the coal bosses could do to make the work environment more safe?

Dennison: There's good bosses out there […] and a lot of them really do what they're supposed to do to protect you, because the only thing they can do is make their rounds, check for methane,[24] check the tops, but when you don't sufficiently bolt an area, […] you're supposed to [reinforce the bolting within] seventy-two hours. I've seen Bob Murray go four or five days before he bolts up [the] center bolt, you know, supplementary bolting. And you're supposed to do it within seventy-two hours. That's the kinda stupid stuff that they'll do, you know what I mean?

Or, like, when I was a pumper,[25] they would send me back around the wrap-around bleeders[26] alone. You know, there's no communication back there […] a couple miles by yourself. If anything would happen, they're not going to know nothing about you until the end of the shift. You should never be alone in the coal mine. I was always alone. I worked alone all the time. Just how it was. And they, as long as your boss takes his readings[27] and does what he's supposed to, they cut corners on stuff they shouldn't cut corners on. That's just how they are.

Mr Dennison also described a significant safety violation that he discovered while mining.

I was a mechanic. I […] walked up to the miner because I got there a little late because I had to fix something in the bottom. Well, I told the boss […] 'we'll stop for fifteen minutes, I'll grease the miner, do my little service check on it, and you get back in the coal and I'll do each piece.' 'Yep, no problem' [he said], so I get up there on the mains, and I walk up to the miner, and I'm looking at the sniffer[28] gauge, it's reading zero [and] my spotters[29] [are] going off. So I'm like, 'sniffer's bad'. [Be]cause it's not reading and […] I was right at 1%, which [mandates] you shut the miner[30] down, and it gets to a certain point, then you gotta clear the section while you fix it. So I hit the E[mergency] Stop on the miner. I said [to the crew], 'don't do nothing.' 'I'll be back, I'm gonna go get my kit and were gonna check this [sniffer]. I'm gonna recalibrate the sniffer cause my spotter's going off.' And I asked [another miner], I said, 'where's your spotter?' [He replied,] 'Oh the boss took it.' I was like, 'OK.' That's when I said, [I'm] 'gonna calibrate this sniffer', which […] I already knew what I was gonna

> see when I opened that [sniffer] up. I was gonna see something covering the sniffer head, so they don't read off methane and they can just cut, cut, cut, cut, cut, cut, cut [coal]. That's the kinda law breaking. It's very stupid. So I went back to the section, I come back and [the crew is] out bolting. I said, 'get off that.' Well, when they did, [I found] a Ziploc bag over the sniffer. I took it off [...] phew!!! I said, 'now, only thing we gotta do is go right back here to this checkup [and] tighten it.' Once we tighten that checkup, the air came up [and] everything went back to hunky dory. [It was a] fifteen-minute job to fix [the problem] yet, they spent ten minutes taking the cover off, five minutes wrapping it up, and another ten minutes to put it back on [just] to run illegal the rest of the day. Is that smart? That's stupid, ain't it? That's the kinda stuff you see, and it's with younger bosses [...] oh they got 'em so brainwashed that they just want coal, coal, coal, coal, coal [...] [because] they get bonuses off of it.

Mr Dennison further explained that, notwithstanding the risk of losing his job, he frequently reported safety violations to managers. Among other things, he complained about 'readings, air readings, [and] samples'. As he explained in further detail, he

> call[ed] out fire boss[31] reports [...] and that was one of the reasons I left Bob Murray, because like two or three different times, I called out a fire boss with bad air, bad gas, which is bad! I come out and [the air quality readings are] not in the book. They put it in this book [...] [a] special book and I would write [the air sample readings] in the book, and they hated that, and [said]: 'you're fired!' I said, 'whatever, fire me, I don't care.' [...] I've been threatened, actually I got sent home three days, without pay, pending termination. When I came in on the third day, I had my buddy, Jeremy Deshin, whose [...] an MSHA inspector, standing right beside me. [I h]ad a map drawled out of where I was gonna send him when we were done. [We] walked in[to the coal operator's] office, and I said, 'am I fired or not?' [He said,] 'what's he doing here?' Well, I said, 'you fired me because I put stuff in this book [...] that's MSHA. That's what they want.' [He said,] '[w]ell you're not fired, go back to work.' [They] [p]aid me for [the] three days [I had been sent home without pay].

You definitely seem to [have] dislike[d] [...] working for [Bob] Murray [the most]. What was different about that?

Dennison: Cause he didn't care [...] I mean [...] we needed parts for equipment and things for safety and he refused to buy them for us.

Why?

Dennison: I don't know…I honest to God don't know why. Like your safety glasses and our gloves. He would buy 'em […] then he went to where, you're only getting so many, and then, like, 'I'm not gonna buy 'em'. […] Stuff like that, he kept doing this to [us], [you] know what I mean?

Was there anything that the union could do about it?

Dennison: Unfortunately, our union, I don't wanna say it, but I think they sold out a long time ago. […] I know they did and […] you have no respect for people like that […] I don't. Bob Murray, when he first came, I was excited. Because Consol was […] all about coal, they didn't care about their people a lot. I mean they did but they didn't, know what I mean? Bob Murray, he comes in, you know […] I'm gonna change this and do this and do this and do that.' Then he came in, and instead of [implementing his promises], he took […] [things away from the miners]. [He] started to take our vacation days […] tried to take our sick days. [He] said, 'we didn't need sick days'. […] Just all kinds of stuff and I have no respect for a man like that […] [who] cares more about what goes in his pockets, like he tells [us]. He used to come to us in meetings […] I'll just tell you how this goes down, you tell me what you would think as a coal miner. [H]e's talking about taking money and vacation days and stuff from you […] [because it] cost[s] […] too much money, but he goes to each one of these mines, in a helicopter, flies around the parking lot with the nose down counting cars in the parking lot, to see how many people are there. This is God's truth. Then he'll go down and land [his helicopter] where only [the] emergency medivac is supposed to be. [He'd] land his helicopter, have a driver that drove all the way from Ohio, in like an Escalade or something like that, pick him up and drive him up to the meeting and then he gets out [of the car for the] meeting and tells us how he ain't got no money […] we're costing him so much money […] then he goes out, gets in his helicopter, and takes off.

Did he get booed?

Dennison: You didn't say too much because you'd get fired. But you see where I'm going with this? What kinda respect do you have for somebody that can literally come in, in a helicopter, pay another guy to drive and come in, not just by himself, but have four or five bodyguards with him, bringing his priest with him, paying for his priest's hotel room – this preacher rather, whatever – he always went everywhere with him, paid him. This guy was on his salary, on his payroll, but we can't get parts we need to make the miner run safely or efficiently or to fix this belt line or to fix this fall that happened that was half-assed [and] got blocked up because we don't have the right shit to do it right to go in and bolt on it and do it right. But he's gonna fly around in a freaking helicopter? You can't respect somebody like that. I can't, I'm sorry. And he always started off, 'I've broke my neck three times, I've had my back broke once, I've had six strokes, ten heart attacks.' And I ain't kidding you […] I mean that's the kinda crap he used to say. […] I was at one of the meetings one time, this was probably the seventh or eighth one we'd had […] and, you had to be there, [if he] didn't [hold the meeting] on your shift, [you] had to come in off-shift to do it. You'd come and […] listen to him […] I was sitting there one day, God forgive me for saying it, because I shouldn't have, because I swore I'd never do nothing like that ever, again, […] but, I was sitting there and [he says,] 'I've had my neck broke blah, blah, blah', and […] I said, 'if I broke your fucking neck you wouldn't be standing up there!' […] [T]hey don't wanna hear what you have to say, like when they ask you if you got something to say, well, I go to say what I wanna say and I'm asked to leave because I'm disrupting the meeting.

Do you think that Murray believed that he was giving the miners a motivational speech?

Dennison: Well, that was a union mine […] and he wants it gone. That was the whole thing, he bought them union mines and his sole purpose is to bust up the union. [L]ike I told them younger guys, I said, 'yeah, they took this and that away from you', but, I said, 'listen to me, I worked them non-union mines [and] I went from ten dollars […] to sixteen dollars an hour and […] when the coal prices went down, I went back to eleven dollars an hour. Then I was up twenty some[thing] an hour and [then] went back to twelve dollars and fifty cents an hour. [The non-union coal operators] can change your pay anytime they want. [They could] do anything they wanted to [do to miners].' Well, 'you're not gonna do this, you're gonna go on this shift, and you're gonna work every Saturday and Sunday, take off Monday and Tuesday, or take off Monday and Wednesday.' [That's] how it is.

Did you feel that Murray came to these meetings to threaten miners?

Dennison: Oh yeah, he does threaten [miners] all the time. Everything he says is a threat [be]cause he'll tell you, 'I'll fire you, I'll close [the mine].'

He's telling us, 'if you don't do this, I'm going to shut this place down.' What kinda man is that? He needs to work on his motivational speaking.

Would you encourage your children to become coal miners?

Dennison: No. My children both been told if they ever work in a coal mine I'll take my hand to them [...] I am very serious. I don't want them [to] because it's too dangerous. I don't want them to have to work like that. I want my kids [...] to go to school and have [things]. I want them to work for what they get, but I don't want them to have to go to work wondering if they're gonna come home alive or missing [a] hand, or with lung disease. I want them to go enjoy life cause there, coal mining, you don't have a life. You work six days a week, guaranteed and you work twelve to sixteen hours a day, guaranteed. [...] It gets old after a while.

Matt Wiseman was born in Elkins, West Virginia, and raised in Belington, West Virginia. At 18, he enlisted in the US Navy. Matt served as a gas turbine electrician from 1999 to 2003 aboard the San Jacinto, during which time he earned the ESWS, Navy Achievement Medal, Good Conduct Medal, Battle Effectiveness Award and the Overseas Expeditionary Medal. He returned to Belington after receiving his honourable discharge from the navy in 2003. Three years later, he went to work in the West Virginia coal mines. He worked as a roof bolter at Mettiki located near Davis, West Virginia, from 2006 to 2007 and as a roof bolter for Anchor, ICG and ArchCoal at numerous mines across the state, including Sago and Philippi, from 2007 to 2014. While working for Arch Coal in 2011, he injured his mouth, eye and shoulder in a mining accident. He currently works as a claims specialist at the Veteran's Administration. He was interviewed at his home in Belington during the summer of 2017.

Wiseman: [discussing his accident at Arch Coal]: We had to build a wall with belt and power, because that's what keeps your air in front of your headings. We built the wall. We didn't have any mud, no headers, no wedges. Nothing to tighten the wall up. They told us to go ahead and build it. We built it. We called out. We had three-quarters of a wall built and no way to hold it up. So, they sent someone with wedges[32] and mud and headers on a man trip,[33] which wasn't allowed. When it got there, I took it in to wedge the wall in, but the wall blew over. Knocked out some teeth, detached my retina, crushed my shoulder. We get outside. I go to the doctor. [...] They stitch up my eye. When I came back to work the next day, they let me go to work. Nothing said. Came in the second day, and they said, until they have a meeting with me, they can't let me work. So, they put me off work for a week without pay after letting me work a night, because

I was hurt and they wanted to have a meeting. We have a meeting. I ended up off on compensation because they wouldn't work with my doctor saying, well, he's a roof bolter. He can't roof bolt or he can't do this. So, they just put me out of work. You have to be off of work for a year on compensation in a case like this before you're terminated. Granted, no one's going to stay off work a year. So, then we got a lawyer and it turned into a compensation battle. It took over two years for them to pay me the money they owed me. To me, it was a bullshit thing. If you want to get down to brass tacks, you're not even supposed to have wood [wedges] in a [mine] wall. I never fought them on negligence. I never fought them on nothing. I just wanted my money through compensation. Then we went our separate ways. I still have friends down there, but I haven't talked to anyone from Arch [Coal]. Right after I was hurt, the safety man did send me a text message that I showed my lawyer: 'Go ahead and come to work. Just keep your doctor's note so nobody sees it.' Stuff like that coming from a safety man is not what I'd call safe. You're telling me to hide it, but when something happens, you're not there to tell them, yeah, I told him so. So, me and Arch [Coal] don't have a good relationship after this.

Why do you think the wall that injured you fell down?

Wiseman: We built the wall. There's always air pressure on your belt line. There's air pushing against it. Theoretically, the way you should build a wall is once you get one side to the top, you put wedges in it. That holds it. And when you get to the next spot, you just wedge it clear across. It's always tight. It's always solid. They didn't have all the block. They didn't have all the stuff down there. They told us, go ahead and build it. They'd get the stuff later. In my opinion, that should have been a priority. We should have gotten a tractor down there and got this equipment in. We're told to build the wall and we did. We did just what we were told. When I went in, it had all the wind it could take. When it blew over, that was it. There was absolutely nothing holding that wall to the top. They should have said, don't build the wall until we get this stuff there. That was their call. We were just following orders.

Have you witnessed other miners injured or killed on the job?

Wiseman: Yeah. There's a lot of them that I can't even remember being on section.[34] We had a red hat[35] killed underground and that's bad all around. His dad was a boss, so he was there. It's a bad way to end your day especially being there. We had three guys run over with a scoop.[36] I don't [know] any one [that] was killed in that, but you'll never heal completely. You had a lot of falls. Or a rock falling and hitting your hand or back. You've always got injuries.

Was your coal mining father ever injured on the job?

Wiseman: He ended up having back surgery. [I]t had something to do with the belt line. He ended up getting hurt at work. He used to get up and have my mom put his boots on because he couldn't bend over and tie them and would go to work. And, finally, he got stuck in one of the pieces of equipment. He couldn't get himself out, he hurt so bad. So, they had to take him out and made him get surgery. Other than that? Smashed fingers. Cuts. Now, his dad, my grandpa, was trapped for two days underground. [...] I wouldn't recommend that to anybody. Doesn't sound like it'd be too much fun.

What would you like to see your children do in the future?

Wiseman: Honestly, I'd like to see both of my kids go to college and do something like you guys are doing. Something that's not putting them in a bad job every day. I'm working at the VA now. It's a great job with great benefits. I love it. I'm not worried about the roof falling on me anymore. My boys growing up were going to be coal miners because dad was a coal miner. Now that they're older, they don't really say anything. I would not want my boys underground. I see the ways it works down there. I've seen the guys that bring in alcohol and liquor. We've come out and had to take breathalysers. That's pretty bad to get a breathalyser after your shift or before your shift. I don't want my boys down there. I want them to get an education and do something that's going to be productive to the world and [...] not going nowhere. Computer skills? Nursing? My wife's a nurse. They could follow in her footsteps. Even the railroads are a good job. They're not going nowhere.

Steven Lipscomb was born and raised in Elkview, West Virginia. At 19, he enlisted in the United States Marine Corps (USMC). He served as a marine infantryman from March 2002 to April 2005 at Fast Company, Yorktown, Virginia, and Twenty-Nine Palms, California. While in service, he earned the Pistol and Rifle Expert Medal, Purple Heart Medal, War on Terrorism Service Medal, Navy Achievement Medal and a Good Conduct Medal. He returned to Elkview in 2005 after receiving his honourable discharge from the USMC and went to work in the West Virginia coal mines. He worked as a roof bolter at Mammoth Coalmine located in Mammoth, West Virginia, beginning in October 2006. He currently works as an underground fire boss at Alpha Natural Resources. He was interviewed at his home in Elkview during the summer of 2017.

Would you encourage either of your daughters to work in the mines?

Lipscomb: If you would meet my daughters, they know darn well neither one of them would ever go in there. […] Hypothetically, I don't think a coal mine is a place for a lady. [The] reason I say that because it is the most unprofessional profession there is. Coal miners, I mean […] they draw stuff that […] Coal miners act like a bunch of kids at times.

If you had a son, would you encourage him to work in the mines?

Lipscomb: I would try to encourage him to do something a little bit more secure […] I want my kids to go to college.

The veteran miners were quick to point out that military service and mining share several distinctive cultural commonalities, such as a demanding appreciation of solidarity and camaraderie in the face of near-constant risk, danger and uncertainty. Moreover, several of the veteran miners spoke frankly about opioid misuse, a public health epidemic that has disproportionately impacted Appalachians generally and Appalachian veterans and coal miners, specifically. Mr Carter attributed this disparate impact to the significant mental and physical health risks attendant to both military service and mining. In fact, he described the cycle of miners incurring work-related injuries, receiving prescription opioids from a doctor in order to continue to work and, ultimately, abusing the medication as 'the coal miner's story here in West Virginia, in which so many of us have dealt with'. He went on to say,

> You know, if you miss work because you're hurt, well, you're not gonna be there long. So what do you do? You gotta get up and go to work. You're hurting so bad. Doctor gives you pain pills and I'll take one, go to work. Well tomorrow, gotta get up and take two to get up to go to work. Next day, I gotta get up and take three to get up to go to work.
>
> [This dynamic] […] fuels the heroin epidemic because once you get cut off from your doctor for your pain pills, heroin is cheaper than the pain pills. So, you paid ten dollars per pill, takes you ten pills to get high. So, that's a hundred bucks. Well, that hundred bucks, you can get high ten times with heroin.

> I've watched my own family destroyed by it. [...] I probably lost [...] one of the most important people in my life because of opioid addiction, because of the coal mining industry [...] I won't ever get that person back in my life again [...] I feel that our government should honestly do something more about it.

When asked, 'is this also something that happens to veterans who are injured' in service, Mr Carter replied, 'Yes, ma'am, it does. Every day, and I see it every day. I've seen a lot of soldiers effected by that situation. That's what they do to us coal miners, too.' He even related that he left Campbell's Creek due to the havoc that opioid abuse has wrought on his home town:

> I removed myself from that place [...] and that's a big part of the tough time that they're going through right now [...] it's because of the opioid problem that we have in our region [...] men and women that worked in the coal mines [...] not only are most of the coal mines shutting down [...] lot of them guys when [...] coal did open back up for some kinda work, they were so hurt and beat up, and so strung out on the pain pills that these doctors prescribed us [...] companies wouldn't take them back. They couldn't, I mean [...] legally [...] it would have been a suicide note for most of them guys to go back down there. They were so high and strung out on these pills.

Mr Dennison conceded that he had taken prescription painkillers in order to work in the mines with a dislocated shoulder and elbow. He said, 'I'll bet you 90% of your coal miners is on pain meds.' In response to a query about the rampant use of prescription painkillers in the mines, he paused and then remarked, 'It's scary, but you do it. Everybody functions. Just how it works.' Mr Lipscomb also admitted that he takes medication on a daily basis to manage his service-related PTSD:

> I went to Iraq and [...] I was [...] there and right around April 12, 2004. I hit an IED. [...] We got ambushed and [...] a whole Humvee of guys got hurt, one guy got killed. He was my roommate. Had a lieutenant; his daughter was born while were in Kuwait. He lost both his legs.
>
> ...
>
> I'm medicated through the VA, so I take my medication every day. [...] I'm not gonna say I'm a ball of sunshine every single day because I'm not. I mean, there's days that I'm a complete butthole and I mean [I] just have days like that. [...] [T]here's days you know, nights I can't sleep through. There's nights that I've had flashbacks there you know but a positive support

network is the main thing, as I said. I have a great wife. She's always been there, no matter what, you know. No matter how I've acted, she's never judged me any different.

Environmental and Community Impacts

Several of the veteran miners subscribed to the philosophy that environmental regulation – as opposed to mechanization or the inability to compete with cheaper natural gas – had significantly contributed to the Appalachian coal industry's decline. Those miners expressed their dissatisfaction with lawmakers they perceived as over-regulators, including former president Barack Obama. In addition, the majority of the veteran miners espoused the view that environmental pollution is simply the price that coal communities must pay in order for people to make a living. At least two of the miners, however, expressed concern about the impact of coal mining and the other extractive industries on West Virginia's natural environment.

What poses the greatest threat to coal production in Appalachia?

Lipscomb: Environmental. Well, you know, I mean, they came up with… global warming, and you know, apparently it was a hoax and then they just changed the name of it to climate change and […] the coal put off something in the air? Yeah, probably, but what doesn't? Everything does. You think God would put something on this Earth that would destroy one of his greatest creations?

…

I think Trump is doing a tremendous job for the coal industry and […] I don't wanna talk about politics but, it's like, whenever you have a Republican in office, the coal market is up, whenever you have a Democrat in office, it's down. And […] you can see whenever Bush was in office, it was up, when Obama got in, it was low, and you know now that Trump's back in – and it's just like whenever Trump was elected, we went from working forty hours to working fifty hours in a matter of a week. From the day the election results came out, we went back to work.

Carter: Obama really had his way and started affecting all the coal miners in West Virginia, Pennsylvania, Kentucky, Virginia […] just, basically all-out war on the working man […] laid a bunch of us off, got rid of us, didn't care how we fed our families. You know, we made a decent wage but, for what we did for the work, and what we supplied for the country, you know, we put our lives on the line every day, to be out of work like that to watch your family start falling apart, kids suffering [...], it's just [...] kinda something I really wasn't ready for.

Does mountain top removal pollute rivers and streams?

Wiseman: I'm sure that's possible. Just like everything else, you have rules to run by, but does that mean everybody ran by them at that time? No. For the most part, we put in our own cleaning plants/systems that are usually pretty well taken care of. But at the same time, you're only going to have so much equipment and so much work done somewhere without some consequences. I've never been involved with any of that mountaintop removal method. I've steered clear of that direction.

Are you concerned about the environmental impact of coal mining on West Virginia communities?

Dennison: Yeah. I worry about it all the time, because I see what they do. And I know what they do, and that's why [...] back when I was a kid, you could go to the stream, take a cup full of your hand and drink the water. Can't [now]. You don't know what you're drinking. I've seen the crap that goes in coal mines and what comes out of a coal mine. I had to go [...] and get shots for hepatitis – just to make sure I didn't get hepatitis, you know what I mean? The boosters for them. I've seen when it was in the news when that sanitation place over in Blacksville [, WV] [...] that guy got busted and fined all that money for [...] dumping that raw sewage. [...] They dumped it down [...] a sealed shaft at Consol [Energy]. I saw them do it, and I went to the mine and told them they were dumping it because we pump that water out from behind the seal and it always smelled like a sewer. They didn't believe me. They found out what was going on [and] then we all had to take the shots and get tested for this and that. [Consol] got fined like [...] three point something million dollars over that and, God, I watched [a Consol employee] dump [sewage] right down there in the Mooresville shaft. I followed him up there.

What do you think about surface mining[37] and its impacts on the environment?

Dennison: I think, if they would go back and fix what they tore up, I wouldn't be against it. I don't like surface mining [...] and it's not just cause I was an underground coal miner, I don't like it because of the way they tear up the Earth […] and they do. I mean […] we're underground but everything we do, is […] supported, to keep from affecting up here and down there. [Then] up here they go in the surface [and] you can't control all the overflows from the crap that they dug out, and the diesel from your equipment, the oil. You can only keep so much of that out of the environment and then it's back in anyway. And then they leave it, it don't look like it did when they came. Not even near. And, usually, [they leave old] equipment laying [around]. You'll still see tore up equipment laying there, and, I just don't like surface mining, never did.

…

And like, with the natural gas […] I don't mind the natural gas except for the fracking. I don't like the fracking […] [be]cause they can say whatever they want to say, and I've worked underground, and I know that when you shut off an explosion underground, it affects […] wide areas. So […] they can say whatever crap they want to say [about fracking being safe for the environment], I don't believe it. I don't believe it.

Returning Home from Service and Mining Coal

As noted above, the veterans who returned from service to work the West Virginia mines explained that they did so because their significant personal and family financial obligations precluded them from taking advantage of the G.I. Bill and attending college or finding any other work in the state that was as lucrative for an individual with only a high-school education.

Why did you go work in the mines when you returned home from military service?

Carter: [I] […] went back to Campbell's Creek […] things weren't working out right, so I went back into the Army again and got married, had a child on the way. I decided I better do something and straighten myself out, so I decided to become a coal miner.

…

I heard a lot of people say back then […], 'I'm not the coal mining type.' Well you know what, I wasn't either. I had a kid to feed, man. I had a pretty woman to take care of […] I had to do something. I had to be a man. You know […] watching my great grandad and pawpaw […] to me was high expectations. As a man you know. How they treated their wives, how they got up went to work every day. Blood, sweat and tears, didn't matter. Doesn't matter if [you're] hurt, sick, whatever. You got to get to work every day and provide for your family. That's what I had to do, provide for that little boy [points to his son].

...

I didn't [mine coal] for me. I didn't go get up and go every day to put [...] myself through that bullshit. If I didn't have a beautiful wife and kids, I'd go out here and flip burgers somewhere.

Why did you turn down a recent offer to return to work in the coal mines?

Carter: I was trying to figure some stuff out at that point [...] after being a coal miner for all that time [...] figure out where I was gonna head in life, so I just sat my little boy down and said, 'you know, got this guy aggravating me, wanting me to work back in the coal mines son.' [He] kinda put his head down a little bit. I said, 'but I've already got a job lined up over here at the VA hospital, [...] daddy would be right here in town every day, and you could call and daddy would be right here.' 'Or I can go back to the coal mines and I could buy you all that nice stuff we used to have. Do you want more money or do you want daddy every day?' He said, 'well, I want my daddy every day.' I said, 'so you want me to take the job over here?' He said, 'yeah, I don't like you working in the coal mines.' I said, 'alright, buddy, that's what daddy will do', so I walked away from the coal mines. As long as I live it will be up to them kids in there whether I go back to the coal mines or not because they're the ones who [have] seen daddy suffer, struggle, grouchy, hurt.

What did your wife think about your decision to work in the mines?

Dennison: She hated it [...] and my kids never liked it. I missed the first five years of my son's life in the coal mines.

Did you consider using your G.I. Bill benefits to earn a college degree post-service?

Dennison: Yeah, I did once [...] and, when I did think about it, I was working because I had a kid and I didn't have the opportunity for the capability to just stop working and […] go to school […] I want my kids to go to school and do what they want to do. After that I don't care [be]cause […] they're not to go in the military and they're not to go in the coal mines.

Why did you go work in the mines when you returned home from military service?

Lipscomb: I mean, I came home, you know, and I had a few small jobs and wasn't making any money. You have a brotherhood you form in the military. I mean people say especially combat guys. I mean, they literally are like your brothers […] you know, then my brother was talking about he was in the coal mines and he asked me […] And, a few months later, I go do it because […] unfortunately […] I fell in love. I didn't wanna go to school because I wanted to marry [my wife] and I can't be married and going to school. I have a wife to support so I was like, 'I'll do that.' And I've been doing it now for like eleven years.

So, you were motivated to go into the mines because of the money?

Lipscomb: The money. That was it. I mean, I don't get to see the sun pretty much for like two weeks out of the month, but […] you still get to make a good living. You get to provide for your family.

What would you have done when you returned home from the military if you had not started a family?

Lipscomb: When […] I got out of the Marine Corps, I wanted to go into the dental field. […] I was the guy in Iraq that always had dental floss, mouthwash, and they all laughed at me. But you know what […] I had crooked teeth as a kid. My mom got me braces […] and now I got a nice smile, so I wanted to keep it.

Would you utilize the G.I. Bill today if you were still eligible for that benefit?

Lipscomb: I don't think I would leave the coal industry. There's a lot of jobs now […] they want some type of degree. Just like I tried to apply for Homeland Security. Well, I didn't have a degree, but I had experience. Well, the degree, apparently, surpasses experience. I don't know why but OK. So, I wanted to do Homeland Security. I wanted to do something like that.

Why did you go work in the mines when you returned home from military service?

Wiseman: My whole family is miners. My wife's family is miners. And the money, because I went to school and got my electrician's license, but you had to have so many years in it before made any real money. So, I just went with the money.

Do most miners go into mining because of the pay?

Wiseman: That's why everyone does it. They say you need to have coal for energy. You need lumber for your house. Why does a sawmill make nine dollars an hour and coal mine make twenty-nine? Swap that around and where do you think the coal miners are gonna go? Coal miners will follow the money. A lot of people around here didn't even graduate high school. They went to the coal mines to help the family. It used to be a family thing. The money wasn't that great. You had company stores,[38] but it was a job and you supported your family. Then it turned into a pride thing. Then you get these big companies that come in and took away the pride. Now, you're just there to get the money and get out of that hole. It's like pulling teeth to get people to come to work, let alone stay another hour. So, it was money. It wasn't a pride thing. I wasn't trying to follow in anyone's footsteps.

Would you ever go back to the mines to work?

Wiseman: If something happened to my job now and it was the only thing I had, yes. I'll do whatever to support my family. Would I ever go back to the mines unless it was an absolute you have to? No. I miss the mines like you miss a toothache. Not at all. […] I'll never go back underground.

What's the best part about no longer working in the coal mines?

Wiseman: The headache and the worry. And when I got crushed, I was in the ER […] and my wife comes down from the second floor without a clue […] and I'm lying there getting my eye cleaned up and stitched. I don't have that worry anymore. Am I going to come home tonight? Am I gonna have to write notes and put them in my dinner bucket for when they find and dig us out? Now, I've got a great job. I've got my federal benefits, my 401k. I get six hours vacation every two weeks and four hours sick leave. The stress relief of not being down there. I got to the point when I'd be miserable in the morning. I don't miss it. Not one little bit. Not at all. [Response to statement 'your wife probably doesn't miss it, either']: No. The black coal dust in her dryer. The worrying about whether I was coming home. But the money was great. I made $29 per hour working 10 minutes from home. The money wasn't everything. I'll never go back. The next time I go underground will probably be when they bury me.

Conclusion

For 10 days at the end of April and beginning of May 2013, the UN Working Group on Business and Human Rights carried out a country visit to the United States.[39] West Virginia was among the states that they visited while they were there. During their stay, members of the Working Group met with government officials, representatives from coal companies and members of the communities directly affected by coal mining activities to discuss the issue of coal mining (specifically surface mining) and its impact on human rights. In the subsequent report that they submitted to the UN Human Rights Council discussing the issues, the Working Group noted that 'according to information received from both industry sources and community representatives, many coal-mining communities are deeply divided about the significance of surface mining and its impact'.[40] In that same report, the Working Group also met with community representatives where they heard 'allegations of significant adverse human rights impacts arising from surface mining, most notably related to physical and mental health'.[41]

The conflicted nature of coal mining seems best amplified by the stories told in this chapter. On the one hand, coal provides good wages and stable employment for many who otherwise would not have access to that opportunity. In the short term, for veterans returning to their homes, coal mining provides for an immediate entry into income. On the other hand, the long-term costs of mining are often extended into the miners' next generation and their community. The toll outlined here is heavy and the cost of the black dollar is mighty indeed.

Notes

1 Shannon Elizabeth Bell and Richard York, 'Community Economic Identity: The Coal Industry and Ideology Construction in West Virginia', *Rural Sociology* vol. 75 (2010), 111, 111–12.

2 Ibid., 112.

3 James Van Nostrand, 'Why the U.S. Coal Industry and Its Jobs Are Not Coming Back', *Yale Environment*, 360, 1 December 2016, https://e360.yale.edu/features/why_us_coal_industry_and_its_jobs_are_not_coming_back (accessed 21 November 2019).

4 West Virginia Geological & Economic Survey, 'History of West Virginia Mineral Industries – Coal', http://www.wvgs.wvnet.edu/www/geology/geoldvco.htm (last accessed 21 November 2019).

5 Philip Bump, 'There are Fewer Coal Miners Than You Might Realize', *Wash. Post*, 20 March 2017, https://www.washingtonpost.com/news/politics/wp/2017/03/20/there-are-fewer-coal-miners-than-you-might-realize/?utm_term=.0aa164c79071 (explaining that, as of 'May 2015, there were 69,460 jobs in coal mining itself – only 15,900 of which were extraction workers or helpers, mining machine operators or earth drillers', which amounts to '0.019 percent of the American workforce'). West Virginia only employs approximately 12,000 coal miners out of a population of 1.8 million people. Bill Raney, president of the West Virginia Coal Association, 'West Virginia Coal Will Overcome Challenges', https://www.wvcoal.com; see also James A. Haught, 'A Short History of Mining – and Its Decline – in West Virginia', *The Register-Herald*, 30 March 2017, http://www.register-herald.com/opinion/columns/a-short-history-of-mining----and-its/article_4c968cfd-8d8b-51c7-bccb-77e186ea61f7.html.

6 Bell and York, 'Community Economic Identity', 112.

7 W.V. Dep't of Veterans Assistance, 'WV Veteran Statistics', 2013, https://veterans.wv.gov/resources/Pages/WVVeteransStatistics.aspx.

8 W.V. Pub. Broadcasting, 'Vietnam: West Virginians Remember', https://tv.wvpublic.org/vietnamwv/ (last accessed 21 November 2019).

9 S. Walker, 'Assessing the Mental Health Consequences of Military Combat in Iraq and Afghanistan: A Literature Review', *Journal of Psychiatric Mental Health Nursing* vol. 17 (2010), 790, 794.

10 'Leave No Veteran Behind', *Economist*, 2 June 2011, http://www.economist.com/node/18775315.

11 US Gov't Accountability Office, 'Veterans Affairs: Better Understanding Needed to Enhance Services to Veterans Readjusting to Civilian Life', 6, 2014, http://www.gao.gov/assets/670/665725.pdf.

12 Ken Ward, Jr., Charleston Gazette-Mail, Deaths at UBB 'entirely preventable', MSHA says," 6 December 2011, https://www.wvgazettemail.com/news/special_reports/deaths-at-ubb-entirely-preventable-msha-says/article_fe12c41f-fcdb-519b-a12d-7c6896c961a7.html (last accessed 21 November 2019).

("In that [...] report, MSHA concluded that the April 5, 2010, explosion that killed 29 miners was 'entirely preventable' and could have been avoided if Performance and its then-parent company, Massey Energy, had followed long-standing and well-known safety standards."); ibid. ("MSHA investigators also focused their report on a wealth of evidence that Massey covered up safety conditions at Upper Big Branch, by keeping hazards out of official record, warning workers underground of impending inspections, and intimidating miners to keep them from reporting safety concerns to the government.")

13 United Mine Workers of America, 'Industrial Homicide: Report on the Upper Big Branch Mine Disaster', 12, 25 October 2011, https://miningquiz.com/pdf/Disasters/134334-Upper-Big-Branch.pdf.

14 Ibid.

15 Ibid., 13.

16 Ibid., 14 (emphasis in original). The UMWA further surmised that 'had Massey Energy been in compliance with all the mandatory health and safety standards related to the conditions that contributed to the explosion on April 5, 2010, the explosion would not have occurred'. Ibid., 15.

17 US Dep't of Labor Mine Safety and Health Admin., 'Upper Big Branch Independent Investigation Report Executive Summary 2', 2011, https://www.msha.gov/sites/default/files/Data_Reports/Fatals/Coal/Upper%20Big%20Branch/ExecutiveSummary.pdf (last accessed 21 November 2019).

18 Ibid.

19 Ibid.

20 A 'cut plan' is a plan of operation and procedure regarding where miners will cut for coal. The plan should insure that there is proper ventilation for the miners. See U.S. Department of Labor, 'Procedure Instruction Letter No. I12-V-11', 30 April 2012, https://arlweb.msha.gov/regs/complian/PILS/2012/PIL12-V-11.asp.

21 Robert E. Murray is the founder and chief executive officer of Murray Energy Corporation. Dominic Rushe, 'Top US Coal Boss Robert Murray: "Trump Can't Bring Mining Jobs Back"', *Guardian*, 27 March 2017, https://www.theguardian.com/environment/2017/mar/27/us-coal-industry-clean-power-plan-donald-trump. Murray Energy Company self-characterizes as the 'largest underground coal mining company in America', http://www.murrayenergycorp.com/.

22 J. J. Sammarco et al., 'An Analysis of Roof Bolter Fatalities and Injuries in U.S. Mining', *Transactions of Society for Mining, Metallurgy, and Exploration* vol. 340, 1, 2 (2016). ('Roof bolting is a critical activity following the extraction of commodities such as coal, metal ore or stone, to help keep the roof from collapsing. Mining results in a section of unsupported roof. This unsupported roof is secured by roof bolting to help prevent roof cave-ins.')

23 A 'spotter' is a coal miner who assists with roof bolting by identifying spots on the roof strata that require additional reinforcement.

24 'Methane [is] a gas composed of carbon and hydrogen [...] High concentrations of methane [...] can accumulate in confined spaces and act as an asphyxiant or become flammable. These dangers can be mitigated through enhanced venting of the well casing or venting confined spaces [...] and removing any ignition sources.' US Dep't of Interior Geological Survey, 'What Is Methane and Why Is It a Safety Concern?' https://www.usgs.gov/faqs/what-methane-and-why-it-a-safety-concern?qt-news_science_products=0#qt-news_science_products (last accessed 21 November 2019).

25 'Pumpers' used machinery to remove water and other liquid mining by-products from the coal mine.

26 'Bleeders' or 'bleeder entries' are '[s]pecial air courses developed and maintained as part of the mine ventilation system and designed to continuously move air-methane mixtures emitted by the gob or at the active face away from the active workings and into mine-return air courses'. Kentucky Coal and Energy Education Project, *Glossary of Mining Terms*, http://www.coaleducation.org/glossary.htm [hereinafter *Glossary*]. A 'gob' is the 'term applied to that part of the mine from which the coal has been removed and the space more or less filled up with waste'. Ibid.

27 'Readings' are the readings on the various instruments in mines that monitor the levels of various potentially dangerous airborne chemicals, including methane and natural gas.

28 A 'sniffer' is a methane monitor, which is 'an electronic instrument often mounted on a piece of mining equipment, that detects and measures the methane content of mine air'. Ibid.

29 A 'spotter' is a portable methane monitor. Ibid.

30 A 'miner' is a 'continuous miner', which is 'a machine that constantly extracts coal while it loads it. This is to be distinguished from a conventional, or cyclic, unit which must stop the extraction process in order for loading to commence.' Ibid.

31 A 'boss' is 'any member of the managerial ranks who is directly in charge of miners.' Ibid. A 'fire boss' is 'one who examines a coal mine to determine whether firedamp is present, to search for fires caused by blasting, and to check on the general safety of the mine.' Merriam-Webster Dictionary, https://www.merriam-webster.com/dictionary/fire%20boss.

32 A 'wedge' is 'a piece of wood tapering to a thin edge and used for tightening in conventional timbering'. Kentucky Coal and Energy Education Project, *Glossary of Mining Terms.*

33 A 'man trip' is 'a carrier of mine personnel, by rail or rubber tire, to and from the work area'. Ibid.

34 A 'section' is any 'portion of the working area of a mine'. Ibid.

35 The term 'red hat' applies to a new or apprentice miner whereas the term 'black hat' refers to certified or veteran coal miners. Suzanne E. Tallichet, 'The Underground Proving Ground: Women and Men in an Appalachian Coal Mine', in *Women Working in the Environment: Resourceful Natures*, ed. Carolyn E. Sachs (New York: Taylor & Francis, 2017), 32.

36 A 'scoop' is 'a rubber tired-, battery- or diesel-powered piece of equipment designed for cleaning runways and hauling supplies'. Kentucky Coal and Energy Education Project, *Glossary of Mining Terms.*

37 'Surface coal mining involves [...] removing parts or all of mountaintops to expose buried seams of coal, and [...] disposing in adjacent valleys the excess [...] "overburden" (rock above the coal seam), and "interburden" (rock between coal seams). Overburden and interburden are disposed of in adjacent valleys because the broken rock will not all fit back into the mining pit, and disposal alternatives are limited.' US Environmental Protection Agency, *Basic Information about Surface Coal Mining in Appalachia*, https://www.epa.gov/sc-mining/basic-information-about-surface-coal-mining-appalachia#what (last accessed 21 November 2019).

38 Until the 1950s, coal companies frequently paid their laborers in company 'script' instead of US currency. Miners, in turn, were then limited to using the script at the local store owned by the coal company – the company store – in the company town. See Price V. Fishback, 'Did Coal Miners "Owe Their Souls to the Company Store"?: Theory and Evidence from the Early 1990s', *Journal of Economic History* vol. 46 (1986), 1011; see also Hardy Green, *The Company Town: The Industrial Edens and Satantic Mills That Shaped the American Economy* (New York: Basic Books, 2010).

39 'Statement at the End of the Visit to the United States UN Working Group on Business and Human Rights, Washington D.C., 1 May 2013', *United Nations Human Rights Office of the High Commissioner*, 1 May 2013, https://newsarchive.ohchr.org/EN/NewsEvents/Pages/DisplayNews.aspx?NewsID=13284&LangID=E.

40 Working group End of Country Report United States, HRC/2625/Add.4 at p. 16, 06 May 2014.

41 Ibid.

Chapter 10

ABANDONED: A TALE OF TWO MINE CLOSURES IN SOUTH AFRICA

Michael Clemens and Maria Isabel Cubides

Boitumelo and Nambitha, residents of the now-defunct mine villages of Durban Deep and Blyvooruitzicht, recall with nostalgia the time when their families first moved to these areas. The men of their respective families had secured employment with the mines, which provided them with access to electricity, running water, education and housing. 'Life was vibrant', said Nambitha. 'We had everything we needed and we thought that the future was bright.'

But their lives would rapidly, and unexpectedly, change when the mines suddenly ceased operation, leaving them breathing toxic air, stuck with few employment opportunities and struggling to find answers about the future.

The similarities between the women's stories, which occurred in the major South African gold mining belt within 10 years of each other, illustrate the persistent human rights challenges of the mining industry in South Africa in respect to proper mine closure, despite recent reinforcement of the domestic legal framework. Against the background of a rapidly declining gold mining industry, serious questions arise around the long-term sustainability of this extractive industry model: who will bear the costs of rehabilitation and undertake responsibility for the environmental and human rights impacts once these companies are gone?

The stories of the Blyvooruitzicht and Durban Deep mining communities, located in the gold mining belt of the Gauteng province of South Africa, offer a damning portrait of the systemic marginalization that many communities, having grown up around major mining operations in the country, experience

Inga Tshayisa conducted the interviews contained in this chapter and contributed valuable research and drafting for this work. The communities of Durban Deep and Blyvooruitzicht were enormously generous with their time and in sharing the stories that shine a light on the problem of improper mine closure in South Africa today. We are grateful for these contributions.

in the aftermath of the improper closure of those operations. The inability of these communities to access their rights to environmental health and to socio-economic well-being, once these operations have been abandoned or put on hold, has significant consequences for those communities in accessing other rights: namely, the rights to equality, dignity and life – despite the fact that these represent fundamental guarantees of the South African constitution and are an integral part of the international human rights framework.

Commitment by mining corporations and state regulators to respect and fulfil human rights throughout the full business cycle means that proper mine closure must be viewed as an integral part of this commitment. Planning for and addressing the end of a business cycle must, in the context of mining, include robust contemplation of the enormous physical, social and economic zones of impact associated with these operations. In sum, proper mine closure must give the communities left behind the chance at a healthy environment and socio-economic stability.

Importantly, the South African legal framework clearly contemplates management of mine closure processes and impacts, theoretically in pursuit of just this aim. But the experiences of mining communities such as Blyvooruitzicht Mine Village and the Durban Deep are emblematic of the fact that this framework is, in many respects, inadequate. Instead, where comprehensive planning and implementation of a mining plan does not occur, the consequences for the communities left behind are intractable and grow progressively worse with time. These inadequacies are amplified by ambiguities regarding which roles and obligations are the responsibility of mining corporates and which are the responsibility of state regulators. International human rights law is useful in considering the gaps in the domestic legal framework that must be filled in.

Community Experiences: From Durban Deep to Blyvooruitzicht

Durban Deep: The decline of the Grand Old Lady

The nature of gold mining in South Africa is well-known: the geological character of the country's primary gold reef, which contains thin, mineral-rich seams running deep into the earth, requires a massive workforce to toil kilometres underground in order to extract the valuable resource. The resultant labour model, which became the unseemly hallmark of the industry in modern times, was based on groups of black manual labourers overseen by a coterie of white supervisors – facilitated by the ideological particularities of the apartheid regime that the industry both benefitted from and, in many respects, propped up. Technological innovation has little altered the reality at the core of this industry: it is back-breaking work to this day.

The nature of the work also led to the development of vast mining settlements, built and serviced by these mining operations, as the industry became increasingly dependent on a migrant labour force. Over time, the communities grew deep roots given the decades-long lives of the operations that prompted their development and sustained them over time. Thousands of workers and, in some instances, their families still live in these communities today.

But many of these operations are rapidly approaching the end of their economically productive lives across the gold belts of the country; the need for a sustainable model of transition from mining to post-mining for these communities is therefore acute. But the experiences of the Durban Deep community reflect the opposite of what is necessary: years of apparent side-stepping of proper mine closure procedures have resulted in devastating consequences for the residents left behind.

Located on the West Rand, just outside of Johannesburg, the Durban Deep community exists at the intersection of a series of mining rights and abandoned mining properties. Today, the shells of old mine buildings and mine headgear rise from the ground, largely stripped of their valuable steel components. Families live together in abandoned mine hostels or in informal settlements that have sprung up around this decrepit infrastructure. Raw sewage flows in rivulets through the community and lines form around large water tanks whenever trucks contracted by the municipality to provide water to the residents deem fit to arrive. Violent crime is a regular feature of life. Scant evidence of the glory days of a vibrant mining community remains today.

And glory days they were. The Durban Deep Mine itself – around which the community was constructed – was established in the late nineteenth century. Over its lifetime, the mine produced more than 37 million ounces of gold, living up to its moniker: the 'Grand Old Lady'.

The Grand Old Lady nevertheless began to experience operational difficulties in the mid-1990s; by 2000, management had decided to cease production but avoided full and proper closure of the mine. Instead, the company reported, it would 'mothball' its shafts. Then CEO Mike Prinsloo reported that mothballing allowed the company to 'avoid the costs associated with environmental rehabilitation when a mine is closed' even though the company would incur significant retrenchment costs.[1] As Prinsloo stated, 'Despite the losses involved, [mothballing] is still a better alternative to closing the shafts completely as, once a shaft is closed, it is difficult to reopen.'[2]

'Mothballing' mine shafts, or putting them on 'care and maintenance'," essentially means pushing pause on an operation without actually closing it; in other words, while production is ceased, and the labour force is typically at least partially retrenched, the costly process of permanently closing the mine is put off for another day. While the business imperative behind mothballing may be sound – indeed, it is intended to safeguard the later opportunity to restart a mine – the consequences for surrounding communities can be severe. This is in part because South African law does not explicitly govern such a process. Instead, in these scenarios the environmental and socio-economic mine closure obligations required by law are routinely disregarded, since the mine is not technically closing. The lack of regulation of the mothballing process effectively allows a mine to circumvent closure requirements and associated costs, sometimes in perpetuity. The community consequences of keeping mining operations in such a state are real: environmental deterioration becomes the norm, while the socio-economic safeguards meant to be instituted by the mine at closure are simply never implemented. Surrounding communities frequently lose out.[3]

In the case of Durban Deep, it is today clear that certain rehabilitation measures were, over time, implemented. But as the mine remained at a standstill, the surrounding area nevertheless began to deteriorate. In 2007 the mine's parent company, DRDGold – former parent of the Blyvooruitzicht Mine, as detailed below – partnered with various other companies to consolidate their various gold mining projects. The purpose was purportedly to 're-evaluate and re-start mining in the West Rand goldfield'.[4] Mintails Mining South Africa (Pty) Ltd was a key partner in this endeavour, targeting the revival of the Durban Deep Mine itself,[5] although the revival does not seem to have occurred.

Instead Mintails 'teetered on the verge of collapse for years' and, in 2015, initiated the beginning stages of liquidation, which process is still ongoing today.[6] According to documents associated with the liquidation proceedings, Mintails owed various creditors more than $1 billion R, including a roughly $300 million R shortfall in environmental reclamation funding.[7]

Today, remnants of the historically vibrant Durban Deep Mine Village are barely evident. Most in the community live in abandoned mine hostels, the dilapidated homes of former mine managers or have erected shacks on the property. Municipal services were discontinued in 2014, and residents live without running water, access to sanitation services or electricity.[8] An undercurrent of tension regularly cuts through the community, driven largely by high unemployment rates.

Resident Boitumelo[9] recalls the period during the mine's operation as 'stable'. While in operation, the mine provided the community with access to housing, electricity and sanitation, though community members had to pay for these utilities. Boitumelo moved to Durban Deep to live with her partner in 1996. She secured a job as a domestic worker in the area upon arrival. Her partner worked for the mine as a driver and remained in the mine's employ for many years.

'We lived in house No. 51. Our children attended school. We always had enough to eat. It was a nice life, a simple life', Boitumelo recalls.

When the mine closed in 2000, it was a surprise to both Boitumelo and her family as well as many fellow mine employees. The mine did not inform people of its intention to cease operations; 'it just closed. It's like the owner was running away', she says. There was no transition period, no access to skills training. 'Just many men left with no other skills besides the ones that are no longer needed.'

Suddenly unemployed, she and her partner were forced to move from their home into an abandoned mine worker hostel, where they remain today, because they could no longer afford to pay rent. Some of their neighbours in the community weathered mass evictions of the area by the former mine operator in 2007 before also crowding into their hostel and others like it.

Boitumelo regularly surveys the damaged, damp walls of her room, where she lives today with her partner and their two children. 'I am coughing because of the fungus on the walls. We need to paint over it but we cannot afford to buy paint because the money that my partner makes is not enough. We can just afford to buy groceries and pay school fees for the kids.'

The family, like those around them, has no electricity and no running water. Boitumelo describes regular community protests to try and force their local government to assist them. 'The municipality sometimes delivers water in [large tanks], but the water is not safe. We know it is not healthy because it smells bad and you sometimes find hair and other things in it. We know the water is straight from the dams. It is untreated and the children become very ill.' She recalls that a nurse from a nearby medical clinic warned Boitumelo not to allow her children to drink the delivered water, after she arrived seeking treatment for her sick daughter's severe stomach cramps.

Lack of access to sanitation services further compromises the dignity of the families that live in the area. Raw sewage pools around the homes of community members are the result of a collapsed sewage system. 'The toilet situation is very bad', says Boitumelo. 'There are outside toilets made of plastic that are serviced by the municipality once per week. There are not enough of these. No running water. It's a mess. It's such an unhealthy environment, especially for our children.'

Boitumelo notes that as a woman, she sees the impacts of the collapse of the mine from a particular perspective: while men in the area often raise unemployment as the primary after-effect, women suffer more directly the impacts of environmental degradation, from sanitation crises to heavy dust that blankets the area due to the surrounding un-rehabilitated mine dumps. 'We take care of our sick children and are unable to cultivate gardens to feed our families because the soil is sick. We bear these heavy burdens.'

Boitumelo feels the lack of services also leads to increased crime levels: 'it is easier for [people] to commit crime because it gets extremely dark at night as there is no electricity. They rob houses and they rape.' The local police have been unresponsive to the community's complaints against these crimes. This has led aggrieved community members to march to the police station demanding adequate delivery of police services. Boitumelo notes that this action yielded few results.

'It is hard to believe that this is our life now', says Boitumelo, who is unemployed and relies on her partner's meagre salary to maintain herself and their children. 'He has extensive mining experience but this is all he knows how to do, and those jobs just don't exist here anymore. He has to take very low paying contract work.' She tries to supplement her partner's efforts by growing crops to feed her family. But 'the crops get eaten by big rats. There's so many because of the mountains of garbage that surround us.' She cannot recall the last time rubbish was collected.

'That was another lifetime ago', she says.

Blyvooruitzicht: From riches to rags

Since the closure of the Grand Old Lady Durban Deep Mine, mining and environmental legislation regulating mine closure in South Africa has grown progressively more robust, and particularly over the course of the last several years. Such changes would indeed seem precisely targeted at preventing the development of further 'Durban Deeps', as the South African gold mining industry moves into its twilight years.

And yet in 2013, the sudden closure of the Blyvooruitzicht Mine, another major gold mining operation located outside of Johannesburg, raised alarm among mining communities and activists across the country, as the surrounding community there began to bear the brunt of the systemic failure of this revised regulatory regime.

Indeed, the situation faced by the Blyvooruitzicht Mine community today resembles nothing so much as that of the Durban Deep residents, despite revisions to the regulatory framework intended to ensure that that the constitutional and human rights of post-mining communities are protected. Instead, Blyvooruitzicht residents find themselves at the intersection of private sector abdication of responsibility, gaps in the legislative framework and state enforcement effort, and an underestimation of all role players of the scope and severity of a sudden liquidation of a major mining operation on the surrounding community. The story of the Blyvooruitzicht Mine community is eerily similar to that of its cousin, Durban Deep.

Situated in Carletonville, Gauteng, the Blyvooruitzicht Gold Mining Village is today home to some 6,000 people, historically comprised of mine workers and their families and who today exist, largely unemployed, on the edge of the defunct Blyvooruitzicht Gold Mine (the 'Blyvoor Mine'). For over seven decades, the Blyvoor Mine was one of the world's largest and most profitable mining operations, yielding approximately one million kilograms of precious metals and other commodities over its lifetime. The village grew up around this operation: a thriving, relatively integrated community of mine employees, their families, schools, health clinics, churches, playgrounds and meeting spaces. As is typical in mining towns across South Africa, the mine provided access to all basic services, including water, sanitation, rubbish collection and security, even though these services fall within the legal responsibility of the state.

Blyvooruitzicht village resident, Nambitha, describes life during this era as 'comfortable'. Nambitha arrived in Blyvooruitzicht with her mother and two siblings, in 2002, to live with her father, who had moved to Blyvooruitzicht a few years before to work as a general labourer for the mine. According to Nambitha, the primary motivation for her family moving to Blyvooruitzicht was to curtail the challenges that the family faced by being separated from her father, as the breadwinner of the family. Upon arrival in Blyvooruitzicht, Nambitha and her family lived in a family housing unit in an area designated for new employees of the mine.

Nambitha admits that she had a difficult time transitioning from the rural Transkei area to Blyvooruitzicht. To Nambitha, the move highlighted fundamental differences in lifestyles, with Blyvooruitzicht representing a more vibrant and modern environment: 'We had electricity, running water, a house to live in […] and we could even report maintenance problems at the offices of the mine and it would have repairs [to our house] done. The mine paid for all those things. […] We had our basic needs taken care of.' Nambitha explains that community members were only required to cover expenses such as school fees and transportation, out of pocket. Other living costs, including rent and basic services, were covered through a modest deduction from employee pay checks.

She recalls moving around within the Blyvooruitzicht Village as her father moved up the employment ranks. 'We ended up in the "New Village" neighbourhood of the Village, where we currently reside. This is where the white people lived. My father had been promoted to "team leader" so we moved to this nicer neighbourhood. Life was comfortable. We could afford things.'

From this perspective, the development that mining brought to the Blyvooruitzicht area seemed to support the South African constitution's explicit aim to redress past discrimination. The right to equality entrenched in the constitution must be interpreted as a response to the oppression of the apartheid regime, which promoted the socio-economic development of the white portion of the population, to the exclusion of marginalized groups and communities. As such, the constitution safeguards a number of specific rights related to ensuring continuous improvement of the population's living conditions, including the right to secure ecologically sustainable development as well as the use of natural resources while promoting justifiable economic and social development.[10]

The legal framework governing mining, including the Minerals and Petroleum Resources Development Act (MPRDA) and the National Environmental Management Act (NEMA), operationalizes these rights, affirming the state's obligation to protect the environment for the benefit of present and future generations and recognizing 'the need to promote local and rural development and the social upliftment of communities affected by mining'.[11]

This is critical, as remedying the inequality entrenched in the history of the mining industry suggests that marginalized groups and communities should be placed at the forefront of industry beneficiaries in the context of the new democratic order; development must be sustainable and understood to be inexorably intertwined with the health of the environment. The relevant mining and environmental regulatory framework therefore requires not only environmental rehabilitation on closure[12] but also includes various mechanisms for long-term benefit transfer to the communities left behind post-closure; guidelines make clear, for example, that the commitment towards improving the quality of life in these communities 'is expected to persist beyond closure of the business'.[13] The purpose of this requirement is to mitigate the negative impacts of mining activities throughout the business cycle – including its final phases – while promoting economic growth and socio-economic development.[14]

Despite the existence of these regulations, however, the Blyvooruitzicht Mine initiated insolvency proceedings in August 2013 leading to catastrophic consequences for the surrounding community. Overnight, operations halted, thousands lost their jobs and environmental mitigation measures ceased entirely. Nambitha describes the mine's closure as sudden and chaotic, noting there was no warning prior to the end of life as the village knew it, either by the corporate operators or by the regulatory authorities. Suddenly, mass unemployment, crises relating to the termination of water and sewage services and uncertainty about the future led to a rising, collective sense of desperation. 'The situation in Blyvoor quickly declined to a state of destruction. Things really changed very quickly. There was just no order', she says.

In the face of a relatively robust legal framework aimed at ensuring sustainable social development, by anticipating, at a minimum, continued access to social services such as education, water, electricity and sanitation, residents' services were instead immediately threatened, their security of tenure with respect to their homes was thrown into question and an adequate standard of living for the area collapsed. Local government authorities, including the police service and elected officials, declined to intervene in nearly any capacity, characterizing the circumstances as a matter for the private sector, not the government.

Prior to the closure of the mine, there was a designated caretaker who kept note of how many people lived in each household and generally attended to residential planning in the village, Nambitha explains. After the mine collapsed, people were 'forced to arrange themselves in any way they could', as services were terminated in various parts of the village due to failing infrastructure. In addition, because of rising crime levels, certain parts of the village became 'no-go' areas for residents. Families crammed together to deal with their new realities.

Security patrol services, long used to keep the village safe, also immediately ceased. Reports have suggested that after the mine was effectively 'abandoned' with little consideration for the welfare of the surrounding community, the area devolved into a 'Wild West atmosphere, with gunshots at night'.[15] Nambitha confirmed these reports: 'We are not safe anymore', she says. 'Women and girls who dare to walk the streets of Blyvooruitzicht alone risk being violated and harassed.'

Under South Africa's law, sustainable economic development also contemplates – if not long-term employment opportunities – at least the avoidance of economic collapse in areas where mines have begun to close. It is therefore striking that in the case of the Blyvooruitzicht Mine, residents have reported not having had access to any training opportunities, for example, during or after the initiation of liquidation proceedings that would have helped mitigate the impact of the mine's closure and their subsequent unemployment.[16] This is despite the mine's written commitment – just a year prior to liquidation – to actively manage the negative socio-economic impacts of mass retrenchment, downscaling and closure on its employees by deploying a multipronged plan in such events.[17]

Instead, residents reported that, having received no clear communication from the mine of its intention to cease operations, there were no job centres set up and neither training nor counselling provided to employees.[18] In theory, the MPRDA and labour law should ensure that the impacts of downscaling and retrenchments are mitigated, even where operations cease due to business rescue or the initiation of liquidation proceedings, rather than circumstances where proper closure has been a considered business choice. But today Blyvooruitzicht residents live with the aftermath of the mine, having sidestepped these obligations; a staggering unemployment rate and inability to secure alternative employment depict the community's plight.

Sustainable environmental development also guaranteed under the existing legal framework involves enduring preservation of the environment so as not to deplete nature's resources for short-term development benefit. Under NEMA, mining right holders are required to rehabilitate the environment as far as reasonably practicable.[19] Rehabilitation of mined land seeks to restore the land to its original form so as to ensure the use of the land, even if in another capacity. South African law requires that financial provision is made during the course of a mine's life in order to ensure that remediation of environmental damage is theoretically able to take place, even in the event of a sudden, unanticipated closure – or, presumably, liquidation.[20] This requirement remains in force even after a closure certificate has been issued, allowing the minister of mineral resources to compensate communities for any rehabilitation costs they incur after remediating the mining company's damage.

But this did not happen in practice. Given that the initiation of liquidation proceedings meant a sudden end to all environmental mitigation measures, the Blyvooruitzicht community found itself living on the edge of an entirely un-rehabilitated gold tailings storage dam. A fine white powder, which locals call 'motolo', regularly blows through the village, blanketing surfaces, even indoors. Nambitha recalls that when the mine was still in operation, it used to 'pour water on the tailings dam to prevent it from being blown into the surrounding areas. But after the mine stopped, the motolo was not managed. It is like a dangerous soil and it affects people badly. People complain about chest problems, eye problems.'

NEMA places a clear duty of care and remediation for environmental damage on persons who are likely to cause or have caused significant pollution or degradation. Nevertheless, examples of improper closures and communities looking for answers dot the South African mining landscape in force. The latest estimates suggest that there are over 6,000 abandoned mines in South Africa today.[21] In these instances, the historical owners have simply closed the gates and walked away without initiating even basic remediation measures.

It is difficult for the Blyvooruitzicht community to see a way forward. Nambitha and others describe the difficulties associated with having lived in a community where a corporate entity effectively acted as the state, and then vanished overnight, leaving the local government unprepared to take over its constitutional responsibilities. Proper mine closure, which should theoretically contemplate the sustainable survival of the surrounding community, appears to have been entirely sidestepped by the mine's owner in its initiation of liquidation proceedings, leaving the village's residents – many of whom, like Nambitha, grew up in the village – with few employment opportunities, breathing toxic air and struggling to find answers about the future. As Nambitha says, 'Our situation in Blyvoor is nothing like it was before. Many of us have nowhere else to go.'

Today, it is difficult to comprehend how the Blyvooruitzicht community, and others like it, can be forced to resign itself to a life in which the daily struggle for survival is so acute. This is especially ironic, given residents' roles in sustaining one of the nation's largest and most productive gold mines over its operating life.

It is inconceivable that such commitment, in the context of mining communities, only exists so long as a private sector partner remains to willingly facilitate it. It seems equally implausible that we accept a situation where mining communities are left worse off after a commercial entity has reaped profit from South Africa's soil for decades.

The experiences of the Durban Deep and Blyvooruitzicht communities however suggest that industry and regulatory authorities have, over time, simply looked the other way when it comes to the concluding phases of a mining operation's life and the obligations of responsible corporations, to the detriment of the long-term sustainability of the communities that surround these operations.

Nambitha's reflections of Blyvooruitzicht are apt. Despite having built and sustained the Blyvooruitzicht Mine, 'the community at large has deteriorated. There's no meaningful employment here, especially for the skills that people who live here have. The Mine was the main job generator. It shut its doors, and the industry is declining so none of the other mines are hiring.'

'It is frustrating: this is not the Blyvoor that we built or the way we used to live.'

As such, far from reflecting the principles of sustainable development, failure to properly and completely close mining operations undermines the very essence of this concept. The purported benefits that it may be argued mining brings to an economy are simply offset by the cataclysmic impacts on local communities with their inappropriate or disorderly cessation of operations, and the open-ended liability that comes with improperly managed closure.

And indeed, such a pattern would appear contrary to the very essence of the South African constitution, and to the domestic legal framework governing the mining industry, which holds as one of its fundamental tenets, a commitment to mineral exploitation in South Africa that is undertaken for the benefit of all, in order to promote economic and social development and to facilitate the upliftment of communities affected by mining.[22]

Liquidation: Strategies for sidestepping mine closure requirements

Evidence demonstrates that when liquidation proceedings are initiated in South Africa, insolvency practitioners tend to argue that the MPRDA's requirements regarding managing closure impacts are inapplicable, suggesting that insolvency law governs instead.[23] This perspective has real consequences for communities left behind. It effectively results in the mining operation sidestepping all mine closure requirements, including environmental mitigation and rehabilitation.

The implications regarding the failure to implement remediation measures are enduring. Community activists who frequently visit the Durban Deep community have recently reported witnessing unacceptable conditions of people 'living under slime dams and breathing in the dust', which can have a long-lasting impact on the residents' health.[24] In Blyvooruitzicht, the consistent exposure to the 'motolo' – and particularly on windy days – has left many fearing for their health. Residents speak of being enveloped in clouds of toxic dust when shaking out bedclothes in the morning and of crunching down on dust particles meshed into locally baked bread.[25]

Declaring insolvency as a way to walk away from the legal requirements related to environmental clean-up and socio-economic support appears to reflect an increasingly popular method for sidestepping such responsibilities. In 2017 alone, Statistics South Africa reported that eight companies initiated liquidation proceedings in the mining and quarrying industry.[26] As such circumstances grow more common in the context of South Africa's declining gold mining industry in particular – today, newly mined gold from South Africa accounts for only 5 per cent of worldwide supply – thousands of community residents living across the country's gold belts will face uncertain futures.

From a corporate and commercial law perspective, liquidation is one of the most significant changes that a company may face during its lifetime – indeed, it may lead to the birth of new business relations due to the acquisition of the assets of the liquidated company. According to the United Nations Guiding Principles for Business and Human Rights, a new buyer may inherit the human rights risks of its predecessor.[27] As such, the Guiding Principles recommend that due diligence 'be initiated as early as possible in the development of an activity or a relationship'. Specifically, in order to respond to the dynamic nature of the context, due diligence should

> be undertaken at regular intervals: prior to a new activity or relationship; prior to major decisions or changes in the operation (e.g. market entry, product launch, policy change, or wider changes to the business); in response to or anticipation of changes in the operating environment (e.g. rising social tensions); and periodically throughout the life of an activity or relationship.[28]

However, the Guiding Principles are silent regarding implementing due diligence within the context of liquidation. As a result, domestic guidance and enforcement is critical to ensure that companies respect human rights during these types of transitions.

In the case of the Durban Deep and Blyvooruitzicht examples, the extent to which operations failed to meet their due diligence obligations and are thus required to mitigate and redress the adverse impacts on human rights depends on the link between the operations and the companies' activities or business relations. Many of the impacts that the communities are experiencing arose after the relevant companies effectively left the area. As a result, attributing or linking the impacts to the companies' actions or omissions is a complex task.

Helpfully however the Guiding Principles rely on the interrelated concepts of causation, contribution, direct links and complicity. Causation refers to the case where a company's conduct enables, exacerbates or facilitates human rights abuses, while contribution exists when there is only an indirect link. Contribution is related to complicity. In the business and human rights field, complicity refers largely to circumstances where a company knowingly and indirectly contributes to another's abuse of human rights.

The difficulty presented by liquidation is that even when the attribution link is established and could lead to liability and remediation by the company, once liquidation is complete, then the company ceases to exist. As such, holding accountable the actor that inherits the burden of liability proves to be challenging. In short, the concepts of causation, contribution, direct link and complicity are useful from a preventive point of view but corporate law may be ill-equipped to facilitate remediation after liquidation, even when the harms were caused or can be linked to the liquidated company.

In the case of Blyvooruitzicht, the initiation of insolvency proceedings, as opposed to pursuing proper mine closure, effectively eliminated the protections in place to mitigate the socio-economic and environmental impacts of the operation's end of life on both mine employees and the surrounding areas. Indeed, mining rights holders are required under South African law to apply for the issuance of a closure certificate when mining works cease to exist. According to section 43(1) of the MPRDA, the holder of the relevant mining right remains responsible for environmental damage caused by its exercise of the right as well as compliance with the conditions of the environmental authorization and sustainable closure of the works, until such a closure certificate has been issued. The National Environmental Management Act goes further, providing that rights holders under its framework in fact retain liability for environmental damage even after closure.[29] But where those rights holders disappear, such as in the case of insolvency, corporate accountability for environmental rehabilitation can be hard to come by.

In such circumstances, responsibility ultimately falls to the state and to the taxpayers. Insofar as companies are allowed to escape their obligations as a result of regulatory and enforcement gaps, an environment of impunity prevails. If the state seeks to avoid bearing responsibility for a company's wrongdoing, then it must adopt and – critically – enforce laws that ensure the protection of human rights, particularly in difficult cases like liquidation or downsizing of operations. Indeed, South Africa's relatively robust legislation governing mine closure is left without teeth where there is no will or capacity to enforce it. Further lack of coordination and coherence between mining law and corporate and bankruptcy law results in legal gaps that open up the possibility of human rights violations for communities left behind post-closure.

This stands in contrast with the Guiding Principles, which require that states 'ensure that other laws and policies governing the creation and ongoing operation of business enterprises, such as corporate law, do not constrain but enable business respect for human rights'.[30] While the Guiding Principles fail to provide any explicit consideration of the termination of a business enterprise's operations, there can nevertheless be no justification in international law for any scaling down of the state's obligation to protect in such a context. The state's failure to act then constitutes a violation of its obligations and sets a dangerous precedent for the mining sector and affected communities in South Africa – and indeed, on the continent – today.

Conclusion: Challenges and Opportunities in International Law

The stories in this chapter make clear that South African legislative and regulatory authorities must explore new ways to integrate a human rights- and environment-focused approach to domestic law governing liquidation in the context of the extractive sector.

The inherently evolutionary nature of international human rights law may provide some guidance. Its capacity to ensure effective protection derives largely from its ability to adapt to multiple situations. It has and must continue to evolve at the same pace that new governance structures and actors appear. Therefore, while 50 years ago international law primarily addressed state obligations, today it must deal with increasingly complex networks of relationships between public and private actors. These relationships modify, transfer, dilute and transform the roles and obligations of all stakeholders.

Mining villages in South Africa provide a clear example of the need for an evolving approach to human rights law. While such villages are physically located within the jurisdiction of local municipalities, constitutionally charged with provision of basic services, seeing to the provision of housing and providing security in the form of police interventions, the typical South African mining town model sees the local mining corporation serving this role. When that mining entity no longer exists, without proper planning, a vacuum inevitably opens up. As one Blyvooruitzicht resident explained, after asking the local municipality for help, 'the Municipal Manager told us that Blyvoor is a private property and there is nowhere and no way that the municipality comes in [to assist]'.[31] In sum, when the mine closed, the municipality suggested that it had no duty to provide water and electricity to the private property on which the mining village was located, nor to facilitate continued access to housing for the residents.

Insofar as the transfer of authority to a private actor allows the state to fulfil its obligations, by providing basic services, education and sanitation to places the state would not otherwise have had the capacity to reach, the relationship contributes to the realization of states' duties. But when an abuse or failure to fulfil those duties occurs, can the company be held responsible under international law? More concretely, in these two community examples, where the victims speak clearly about corporate failures to adequately close a mine, who is liable for the damages caused to the communities and the environment? To whom can the victims turn to obtain a remedy?

Despite the growing economic and political powers of business today, state actors remain the main subjects of international law and, consequently, the primary duty bearers. The scope of their negative (do no harm) and positive (ensure the effectiveness) obligations have been developed by international and regional jurisdictions and mechanisms.

For instance, the Committee on Economic Social and Cultural Rights has affirmed that states' obligations with respect to the right to water are not limited to 'refrain[ing] from interfering directly or indirectly with the enjoyment of the right to water' but also entail an obligation to protect and fulfil the right.[32] The obligation to protect includes 'prevent[ing] third parties from interfering in any way with the enjoyment of the right to water', for example by 'restrain[ing] third parties from denying equal access to adequate water'.[33] Despite the clarity of the law, the stories of mining villages in South Africa demonstrate that the devolution of authority to corporate actors can open spaces for the state's later abdication of responsibility.

In the case of Blyvooruitzicht, the company provided the village with its basic services throughout its operations. But the state's duty to provide access to these services was never discharged. It continued to exist, despite the company's actions. When the company stopped providing the village with access to basic services, the state was obliged to act. Continued access to basic services is crucial. As Katrina Mokgoto, resident of Blyvooruitzicht, explains, 'Without water or electricity, we won't survive.' In failing to provide these services, the state violated the affected communities' residents' human right to water.

In sum, it is not enough for the state to simply refrain from harming human rights. The state can, and must, be held responsible when no action is taken when private actors, such as companies, interfere with the full realization and enjoyment of these rights.

Despite the role played by companies with respect to mining villages, which could be easily compared to that of a government, their obligations and liabilities cannot be compared to those of the state. Strictly speaking, international liability is allocated under a cascade framework – the state must adopt the necessary legislation to protect human rights, and then if a private actor, such as a company, violates human rights, the state must ensure the wrongdoer is sanctioned and the harm remedied. In failing to do so, the state can be considered internationally responsible for the harm inflicted by the private actor. However, this does not mean that companies are free of human rights obligations. Since 1948, the Universal Declaration of Human Rights has declared that 'every individual and every organ of society, [...] shall strive by teaching and education to promote respect for these rights and freedoms and by progressive measures, national and international, to secure their universal and effective recognition and observance'.[34] Consequently, as specialized organs of society performing specialized functions, business enterprises are 'required to comply with all applicable laws and to respect human rights'.[35]

These challenges reveal the need for stronger and clearer regulations, and they raise the question of economic actors as bearers of international obligations. On the one hand, such binding international regulation seems natural to regulate corporate entities that can play roles equivalent to that of the state, and in some cases wield even greater economic power. But the cases of Blyvooruitzicht and Durban Deep also reveal the importance of strengthening local regulations and the state's capacity to implement legislation. Such an approach is essential to preventing and addressing specific human rights violations. To this end, the negotiation of an international treaty on business and human rights must be clear on the allocation of obligations and responsibilities of the state and companies and use real-life examples to ensure that an adopted treaty will respond to the specific challenges faced by victims, such as the ones described above, in order to provide them with concrete avenues for remedy.

For the communities of Blyvooruitzicht and Durban Deep, such changes may be too little, too late, as they continue to struggle for survival. But local regulators must ensure these experiences are not for nothing – and must halt the process of these stories becoming the norm, as gold production in South Africa reaches its natural end.

Notes

1 'Nine Shafts Mothballed', *Mining Weekly*, 19 May 2000, http://www.miningweekly.com/print-version/nine-shafts-mothballed-2000-05-19.
2 Ibid.
3 Troublingly, mothballing appears to be an increasingly common occurrence in South Africa. Recent examples include mining company, Lonmin, which mothballed its K4 shaft near Rustenburg in the North West Province and several other shafts in the Limpopo province for poor production: see David Kay 'Re-Opening Mothballed Shafts May Yield 250koz/year for Lonmin', *Miningm*, 15 May 2017, https://www.miningmx.com/news/platinum/29606-reopening-mothballed-shafts-add-250kozyear-lonmin/; see also Siphiwe Sibeko, 'Toronto-Based Atlatsa to Mothball South African Platinum Mine', *Reuters*, 27 July 2017, https://www.google.com/url?sa=i&source=web&ved=0ahUKEwjjqKal24nhAhWEx4UKHfF-DeoQzPwBCAM&url=https%3A%2Fwww.reuters.com%2Farticle%2Fus-atlatsa-resrcs-amplats-bokoni-mine-idUSKBN1A61WX&psig=AOvWaw18BGeX4J6rm6g35zVtc-L&ust=1552930562002449.
4 'DRDGOLD, Mintails Agree West Rand Gold and Uranium Exploration and Mining Joint Venture', 26 April 2007, http://www.drdgold.com/investors-and-media/media-releases/2007/drdgold-mintails-agree-west-rand-gold-and-uranium-exploration-and-mining-joint-venture-2007-04-26.
5 Ibid.
6 Mintails initiated 'business rescue' proceedings, a feature of South African insolvency law that effectively facilitates a business standstill, theoretically allowing distressed companies time to come to terms with their creditors.
7 Mark Olade, 'Mintails Collapse: A Case Study in How Not to Close Mines', 11 August 2018, http://www.fse.org.za/index.php/item/626-mintails-collapse-a-case-study-in-how-not-to-close-mines.
8 'Murder and Corruption in the Mining Town the World Forgot', 11 January 2018, https://www.groundup.org.za/article/illegal-mining-syndicates-wreak-havoc-durban-deep/.
9 All names in this chapter have been changed at the request of the interviewees.
10 Constitution of the Republic of South Africa § 24 (1996).
11 Mineral and Petroleum Resources Development Act 28 of 2002, Preamble.
12 National Environmental Management Act, § 24 n.7.
13 Department of Mineral Resources, 'Guidelines for the Submission of a Social and Labour Plan', October 2010.
14 Ibid.
15 Federation for Human Rights and Lawyers for Human Rights, 'Blyvooruitzicht Mine Village: The Human Toll of State and Corporate Abdication of Responsibility in South Africa', at 51, last accessed 7 March 2019, http://www.lhr.org.za/publications/blyvooruitzicht-mine-village-human-toll-state-and-corporate-abdication-responsibility-s (herein after referred to the 'Blyvooruitzicht Report').
16 Ibid., 23.
17 Blyvooruitzicht Gold Mine Village Main Reef/DRDGold Social and Labour Plan, 75–76 (2012). It remains unclear whether this document was actually submitted to the Department of Mineral Resources.
18 *Blyvooruitzicht Report*, 23.

19 National Environmental Management Act 107 § 24 n. 7(1998) ('NEMA').

20 NEMA section 24 requires that an applicant for an environmental authorization is required to make financial provision for rehabilitation, closure and ongoing post-decommissioning management of negative environmental impacts.

21 David Oliveira, 'Mine Closure, Rehabilitation Getting More Attention from Regulators', *Mining Weekly*, 27 May 2016, http://www.miningweekly.com/print-version/mining-industry-resistant-to-mine-closure-and rehabilitation-2016-05-27.

22 Mining and Petroleum Resource Development Act 28, Preamble (2002).

23 *Blyvooruitzicht Report*, 23

24 Sheree Bega, 'Residential Mining Raises Questions', *IOL*, 2 June 2018, https://www.iol.co.za/saturday-star/news/residential-mining-raises-questions-15276591.

25 *Blyvooruitzicht Report*, 34.

26 Statistics South Africa, 'Statistics of Liquidations and Insolvencies', December 2017.

27 United Nations Human Rights Council, *Report of the Special Representative of the Secretary-General on the Issue of Human Rights and Transnational Corporations and Other Business Enterprises, John Ruggie Guiding Principles on Business and Human Rights: Implementing the United Nations 'Protect, Respect and Remedy' Framework*, 21 March 2011, UN doc. A/HRC/17/31, 17 (hereafter "Guiding Principles").

28 Ibid., 14–15.

29 NEMA, § 24 n. 7; see also NEMA, § 24R(1).

30 *Guiding Principles*, 8.

31 *Blyvooruitzicht Report*, 49

32 Committee on Economic Social and Cultural Rights, *General comment No. 15: The Right to Water, 20 January 2003* (Contained in Document E/C.12/2002/11), para 21

33 United Nations Human Rights Council, *Report of the Special Representative of the Secretary-General*, at para 23.

34 Universal Declaration of Human Rights, Preamble (1948).

35 *Guiding Principles*, 1.

CONCLUSION

> If a tree falls in the forest does it make a sound? If a business commits a human rights abuse does it lead to remedies? To protections? Will the practices stop if the victim's voices aren't heard?

This edited volume represents a collective effort among scholars, practitioners and affected communities and individuals to give voice to many who have, up until now, not been able to be heard. Whether by recounting the struggles of individual human rights defenders or organized communities, the primary purpose of this book – since its conception – has been to ensure that some of those whose conduct has been impacted by businesses have an outlet to express their frustration, their outrage or their hope, as the case may be. Our task in this conclusion is to coalesce many of the themes that were explored by the individual contributors into an overarching exploration of what their struggles can foretell about the business and human rights agenda. To that end, we have organized our conclusion as follows.

First, we relate the narratives reported and analysed in the preceding chapters to other business and human rights narratives recently covered in the media. Next, we provide a superficial/high-level description of the field of business and human rights while questioning whether the purpose of this edited volume has been fulfilled. Then, we address some of the major themes evoked by the narratives. Finally, we end by offering our thoughts on possible ways to improve the protection of the human rights of individuals and communities affected by businesses.

The narratives contained in this volume are a small subset of the stories about businesses' impacts on individuals and communities and yet, a cursory review of today's headlines show just how timely the stories contained in this volume actually are. For instance, as we write this conclusion, we have been struck by four recent media stories that evoke business and human rights issues.

1. The BBC runs a story about the past and present of human rights abuses in the early twentieth century rubber extraction industry in

Cameroon: European society was outraged by photographic and narrative depictions of the methodologies used to extract higher rubber production from villagers – the death and/or mutilation of workers' wives and children.[1] The outcry led to some relief and changes in business tactics.[2] Today, environmental concerns are a primary issue raised by rubber extraction. Halayan Agri, a subsidiary of Sinochem, a Chinese state-owned enterprise, reportedly the world's largest rubber processing company, is clearing thousands of hectares in order to plant rubber trees in Cameroon – in close proximity to a UNESCO World Heritage site.[3] Reassuringly (?), the company has announced its commitment to sustainability through the creation of a 'Sustainability Commission' with respect to its work in Cameroon. The story's themes evoke many of the issues that were outlined in Chapter 5 (surrounding the issues presented when a Chinese multinational corporation enters parts of Africa).

2. Under the heading 'Is fair trade finished?', *The Guardian*'s Samantha Subramanian reports on companies' withdrawals from Fair Trade International, the standard setting and certification entity whose inaction is also called into question in Chapter 1 of this volume. Subramanian identifies questions about the effectiveness for consumers, primary producers and companies of third-party certification/labelling efforts, businesses' desire for control of certification processes, the confusing diversity of standards flooding the market and the powerlessness of primary producer communities confronting the manoeuvrings,[4] echoing Chapter 1's discussion regarding the alleged human rights abuses committed by a FairTrade-certified company.
3. Activist survivors of opioid overdose victims, devastated communities and prosecutors challenge the role of pharmaceutical companies in the opioid epidemic that has swept through the United States.[5] Alleging that the companies prioritized profit making over public health and safety, and over the lives of their loved ones, and that the federal government failed to exercise regulatory control, the parties have launched criminal and civil actions aimed at establishing the liability of the companies.[6] West Virginia, the state that was featured in Chapter 9 of this volume, has some of the most devastated communities in the United States. In fact, the state is generally considered the hardest hit by the opioid crisis.[7] This is one of the cruellest ironies depicted in Chapter 9: many of the victims of the crisis in this state are miners who turned to opioids to deal with the pain from work-related injuries[8] (where health and safety issues were often ignored) only to be one of the millions of people who, in turn, became addicted.[9]
4. Vale, the Brazilian mining company whose dam was involved in a disaster in January 2019 that killed 300 people, has agreed to pay over US$100 million in 'collective moral damages' as well as pay each of the victim's families

US$186,000 as compensation for the loss of the family's loved ones.[10] This story provides a tragic postscript to the story recounted in Chapter 4 of a Brazilian mining disaster that occurred in 2015 and that also involved the Vale corporation.

The media stories exemplify the depth, scope and challenges of the field of business and human rights by, among other things, demonstrating the linkages between past and contemporary abuses; reporting on questions regarding the efficacy of mechanisms deployed to decrease exploitation of primary producers and provide them with a meaningful share of the profits earned from their efforts; and suggesting that we characterize opioid epidemic consequences of the profit-seeking prioritization of pharmaceutical companies in the United States, a powerful Western country, as an abuse of the human right to life. To that extent, they offer an appropriate overlay to the themes that the contributors have explored in this volume.

Purpose and Summary

As we noted earlier (as well as in the Introduction), this volume's purpose is to provide a forum that will allow us to hear directly from and to amplify the voices of communities and individuals affected by businesses. We have not fully succeeded in this purpose – demonstrating the scope and scale of the challenges of absent or unheard 'voices'. Despite our explicit goal in putting together this volume, the voices collected here are intermediated by academics and NGOs that relay (and necessarily have filtered) the raw voices. While we believe that the contributors have tried, where possible, to provide as much of these narratives first-hand from those affected, one lesson that has emerged from undertaking this project is the logistical hurdles that can arise from trying to help these communities convey their story to the world. Whether it is because of language or cultural barriers, difficulties in finding people who are willing to participate or other unforeseen issues, in many ways this volume suffers from some of the issues that we discussed in the Introduction and that motivated us to undertake this project in the first place – trying to allow impacted communities and individuals to speak directly about their experiences was more challenging than we anticipated. As such, we believe a more accurate characterization of the work we have presented here is that of 'reported narratives' rather than direct first-hand accounts. Nonetheless, we believe that, even with these limitations, this volume represents a substantial step forward in this work: it is, to our knowledge, the first time that accounts such as these have been presented on such a large scale or (we hope) to such a large audience. To that end, we are also hopeful that, in presenting these stories here we can: (1) shed more light on the tolls experienced by people affected by businesses around the world; and (2) provide a starting point for others who are interested in pursuing work in the business and human rights field.

A Note about Business and Human Rights

The vast majority of business enterprises are organized into corporations or other types of legal entities that are designed specifically to limit the liability of the shareholders (the residual owners of the company) so that investors risk the loss of only their initial investments. The legal entities serve society by: (1) raising capital for endeavors without taxing large portions of society and (2) promoting innovation and efficient production that, theoretically, improve standards of living. However, working in tandem, limited liability, profit-seeking, the accumulation of vast financial resources, and the prioritization of shareholder value create risks that others will be exploited and abused – such as workers, consumers, and the environment. How, then, do we ensure that these three characteristics do not eviscerate the benefits that humans gain from businesses? As editor Karen Bravo explained in an earlier edited volume,

> In 2005, UN Secretary General Kofi Annan appointed Harvard Professor, John Ruggie, as UN Special Representative to the Secretary-General (SRSG) for Business and Human Rights. Ruggie served for six years in that capacity. (His initial two-year term was twice renewed.) During his time as Special Representative, Ruggie led an exhaustive process of research and consultation into the subject of business and human rights.
>
> In 2008, he produced a three-pillar Protect-Respect-Remedy Framework (the 'Framework') which was adopted by the UN Human Rights Council. The goal of the Framework was to assist all stakeholders in understanding and addressing their roles in the context of business and human rights. The three pillars – a State's duty to protect, a Corporation's duty to respect, and the role of both in remedying human rights violations should they occur – provide conceptual guidance with respect to the intersection between business and human rights.
>
> The Guiding Principles produced by SRSG Ruggie, following an extensive multi-year global research and consultation process, further developed the field of business and human rights. On June 16, 2011, the United Nations Human Rights Council endorsed the Guiding Principles to serve to operationalize the three-pillar Framework. The United Nations resolution marks the first time that the idea of corporate responsibility for human rights impacts has been explicitly endorsed by the United Nations.
>
> Together, these two documents – the Guiding Principles and the Framework – effectively created the first UN-approved global standards that can be used to

'prevent and address the risk of adverse impacts on human rights that are linked to business activity'.[11]

In sum, the international business and human rights regime recognizes the *state's* duty to protect human rights; *businesses'* role in respecting human rights; and the obligations of *both* states and businesses to remedy any human rights violations that do occur. When the Guiding Principles were first produced, it marked an unprecedented shift regarding how we envisioned businesses' role with regard to an individual's human rights. And yet, somewhere along the way, the focus of the field seemingly shifted from the *individuals* and their rights and protections to the *businesses* and their responsibilities. An understandable shift perhaps – given that the rise of (and attendant impact of) corporations is the key distinction between the international human rights field in general and the business and human rights field specifically – but one that nonetheless led to the subjugation of impacted voices from much of the conversation. It is our hope then, that by providing these narratives, we can once again shift the conversation to the heart of the matter, namely those who have been affected.

These Narratives

These narratives describe abuses and/or threats to individuals' and communities' human rights to health (e.g. Brillo; Cimrin and Demiral; Oliva); to property (Hung; Maher and Bravin; Van Ho); freedom (Parisi and Sims); and life project (Van Ho; Brillo). Those within the businesses' functions (i.e. workers) suffer human rights impacts – as depicted by Brillo (Philippine banana workers are rendered involuntarily sterile by toxic chemicals) and Cimrin and Demiral (workers in Turkish free trade zones suffer occupational disease impacts from exploitative factory conditions). The impacts also extend to the communities within which the businesses are situated or within which they plan to establish operations. Chapters depicting these human rights impacts include Chinowawa's (sect patriarch and extensive extended family – as well as all members of their community – are removed from a diamond-rich zone so as to clear the path for diamond mining by Chinese-owned multinational corporations (MNC)); Maher and Bravin's (the catastrophic failure of the mining dam operated by BHP Billiton's joint venture subsidiary destroys a thriving town, killing some residents and displacing the entire community); and Van Ho (the life plans, social relationships and culture within a community are disrupted and reconfigured as the community combats the threatened siting of La Colosa (a mammoth gold mine) that the members of the community believe will inevitably cause detrimental environmental impact on them and their way of life).

In light of these wide-ranging negative impacts, it is worth pointing out that the narratives do not contest the existence and need for business. Instead, the narrators and authors raise questions about the *way* that business is conducted – so as to dehumanize and exploit. That is, these chapters challenge the 'hows' of business practices, not the 'whys'.

Another striking aspect of the narratives is the ways in which they – together with the media narratives briefly summarized earlier in this conclusion – demonstrate the widespread and endemic scope and extent of business' impacts on individuals and communities. The impacts are far-reaching in terms of geographic locations – from the mountaintops of Peru to the diamond fields of Zimbabwe to the coal mines of the United States. Within the lives of the individuals and communities, the institutional, emotional, cultural, psychological and even biological effects have a permanent rippling-outward effect.

Themes

The narratives offer many themes to unpack. We focus here on three of them: power, impunity and the elusive nature of remedies.

Power

The narratives display the shifting balance of power among businesses, states and targeted individuals/communities. In the narratives, the power never resides within the individuals and communities. In Brillo's chapter, despite coming together with other involuntarily sterilized workers, her narrator is unsuccessful in receiving acknowledgement and compensation for the life-changing harm he has suffered. In Clements and Cubides' chapter, the workers and their families, who, together with the mines, have been abandoned by the mining operators, have no power to demand remediation from the companies or services from the surrounding or nearby municipalities – the local instruments of the state. In Oliva's and Cimrin and Demiral's chapter, despite protective legislation and regulatory bodies, neither coal miners in West Virginia nor free trade zone factory workers in Turkey are empowered to demand safe and adequate work conditions. Instead, with the fear of dismissal and job loss hanging over them, they assist in covering up safety failures in anticipation of bizarrely pre-announced regulatory 'inspections'.

In the interrelationships depicted in the narratives, states have the power of sovereignty and lawmaking – to take the land of its citizens, to allocate licenses and land for exploration, to provide (or not provide) an effective forum for the hearing of claims made within their jurisdictions and to protect the peace through their law enforcement and military forces. At the same time, however, states are disempowered by their lack of fiscal resources and, as a result, their need for infusions of capital through corporate foreign direct investments. In addition, the investor-state protections and dispute resolution mechanisms to which states have committed in bilateral investment or free trade treaties may bind states such as to prevent or hinder implementation of their duties to protect the human rights of their citizens or their environment. Further, corruption of public officials and institutions weakens the states such that the obligations to citizens and protection of sovereign interests are subordinated to the shorter-term, graft-taking incentives of officials and institutions.

The power of businesses also shifts. Popular activism, widespread demonstrations and undesirable negative publicity affect their power vis-à-vis communities, individuals, and states. However, these narratives demonstrate that, in the vast majority of the cases, the financial resources at the companies' disposal shift the balance of power in their favour. The companies can employ lawyers to continue to seek permits and access to land, and they can outwait and outspend in judicial proceedings in multiple jurisdictions. And, finally, if the financial calculations change, the companies can be liquidated and escape responsibility for harmful actions and non-actions.

Private third-party and self-regulation initiatives that purport to increase worker, community or consumer power have not restrained the exercise of that power. Examples in this volume include Hung's chapter (describing the ineffective or non-response of Fair Trade International to alleged violations by a company that it certifies) and Maher and Bravin's chapter (where the authors report that Corporate Human Rights Benchmark ranked BHP Billiton the third best in the world based on its human rights performance while, at the same time, its joint venture subsidiary's neglect resulted in the destruction of an entire town). Finally, Subramanian's July 2019 report in *The Guardian* describes the ways in which companies are moving away from such third-party certification regimes in order to create in-house certification programs which *they* will control.

Impunity

A second major theme that emerges from the narratives is that of impunity for human rights abuses. The narratives display a gap between doctrines (state's responsibility to protect, business's responsibility to respect and joint responsibility to provide mechanisms for redress, for example) and the facts lived on the ground. Individuals and communities such as the involuntarily sterilized Philippine farm workers and Gilberto Torres, Colombian labour rights activist, find that the perpetrators of the human rights abuses they have suffered have acted with impunity (Brillo, Parisi and Sims). Through, among other mechanisms, the complexities and contradictions of legal systems, the courts do not offer true venues for redress. Contributory factors include the contradictions and costs of transnational multijurisdictional litigation – for example, dismissals for forum non conveniens; years-long duration of proceedings; witness inaccessibility and memory losses; and simultaneous corruption and lack of power of courts in weak governance zones. Additional power is provided by entangled and/or Russian nesting doll-like corporate structures designed to obfuscate ownership and avoid legal responsibility.

Elusive/illusory remedy

This leads to the elusive, incomplete or illusory remedies shown in these narratives. Where communities and individuals have received remedies, they have been hard-fought or illusory. For example, Chinowawa demonstrates that, even after multiple attempts by the company involved, the redress finally accepted by the exhausted community (after years of struggle) remains inadequate. As a result of the displacement they suffered, the family and community struggle to make a living (their productive farmlands were never adequately replaced), with consequences for gender rights; children's rights (lack of education, early marriages); health (prostitution, hunger, starvation, HIV infections); loss of economic resources; loss of culture; and endemic conflict with the new local community to which they have been relocated.

In the Maher and Bravin chapter, where the neglect of the mining company led to a devastating breach of the mine tailing dam, accountability has thus far taken the form of payment of fines to the Brazilian state. However, the redress desired by the affected (*Atingidos*) – to return to and rebuild their lost town – has not been achieved and may not be on the table. Thus, even a seemingly responsive reaction is flawed by power disparity, lack of or insufficient individual or community voice at the table and slow, cumbersome processes, even with respect to compensation for lost personal property.

For now, the business and human rights regime appears to offer slight comfort. To facilitate implementation of the principles and guidelines, the UN Human Rights Council approved the formation of a Working Group on Business and Human Rights. The ultimate goal of this 'Working Group' (composed of five independent experts) is, in part:

1. To promote the effective and comprehensive dissemination and implementation of the Guiding Principles;
2. To identify, exchange and promote good practices and lessons learned on the implementation of the Guiding Principles and to assess and make recommendations thereon and, in that context, to seek and receive

information from all relevant sources, including Governments, transnational corporations and other business enterprises, national human rights institutions, civil society and rights-holders;
3. To provide support for efforts to promote capacity-building and the use of the Guiding Principles, as well as, upon request, to provide advice and recommendations regarding the development of domestic legislation and policies relating to business and human rights.[12]

Three of the narratives (Maher and Bravin; Bertrand and Toval; Oliva) include descriptions and discussions of visits by the UN Working Group during the events recounted and analysed in the chapters. In none of the three cases does the Working Group's visit appear to have substantively changed the power dynamic and/or resulted in any meaningful remedy for the affected individuals or communities.

Solutions?

The narratives contained in the 10 chapters of this edited volume are salutary, in that they bring us into the homes and lives of individuals and communities who have been affected by businesses. Through the chapters, they speak to us. However, the salutary nature of the chapters does not extend to offering pathways to prevent or remedy human rights abuses by businesses. Instead, the reader is led to the realization that s/he is a consumer-victim-participant in endemic exploitation and unsustainable resource extraction. With every fruit – every banana – that we eat (produced and exported to our local grocery store), we may be eating death – of individuals, of individuals' dreams and their right to procreate, of the life of communities that are not as distant as they appear. With the oil, gold, precious stones, metals and plastics that make up the goods that we consume, we may be involuntarily complicit in and beneficiaries of exploitation and must bear the consequent psychological pain.

Are there ways to prevent these abuses? Can we design a modified or completely different system? Some ideas include the following:

1. Creation of an international judicial or arbitral body that would have the power to exercise jurisdiction over businesses, wherever they are located or are operating.
2. Harmonization of domestic liability and jurisdiction regimes (through the creation of special domestic courts, for example) that could apply liability and compensation standards in each jurisdiction.
3. Prior attachment of resources for remedies: host states could require that businesses – whether domestic or international – agree in advance to the

imposition of jurisdiction and identify funds/resources from which compensation would be paid in the event of the commission of human rights abuses.

4. Import jurisdictional concepts from the field of tax law[13] such that compensation for adjudicated or consensually determined human rights abuses can be assessed jointly and severally against affiliated companies, wherever located or operating.
5. Criminalization and penalties against individual actors who are agents of corporations. Jurisdiction to adjudicate would be conceded in advance, and criminal penalties would be served within the state of the affected individuals and communities.
6. Use of indigenous/traditional systems of dispute resolution such that the traditions and cultures of the affected persons and communities will have a voice in designing the redress.
7. Implementation and meaningful enforcement of due diligence and community consultation best practices as a prelude to and integral part of launching new business investments.

The potential solutions that we list above are but a few of the many potential mechanisms to meaningfully address the types of human rights abuses described in this volume by those who have been affected. We prioritize mechanisms that would increase their 'voice' such that the points of view and experiences represented at the table are diverse and the hierarchies of power are flattened to facilitate meaningful protection and access to remedies. If we do this, we can highlight their struggles and amplify their voice regarding the fate of their own communities and life projects.

We can't afford not to.

It is incumbent upon us to try.

Notes

1 Tim Harford, 'The Horrific Consequences of Rubber's Toxic Past', *BBC News*, 24 July 2019, https://www.bbc.com/news/business-48533964.

2 Ibid.

3 Ibid.

4 Samantha Subramanian, 'Is Fair Trade Finished?', *Guardian*, 23 July 2019, https://www.theguardian.com/business/2019/jul/23/fairtrade-ethical-certification-supermarkets-sainsburys?CMP=Share_iOSApp_Other.

5 Angie and John Minchillo, 'Buried in Opioids, Sickened Community Eyes Drugmakers' role', *Washington Post*, 18 July 2019, https://www.washingtonpost.com/business/rural-ohio-county-shows-the-impact-of-opioid-influx/2019/07/18/00330380-a973-11e9-8733-48c87235f396_story.html?utm_term=.a5591441d132; Beth Macy, 'The Four Ordinary People Who Took on Big Pharma', *New York Post*, 20 July 2019, https://www.nytimes.com/2019/07/20/opinion/sunday/oxycontin-purdue-sacklers.html.

6 Ibid.

7 Clay Marsh, 'Facing Deaths of Despair from the Depths of Despair in West Virginia', *Stat*, 18 July 2018, https://www.statnews.com/2018/07/12/despair-deaths-opioid-crisis-west-virginia/.

8 Kan Nishida, 'How Coal Mining Employment Has Impacted on Opioid Epidemic in America', *Medium*, 20 August 2018, https://blog.exploratory.io/how-coal-mining-employment-has-impacted-on-opioid-epidemic-in-america-69cd0156a50d.

9 American Psychiatric Association, 'Nearly One in Three People Know Someone Addicted to Opioids; More than Half of Millennials Believe It Is Easy to Get Illegal Opioids', 7 May 2018, https://www.psychiatry.org/newsroom/news-releases/nearly-one-in-three-people-know-someone-addicted-to-opioids-more-than-half-of-millennials-believe-it-is-easy-to-get-illegal-opioids.

10 'Brazilian Mining Company to Pay Out £86m for Disaster That Killed almost 300 People', *Guardian*, 16 July 2019, https://www.theguardian.com/world/2019/jul/16/vale-brazil-mining-dam-collapse-brumadinho.

11 Karen E. Bravo, 'Business and Human Rights: A Call for Labor Liberalization in the Business And Human Rights Landscape: Moving Forward, Looking Back' (Jena Martin and Karen E. Bravo, eds,. October 2015) (citations omitted).

12 See United Nations Office of the High Commissioner for Human Rights (OHCHR), 'Working Group on the Issue of Human Rights and Transnational Corporations and Other Business Enterprises', http://www.ohchr.org/EN/Issues/Business/Pages/WGHRandtransnationalcorporationsandotherbusiness.aspx (last accessed 22 November 2019).

13 Worldwide combined reporting, which allowed host jurisdictions to base tax liability on the income of the entire corporate entity.

APPENDICES

Mr Youpa presented several documents to corroborate his story. These documents are included at the request of Mr Youpa.

1. A paper documenting Mr Youpa's release from prison for the crime of 'petty theft' (2002)
2. A list of materials taken from Mr Youpa, as assembled by the general prosecutor upon inspection of the PHP warehouse (2002)
3. A letter from the court sent to PHP detailing the materials stolen from Mr Youpa and claiming Mr Youpa as the rightful owner (2002)
4. A paper documenting PHP's receipt of Appendix C, signed by PHP's director of external affairs (2002)
5. A response from the director general of PHP (2003)
6. A summary of the court proceedings from the Court of First Instance in Mbanga during which Mr Youpa was pronounced 'not guilty' (2005)
7. A certificate of non-appeal from the Court of First Instance in Mbanga (2005)
8. A letter from Mr Youpa requesting audience with the director general of PHP (2015)

Appendix A

(TEO/ET)
MINISTERE DE L'ADMINISTRATION TERRITORIALE

DIRECTION DE L'ADMINISTRATION PENITENTIAIRE

PRISON PRINCIPALE DE MBANGA

REPUBLIQUE DU CAMEROUN
PAIX-TRAVAIL-PATRIE

N° 056 / BLE/RG/PP/MBGA

BULLETIN DE LEVEE D'ECROU

LE REGISSEUR DE LA PRISON PRINCIPALE DE MBANGA

Certifie que le (la) nommé(e) NGAMENI YOUPA Pierre

Fils (~~fille~~) de F. YOUPA Emile et de KOUANOU Anastalasee

Né (e) le 20/02/56 à [illegible] département Haut-Nkam

Arrondissement de Bandja Incarcéré (e) à la prison principale de MBANGA le 16/11/2001

—— sous le N° D'écrou 401/2001 Motif de l'incarcération Coaction d' Vol Simple

Condamné (e) le —— a —— d'emprisonnement ferme

Et à la contrainte par corps de —— suivant ordre d'incarcération N° ——

Du —— du jugement N° —— du —— rendu par le

Tribunal de Mbanga

Est libéré (e) le —— Est mis (e) en liberté le 01/03/2002

Après avoir purgé la peine de —— après avoir bénéficié de la remise de peine de ——

Suivant Décret N° —— du —— suivant décision d'audience du ——

—— suivant ordre de mise en liberté du 01/03/2002 suivant main –levée du mandat

de dépôt du 16/03/2001 de Monsieur le procureur de la République près le tribunal

de Mbanga

L'intéressé (e) déclare se retirer à Njombé Département du

Moungo Arrondissement de Njombé

MBANGA , LE 01/03/2002

[signature]

Appendix B

COUR D'APPEL DU LITTORAL

PARQUET D'INSTANCE DE MBANGA

CABINET D'INFORMATION JUDICIAIRE

N°13/01/0°602./-

Paix-Travail-Patrie

-(O)RDONNANCE DE RESTITUTION -

L'an deux mille deux et le Dix Sept du mois d'Avril ;

Nous, [illegible] Paul, Substitut du Procureur de la République près des Tribunaux de Mbanga ;

Vu l'ordonnance n°72/4 du 26/8/72 portant organisation Judiciaire de l'Etat ainsi que les textes modificatifs subséquents ;

Vu les articles 128 et suivants du Code d'Instruction Criminelle ;

Vu l'article 89 du Code d'Instruction Criminelle

Vu la procédure n°419/RP/01-02 du 11/12/2001 ;

Attendu que l'information judiciaire a révélé qu'au cours de l'enquête préliminaire, certains effets meubles et imobiliers ont été saisis au domicile des nommés KAPCKO Séraphin, NGAMENI YOUPA Pierre, DONGMO Victor n'ayant aucun rapport avec les faits de la cause ;

Que le 19/02/02, un inventaire de ces effets a été commis par le Magistrat Instructeur de céans dans le cadre d'un transport judiciaire ;

Qu'il résulte de cet inventaire que les effets ci-dessous désignés ont été saisis chez les susnommés respectivement ;

01°)- Chez DONGMO Victor :

- Un fer à repasser de marque ARNAYS .
- Un pagne cousu.
- Un drap avec deux taies d'oreillers.
- Une kaba blanche avec chéchia.
- Un drap blanc rayé de bleu ciel.
- Trois taies brodées et un drap blanc.
- Deux pulls et deux tricots pour enfants.
- Un imperméable.
- Deux taies et un drap brodés.
- Un jeu de quatre couteaux-Quatre cuillères-Quatre fourchettes.
- Un cachet"Président de la jeunesse Club Njomb et quatre carnets.
- Un cachet"Association des trois quartiers".
- Deux ensembles pulls pour bébé et un ensemble chaussettes.
- Un petit drap pour bébé surfilé.
- Quatre serviettes pour bébé.
- Trois robettes et un pull pour bébé
- Deux sparadraps.
- Un chapeau traditionnel et un collier.

-Quatre chemises avec divers documents.
-Un carton des divers cahiers usés.
-Huit couches pour bébé-Une paire de lunettes pour soudure.
-Cinq coussins-Une tasse-Une somme de trois mille quinze francs.
-Une moto de marque Suzuki 100-moteur n° 1100-301036 châssis n°A100.
-Dix mini-vels de diverses dimensions-Trois portetout sans roue.
-Un porte-tout avec une roue-Un porte-tout avec deux roues.
-Quatre roues de porte-tout-Un lit sans matelas
-Un pulvérisateur marque TROPIC-Une bâche bleue.
-Un carton de ficelles-Un sac contenant trente neuf sondes.
-Un demi-rouleau de grillage-Une roue usée de moto sport.
-Un demi bidon d'herbicide RONDOR-Un demi bidon d'herbicide PTEIRORON.
-Un bidon de cinq litres de peinture à eau.
-Un petit sac de pluts en plastique 95.
-Quatre vingt dix sept cuillers en aluminium-
-Un stock de nasco.
-Une balance de poche-Un sécateur-Un arrache clous.
-Un rouleau de cable-Deux vieilles radios.
-Un carnet d'épargne postale n°483341-87 au nom de NDOCPO avec un montant de Cinq mille francs.

2°) Chez KAPOKO Séraphin :

-Un poste soudure électrique de fabrication locale.
-Un petit étau avec support-Plusieurs serre-joints de fer.
-Un pince et un marteau.
-Deux tuyaux PVC de 110 raccordés.
-Deux tuyaux PVC de 100 raccordés.
-Deux tuyaux PVC de 50 raccordés.
-Seize tôles de récupération de quatre mètres
-Quatre tôles de récupération de trois mètres
-Trois petits rouleaux de grillage.
-Un demi sac de carreaux-Un lave-mains complet-Un réservoir de WC.
-Un ventilateur-Du masticon-Neuf carreaux de 14 x 14.

-3°)-NGAMENI YOUPA Pierre :

-Un mètre de mastic.
-Un ventilateur.
-Quatre morceaux de carreaux de casse, 179 carreaux de 14cm, 09 carreaux de 30cm, 16 tôles de 5m, 04 tôles de 3m, 3rouleaux de de grillage, un lave main au complet, un reservoir et des tuyaux.

-Que dès lors, il y a lieu d'ordonner d'office la restitution des objets saisis aux prétendants droit ;

.../...

Société S.P.N.P. de Njombé ,

Arrivons sur les lieux à 11 heures 20 minutes

Procédons à l'audition du Responsable de ladite société en la personne de NDONO NGANGA.

Qui s'étant trouvé préoccupé a sollicité le rapport des constations le lendemain ,le 20 février 2002

Arrivons à la société S.P.H.P. à 9 heure 45 minutes

procédons à l'audition de sieur EWANE (représentant de la société) en pré ence de Mr TOKOUMBA

Qui mentionne effectivement que tout le materiel cité plus haut a été reçu par la S.P.HP. par l'intermédiaire du service du garage représenté par Nicolas DAVID ;

Les restitutions se faisent en nature nous avons demandé au responsable susvisé de mettre sous main de justice les effets dont la liste suit ;

- Une paire de lunettes soudure
- 06 Anti-vol
- 05 Porte-tout sans roue
- un porte-tout avec une roue
- un porte-tout avec deux roues
- quatre roues de porte-tout
- une roue usée de moto sport
- un sécateur petit modèle
- une caisse contenant deux burains
- [illegible] clés
- [illegible] tournevis
- une [illegible] pince
- un [illegible]
- 16 tôles de récupération 04 m 05
- 04 tôles de récupération de 03 m
- Un demi sac de carreaux
- un lave main complet
- Un reservoir de voiture
- 09 carreaux 14 X14

Nous terminons les constations à 10 heures 40 minutes plus rien à déclarer , persiste et signe ;

LE MAGISTRAT INSTRUCTEUR LE GREFFIER LE COMPARANT

Bessong Paul
Magistrat

Appendix C

COUR D'APPEL DU LITTORAL

PARQUET D'INSTANCE DE MBANGA

CABINET D'INFORMATION JUDICIAIRE

REPUBLIQUE DU CAMEROUN

Paix – Travail – Patrie

PROCES-VERBAL DE DESCENTE SUR LES LIEUX

L'an deux mille deux et le dix neuf du mois février;

Nous, MESSENG PAUL, substitut du Procureur de la République près le Tribunal de première instance de MBANGA, Magistrat Instructeur ;

Assisté de Maître NYELE Georges, Greffier d'instruction assermenté ;

Effectuons une descente à la Brigade Gendarmerie de Njombé;

Arrivons à ladite unité à 10 heures 15 minutes

Procédons à l'audition du commandant de Brigade :

Qui énumère les objets ci-après (retrouvés chez le nommé NDONGO VICTOR)

- Un fer à repasser
- Un pagne cousu
- Un drap avec deux taies
- Une tenue blanche avec Chéchia
- Un drap blanc rayé
- Trois taies brodées
- Un drap blanc
- deux pulls pour enfant
- deux tricots
- Un jeu de quatre couteaux
- Quatre cuillères
- Quatre fourchettes
- deux ensembles pulls pour Bébé
- Un petit drap pour Bébé
- Quatre serviettes
- Un pull pour Bébé
- deux sparadas (Sandes)
- trois robettes
- Un chapeau traditionnel
- Un collier
- Un carton contenant divers papiers
- deux cachets et quatre carnets (ASSOCIATION –Njo
- huit couches pour Bébé
- Un pulvérisateur de marque TROPIC
- Une tasse
- Une Moto de marque SUZUKI
- Une bicyclette
- deux demi Bidons d'herbicide
- Un petit sac de plats en plastique
- 97 Cuillères en aluminium
- Une balance de poche
- Un étau avec support (chez KAPOKO Séraphin)
- Un poste de soudure électrique de fabrication lo[c]
- Un sachet de baguettes
- deux vieilles poste radio
- Un carnet d'épargne
- Une bache bleue

[illegible] objets étant à la disposition du

S.I.R. Commandant de Brigade : En ce qui concerne le reste des effets , ils ont été reversés à la société S.P.N.P. , entre les mains du chef de service du garage

A savoir les effets suivants :

- Une paire de lunette pour soudure
- 06 bouts de tuyaux
- 04 Perches de 05 mètres
- 03 demi-perche
- 05 anti-vol
- 03 porte-tout sans roue
- Un porte-tout avec une roue
- Un porte-tout avec deux roues
- Quatre roues de porte-tout
- un carton de ficelles
- Un sac de 39 Coudes
- deux demi perche avec coudes
- Un demi -rouleau de grillage
- Une roue usée de moto sport
- Trois morceaux de [illegible] WAX
- Quatre demi tuyaux d'irrigation
- 07 barre de fer rond
- Un secateur (petit modele)
- 46 Perches d'irrigation
- 39 Cornières
- Une caisse contenant deux burains
- [illegible] clés
- [illegible] Tournevis
- 03 grandes plaques avec tiges
- Plusieurs plaques sans tige
- 03 fer de 10
- Un sac contenant des fiches
- Une pince
- Un marteau
- deux tuyaux P.V.C. de 110 raccordés
- deux tuyaux P.V.C. de 100 raccordés
- deux tuyaux P.V.C. de 50 raccordés
- 16 tôles de récupération de 4m,05
- 04 tôles de récupération de 03 m
- 03 petits rouleaux de grillage
- Un demi sac de carreaux
- un lave main complet
- Un reservoir de voiture
- Un [illegible] (panier)
- 09 Carreaux 14 X 14 m

S.I.R. - Commandant de Brigade: A la remise des effets à la S.P.N.P. , Nous avons agi sur instruction du parquet ,

Nous terminons les constatations à 11 heures 15 mn Plus rien à déclarer ,persiste et signe

LE MAGISTRAT INSTRUCTEUR LE GREFFIER LE COMMANDANT BRIGADE

– 3 –

PAR CES MOTIFS –

-Ordonnons au Commandant de la brigade de gen darmerie de NJOMBE et au représentant légal de la S.P.H. P NJOMBE la restitution aux susnommés des objets qu'ils détiennent respectivement telsque ci-dessus énumérés ;

-Ordonnons, par ailleurs, au Greffier en Chef du Tribunal de première Instance de céans la restitutio à ZAPOKO Séraphin de la Caisse métallique mise sous scellé le 16/11/2001 .

LE MAGISTRAT INSTRUCTEUR .

Bessong Paul
Magistrat

Appendix D

COPIE

NOTIFICATION D'UNE ORDONNANCE AVEC SOMMATION DE RESTITUER.

L'an deux mille trois
Et le, Quatre Fevrier

A la requête de Monsieur YOUPA NGAMENI Pierre demeurant à NJOMBE, lequel fait élection de domicile en sa demeure ainsi qu'en étude aux fin du présent exploit ;

J'ai Maître MINKASSO Marie Paul, Huissier de Justice près les Tribunaux de Mbanga et Cour d'Appel du Littoral B.P 112 y demeurant et soussigné.

NOTIFIE ET EN TETE DE CELLES DES PRESENTES LAISSE COPIES A :

La SPNP B.P 05 Njombé en ses Bureaux sis à Njombé où étant et parlant à : Monsieur Ewane qui reçoit tant ladite ordonnance que copie du present exploit.

D'une ordonnance n°13/CI/0602 rendue le 17 Avril 2002 par le cabinet d'information judiciaire du parquet de Mbanga et dont le dispositif est ainsi conçu « Ordonnons au Commandant de Brigade de Gendarmerie de Njombé et au représentant légal de la SPNP Njombé la restitution aux susnommés des objets qu'ils détiennent respectivement tels que ci-dessus énumérés ……… »

Lui déclarant que la présente notification est faite à toutes fins utiles.

Et à mêmes requête, demeure et élection de domicile que ci-dessus, j'ai Huissier susdit et soussigné étant et parlant comme il vient d'être dit fait sommation à la SPNP d'avoir séance tenante à restituer à mon requérant que j'accompagne ses effets visés par l'ordonnance.

CE A QUOI IL RESULTE

je ne peux pas donner une réponse tout de suite, je vais transmettre le dossier à ma hiérarchie

Dont acte.

Sous toutes réserves

4000
1500

Et afin qu'elle n'en ignore, je lui ai où étant et parlant comme ci-dessus remis et laissé copie tant de l'ordonnance que celle du présent exploit dont le coût est de : mille deux cent quatre vingt dix francs

1000
1210

Employé pour copie une feuille de la dimension du timbre à 500F, somme incluse dans le coût de l'acte.

300
3280

Appendix E

PHP
SOCIETE DES PLANTATIONS DU HAUT PENJA
Société Anonyme au capital de 85 500 000 FCFA
BP 1 PENJA

SPNP
SOCIETE DES PLANTATIONS NOUVELLES DU PENJA
Société anonyme au capital de 870 000 000 FCFA
BP 5 NYOMBE

SBM
SOCIETE DES BANANERAIES DE LA M'BOME
Société anonyme au capital de 1 000 000 000 FCFA
BP 5 NYOMBE

Monsieur YOUPA NGAMENI
Planteur à Njombé

Objet : V / L du 11 juillet 2003.

Monsieur,

Nous accusons réception de votre correspondance visée en objet, par laquelle vous avez bien voulu porter à notre connaissance le litige qui vous oppose à notre groupe.

Y faisant suite, nous regrettons de vous faire savoir qu'il ne nous est pas possible d'examiner favorablement votre réclamation, en l'absence d'un procès verbal de restitution des matériaux concernés à son présumé légitime propriétaire.

Au cas où vous seriez en possession de ce document, nous vous remercions de bien vouloir nous le faire parvenir, par tout moyen à votre convenance.

Veuillez agréer, Monsieur, nos salutations distinguées.

NDONO MBANGA
Directeur Administratif

ISO 14001

Appendix F

ANNEE JUDICIAIRE 2004-2005

JUGEMENT N° 693/COR
DU 16 FEVRIER 2005

A F F A I R E

MINISTERE PUBLIC
&
S.P.N.F (Me MAKEMBE)

Contre

- SONI MEKAM Albertin alias SONI Gaston alias TAMBIA David
- KAPOKO Séraphin
- NGAMENI YOUWA Pierre
- DONGMO Victor
- LEKEUFOUET Thérèse
- DEMANOU Norbert

NATURE DU DELIT

Coaction de vol simple, recel simple et recel d'individus

DECISION DU TRIBUNAL

Lire le dispositif.-

REPUBLIQUE DU CAMEROUN

N° DU PARQUET : 419/RP/01-02
du 11 Décembre 2001

—— A l'audience publique du Tribunal de Première Instance de Mbanga siégeant au Palais de Justice de ladite ville, le seize février deux mille cinq, tenue pour les affaires correctionnelles par Mme NDENGUE Florence, Juge audit Tribunal.. PRESIDENT ;

—— En présence de Monsieur SOUAIBOU YOUSSOUMA, Substitut du Procureur de la République occupant le banc du Ministère Public ;

—— Assistés de Mme EPOH Justine, Greffier tenant la plume ;

—— Et de Monsieur EMBOM Pierre, âgé de 24 ans, interprète pour le dialecte local, a prêté le serment prescrit par l'article 332 du Code d'Instruction Criminelle ;

—— A été rendu le jugement ci-après :

E N T R E

—— Monsieur le Procureur de la République, et la S.P.N.P ayant pour conseil Maître MAKEMBE BEBEY, partie civile ;

D'UNE PART

E T

—— SONI MEKAM Albertin alias SONI Gaston alias TAMBA David, fils de MELASSAP Henri ans, comme né en 1980 à Bafang, arrondissement dudit, département du Haut-NKAM, commerçant domicilié à Badounga, célibataire sans enfant, de nationalité camerounaise, prévenu de recel d'individus, libre non comparant ;

2°- KAPOKO Séraphin, fils père non dénommé et de MOTOUOM Jisèle, âgé de 19 ans, comme né le 20 Avril 1982 à Njombé, arrondissement de Njombé-Penja, département du Moungo, soudeur domicilié à Njombé, célibataire sans enfant, de nationalité camerounaise, jamais condamné, prévenu de recel, libre comparant ;

3°- NGAMENI YOUPA Pierre, fils de feu YOUPA Emile et de KOUAHOU Anastasie, âgé de 45 ans, comme né le 20 Février 1956 à Fondjomekwet, arrondissement de Bafang, Département du Haut-Nkam, cultivateur domicilié à Njombé, marié 05 enfants, de nationalité camerounaise, jamais condamné, libre comparant ;

4°- DONGMO Victor, fils KAMEDIONGO Philippe et de ZEMO Régine, âgé de 31 ans comme né vers 1969 à Bamendou, arrondissement de Penka-Michel, département de la Menoua, conducteur d'engins lourd domicilié à Njombé, de nationalité camerounaise, prévenu de vol simple, en fuite ;

5°- LEKEUFOUET CHIENDJUI Thérèse, fille

de feu NZEUKENG Fidèle et de NANFACK Ma tine, âgée de 40 ans, comme née vers 19 à Foréké arrondissement de Dschang, dépa tement de la Menoua, ménagère domiciliée à Njombé, mariée 04 enfants, de nationalité camerounaise, jamais condamnée, pré venue de recel d'individus, libre non co parant ;

6°- DEMANOU Norbert, fils de ZAMBOU Pauline, âgé de 25 ans, comme né le 10 Août 1976 à Bamendou, arrondissement de Penka-Michel, département de la Menoua, mécanicien domicilié à Njombé, célibataire sans enfants, de nationalité camerounaise, jamais condamné, prévenu de recel d'individus, libre non comparent ;

D'AUTRE PART

--- L'affaire a été appelée pour la première fois à l'audience du 29 Octobre 2003 suivant ordonnance de renvoi du 31 Juillet 2002 et retenue à celle du 19 Janvier 2005 après plusieurs renvois utiles;

--- Le Président a donné lecture des préventions telles qu'elles figurent sur l'ordonnance sus évoquée ;

--- Les prévenus NGA ENI YOUPA Pierre et KAPOKO Séraphin ont été interrogés ;

--- La partie civile n'a pas été entendue en sa demande ;

--- L'assistance de l'interprète a été requise chaque fois [illegible]

—— Le Ministère Public a été entenc
ses réquisitions ;
—— Les prévenus NGAMENI YOUPA Pierre et
KAPOKO Séraphin ont été entendus en leur
moyens de défense présentées par eux-mêm
et Maître NTCAMO Etienne ;

—— Nul pour les prévenus SONI MEKA Alb
tin, NDONGMO Victor, LEKEUFOUET Thérèse
DEMANOU Norbert non comparants ;
—— Le Greffier a tenu note des déclara-
tions des prévenus comparants ;
—— Sur quoi le Tribunal après en avoir
délibéré conformément à la loi, a statué
en ces termes à l'audience du 16 Février
2005 à laquelle l'affaire a été mise en
délibéré ;

—————————— LE TRIBUNAL ——————————

—— Attendu que suivant Ordonnance de rè
glement en date du 31 Juillet 2002 du
Procureur de la République près le Tri-
bunal de Première Instance de Mbanga agi
sant en qualité de Magistrat Instructeur
les nommés NDONGMO Victor, KAPOKO Séra-
phin, NGAMENI YOUPA Pierre, SONI MEKAM
Albertin, LEKEUFOUET Thérèse et NDEMANOU
Norbert ont été renvoyés devant le Tribu
nal de céans statuant en matière correc-
tionnelle, pour y répondre des faits de
vol simple pour le Premier, recel de cho
ses pour le deuxième et le troisième, et
coaction de recel d'individus pour les
trois autres : délits prévus et réprimés

par les articles 74, 318 (1,a), 324, 96, 100 et 194 du Code Pénal ;

—— Attendu que seuls KAPOKO et NGAMENI ont comparu ; qu'il y a lieu de statuer contradictoirement à leur égard et de donner défaut aux autres parties non com parantes ;

—— Attendu qu'il ressort de l'ordonnanc de renvoi que dans la nuit du 17 Octobre 2001, un cambriolage a été perpétré dans les locaux de l'IRAD de Njombé par des i dividus qui ont emporté un important lot de matériels de bureau ; que l'enquête o verte a conduit les Gendarmes au domicil de NDONGO le 24 Octobre 2001 où un ordi nateur de l'IRAD a été retrouvé et saisi en même temps que des perches en fer et d'autres effets mobiliers ; qu'une perquisition incidente effectuée au domicil de ses voisins KAPOKO et NGAMENI a permi la saisie des perches en fer, des porte-tout, des tôles et autres matériaux de constr uction, ces autres effets s'étant révélés être la propriété de la SPNP de Njombé ;

I— Cas de NDONGO Victor —

—— Attendu qu'au cours de la perquisition effectuée à son domicile, ce prévenu a pris la fuite en abandonnant sa progéniture et n'est plus jamais retourné à son domicile ; que les effets volés ayant été retrouvés à son domicile, il y a de le déclarer coupable de vol simple, et de le condamner en conséquence ;

II- Cas de KAPOKO et de NGAMENI -

Attendu qu'interrogés sur les matériaux de construction retrouvés dans leurs domiciles, KAPOKO qui est artisan soudeur de son état, a déclaré que les perches lui avaient été remises par NDOGMO pour fabriquer un porte-tout et qu'il n'avait aucune raison d'en soupçonner l'origine délictuelle, puisque ces perches se vendent dans le commerce ; que NGAMENI à son tour a déclaré avoir acheté ses matériaux de construction tant à la "casse" à Douala, qu'au nommé PANGOI MESSI ;

Attendu qu'aucun indice ne permet au Tribunal de déduire que ces deux prévenus avaient des raisons de soupçonner l'origine frauduleuse des effets retrouvés chez eux ; qu'il y a lieu de les déclarer non coupables de recel de choses et de les relaxer pour défaut d'intention délictuelle ;

III- Cas de LEKEUFOUET Thérèse -

Attendu que cette prévenue a été surprise au domicile de NDOGMO le 28 Octobre 2001 alors qu'elle tentait de récupérer les effets vestimentaires de ce dernier ; qu'entendue, elle a déclaré

que c'est SONI MEKAM qui l'y avait en-
voyée chercher une somme de 8.000 Frs,
ainsi que les vêtements de NDOGMO dont el
ignorait en fuite ;

—— Attendu que cette version des faits
a été confirmée par SONI MEKAM ; qu'il
y a lieu de déclarer la prévenue non co
pable de recel d'individu, et de la re-
laxer pour faits non établis ;

IV– Cas de SONI MEKAM et de NDEMANOU
Norbert –

—— Attendu qu'interrogé, SONI MEKAM Al
bertin a déclaré qu'il avait rencontré
NDOGMO à la gare routière de Bafang qui
lui a remis son trousseau de clés aux
fins de récupérer ses habits ; qu'enter
du à son tour, NDEMANOU a déclaré avoi
rencontré le fugitif à Bafang et de der
nier lui a remis une lettre dans laquel
il invitait toute personne qui souhete-
rait communiquer avec lui, de passer p
NDEMANOU ;

—— Attendu qu'au regard de ce qui pré-
cède, il est évident que ces deux prév
nus ont servi de courroie de transmiss
au fugitif NDOGMO pour gérer ses affai
res ; qu'il échet par conséquent de le
déclarer coupables de coaction de rece
d'individu, et de les condamner confor
mément aux articles 100 et 194 du Code
Pénal :

—— Attendu par ailleurs que les dép.
sont à la charge solidaire de NDOGMO,
SONI NEKAM et NDENANOU qui ont succom
qu'en outre, pour une prompte exécuti
de la présente décision, il échet de
cerner contre ces trois prévenus mand
d'arrêt à l'audience ;

——————— PAR CES MOTIFS ———

—— Statuant publiquement, contradicto
rement à l'égard des prévenus NGAMENI
YOUPA Pierre et KAPOKO Séraphin, par d
faut contre toutes les autres parties,
matière correctionnelle et en premier
sort ;

—— Déclare NDOGMO Victor coupable de
vol simple ;

—— Lui accorde des circonstances atté-
nuantes en raison de sa qualité de déli
quant primaire ;

—— Le condamne à un an d'emprisonnem
ferme et aux dépens ;

—— Déclare SONI NEKAM Albertin et NDEN
NOU Norbert coupables de recel d'indivi

—— Les condamne à six mois d'emprisonn
ment ferme ;

—— Déclare NGAMENI YOUPA et KAPOKO Sér
phin non coupables de recel simple ;

—— Le relaxe pour défaut d'intention
délictuelle ;

—— Déclare NGOUTOUKEN Thérèse non coup
ble de recel d'individu ;

—— Condamne DOGMO, SONI MEKAM et NDE-MANOU aux dépens solidaires, et décerne contre eux Mandat d'Arrêt à l'audience ;

—— Fixe la durée de la contrainte par corps au taux légal pour le cas où il y aurait lieu de l'exercer ;

—— En foi de quoi le présent jugement a été signé par le Président et le Greffier approuvant___ligne___mot___rayé_ nul___et___renvoi___en marge/-

DETAIL DES FRAIS

- Enregistrement.....	20.000
TIMBRES............	4.000
Constitution dos...	500
Expédition jugt....	500
Extrait jugt.......	150
B2-B1..............	975
T O T A L....=	26.125

AOUT 2005

Appendix G

COUR D'APPEL DU LITTORAL
RIBUNAL DE PREMIERE INSTANCE DE MABNGA
GREFFE

REPUBLIQUE DU CAMEROUN
Paix-Travail-Patrie

CERTIFICAT DE NON APPEL

[illegible] 693/COR
16 FEVRIER 2005

NOUS, Maître MELA David Greffier en Chef du Tribunal de Première Instance de Mbanga soussigné ;

VU le jugement n) 693/COR rendu le 16 Février 2005 par le Tribunal correctionnel de céans dans la cause

MP. et SPNP
(NDONO MBANGA)

contre : SONI MEKAM Bertin alias SONI Gasto
- KAPOKO Séraphin
- NGAMENI YOUPA Pierre
- DONGMO Victor
- LEKEUFOUET Victor
- DEMANOU Norbert

AJ0893231

prévenus de coaction de vol aggravé, coaction de vol simple, coaction de recel d'individus;

VU le régistre tenu à cet effet ;

VU la requête verbale de monsieur YOUPA NGAMENI Pierre en date du 20 Octobre 2005;

CERTIFIONS

Qu'aucun APPEL n'a été enrégistré à ce jour à l'encontre du jugement susvisé ;

En foi de quoi le présent CERTIFICAT DE NON APPEL lui a été délivré sur sa demande expresse pour servir et valoir ce que de droit./-

FAIT A MBANGA , le [illegible]
LE GREFFIER EN CHEF,

Appendix H

NJOMBE LE 22 MAI 2015

Tel. YOUPANGAMENI
PIERRE
679.66.14.02
698 35 58 74

PHP
23 JUN 2015

A
MONSIEUR LE
directeur du group
PE PHP s/c du
directeur des
Relaction exterieur

Objet: Demande d'intervention

Monsieur le directeur,

J'ai le respect honneur de porter a votre connaissance cette situation qui me met en désacord avec votre chef groupe.

Au courant des années deux mille, j'étais victime d'une injustice lors de la decente du commandant de la gendamerie de NJOMBE chez moi, arrêter pour coalition de vol, Relaxé après quatre mois de prevention. La société n'a jamais restitué mes materiaux detenus depuis la fin des enquettes du juge d'instruction

pieces jointes:

1) Bulletin de levee d'ecrou
2. proces verbal de constat sur les lieux
3- l'ordonnance de restitution
4. la requette du directeur des relations exterieur du groupe PHP
5- la replique du parquet avec la liste des materi
6. la sommation d'huissier.

A l'atente d'une suite favorable, veillez agréer mes sentiments les plus distingués

YOUPA NGAMENI PIERRE

CONTRIBUTORS

Ariadna Tovar Ramírez and Marianne Bertrand were, respectively, researcher and campaigner on human rights defenders for Amnesty International at the time of writing. In this capacity, they documented human rights violations and designed campaigns to end the abuses faced by land and environmental rights defenders in the Americas such as Máxima Acuña. Ariadna is currently working as a Consultant in Human Rights and Strategic Litigation in Latin America and Marianne works as Campaign and Mobilisation Manager for the International Service for Human Rights in Geneva.

The authors would like to thank the following people: Arjun Chaudhuri, Rodrigo Da Costa Sales Gabriela Quijano, Daniel Joloy, Maggie Maloney and Malavika Vartak.

Adriana Bravin is a Professor of Communications at the Federal University of Ouro Preto, located in the city of Mariana, the scene of the Samarco environmental disaster discussed in Chapter 4. Since moving to Mariana in 2009, she has experienced the social and environmental impacts caused by mining, as well as the devastating magnitude of the social disintegration and the profound impacts on the lives of thousands of people as a result of the Fundão dam collapse. On 5 November 2015, while in Portugal on an exchange program for her PhD, the news of the disaster left her emotionally devastated. Upon returning to Mariana in March 2016, she sought out the groups that were organized around actions with victims affected by the disaster. One of these groups was the *Sirene* (Siren) newspaper published to keep alive the memory of the crime and disaster. This is how she was able to meet and connect with people like Monica Santos and share her story, which is now also part of Adriana's.

Daysheelyn Anne P. Brillo grew up with the stories of her grandfather during the Vietnam War where Filipinos had a non-combat role and provided medical and humanitarian aid. During her Civil Procedure class in law school, she read the product liability case about Agent Orange where Vietnam War veterans filed a class action against the manufacturers and the US government. The Philippine government waived the rights of all Filipino war veterans to file an action or participate in the class suit in order to be within the good graces of the United States. The next case in her Civil Procedure class was the story of Filipino banana farmers who were exposed to a pesticide in Mindanao, south of the Philippines. She decided that she would channel her frustration about the exposure of the Filipinos to the Agent Orange case by writing a paper about the stories of these farmers. She searched for the names of the farmers who had filed a case before the Supreme Court through Facebook. She was lucky that a few of them responded and agreed to be visited in their homes. She flew to Mindanao to meet Digong and another banana farm leader. She now works as a lawyer at a government agency administering universal health care in the country. She also volunteers as a community lawyer for indigenous communities fighting for their ancestral domains. She is a graduate of Juris Doctor and Industrial Engineering from the University of the Philippines.

Belinda Chinowawa worked as a public interest lawyer in Zimbabwe at the height of the diamond rush in Marange. One of the issues which constantly occupied Belinda's mind was the disparity between the supposed mineral wealth of the country and the lived realities of the majority of Zimbabweans. One day, she was approached by colleagues from the eastern province to provide an expert opinion on a case they were dealing with, which happened to involve a family affected by the relocations from the diamond fields. That is how she witnessed first-hand how the confluence of corporate greed and government complicity diminished the quality of life for the Kambeni family. She is aware that their much improved living conditions are a result of their own tenacity, but she does hope that telling their story will amplify the importance of community consultations and corporate accountability.

Cigdem Cimrin has been carrying out her PhD studies and advising on business and human rights. She approached Yucel Demiral with a proposal to conduct a joint study about workers' health in transnational companies operating in Aegean region and their access to remedy. They then contacted and interviewed workers who had been diagnosed with occupational diseases by the department and whose employment contracts had been unfairly terminated by their employers due to their poor health status. They narrated the current legal challenges which these workers have been facing and how their rights are being abused by both their employers and the authorities.

Yucel Demiral is one of the coordinators at the Department of Work and Occupational Health of Dokuz Eylul University Faculty of Medicine ('Department') in Izmir, Turkey. He is also a professor of public health. Workers with occupational health problems have been diagnosed and cured at this department.

Madeline Hung is a writer and entrepreneur. She began her career at Oxfam America and the Institute for Multi-Stakeholder Initiative Integrity (MSI Integrity) where she researched the efficacy of voluntary certification programs that set standards for corporate conduct. Madeline met Mr. Youpa while conducting interviews with Fairtrade certified banana plantation workers in Cameroon, and documented his story with the help of local staff at Réseau de Lutte Contre La Faim (RELUFA). Since then, Madeline has worked to build tools to address a wide range of global challenges – from climate change to mass migration.

Rajiv Maher been working with mining and dam affected communities across Latin America since 2008. He specifically researches how these communities experience corporate social responsibility-related initiatives led by extractives firms. Rajiv first visited Mariana in 2012 while researching the perspectives of the local residents to a proposed mine by Vale. He met his co-author Adriana on this visit who was also researching conflicts with mining. In 2016, he felt obliged to collate local narratives from victims of the Fundao Dam collapse and worked together with Adriana on this endeavor. Rajiv made three visits to Mariana over 2019 to speak to as many victims, community members, state authorities, civil society representatives and corporate foundation in order to understand the dynamics of how the environmental disaster is being remedied, remembered and forgotten.

Jennifer D. Oliva is an associate professor at Seton Hall Law where she specializes in health, FDA, evidence, and veterans law. Oliva is an honors graduate of Georgetown University Law Center, earned her MBA at the University of Oxford and was elected as a Rhodes and Truman Scholar while a cadet at the United States Military Academy. Oliva is also a US Army veteran who completed this project while directing the Veterans Advocacy Clinic, which provided pro bono representation to veterans entitled to service-connected benefits, at the West Virginia University College of Law.

Piergiuseppe Parisi is a research associate at the Centre for Applied Human Rights, University of York, where he works for the Human Rights Defenders Hub, and an associate lecturer at York Law School. He first met

Gilberto Torres through the Colombian Caravana, a London-based charity that supports human rights lawyers at risk in Colombia, for which Piergiuseppe serves as advocacy director and trustee. When they first met, Gilberto was litigating his case before English courts. Piergiuseppe has participated in the advocacy campaign built around Gilberto's case and met with him and his lawyers on several occasions. He keeps in touch with Gilberto on a regular basis and monitors his situation.

Maria Isabel Cubides Sanchez and Michael Clemens work for the International Federation for Human Rights (FIDH). Their work is guided by multidisciplinarity and an inclusive and bottom-up approach, which ensures rights holders are the center and motor of documentation, judicial and non-judicial actions in defense of human rights and the environment.

In 2016, the case of Blyvooruitzicht was the first FIDH community-based human rights impact assessment in Africa, and the only one to have dealt with human rights impacts at the dawn of investment projects. In the male-dominated mining sector, the challenges to bring a gender perspective to the study were great. But after more than a year of collaboration, Maria Isabel Cubides and Michael Clements, together with FIDH and LHR teams, organized a workshop with representatives of numerous communities from all over South Africa suffering the impacts of sudden mine closure. In these workshops the voices of women were particularly strong, emphasizing the environmental and collective dimensions of human rights violations. Those voices were the key inspiration for the chapter 'Abandoned: A Tale of Two Mine Closures in South Africa'.

Gareth Sims is an environmental and human rights lawyer based in the UK. He qualified with Deighton Pierce Glynn, a leading UK-based law firm specializing in various areas including human rights, public law, and claims against multinational companies for human rights abuses committed in the global south. He met Gilberto Torres when Sue Willman, a senior partner at the firm, took on Gilberto's case against BP for his kidnapping and subsequent torture. A national campaign ensued involving various UK-based organizations, and obtaining widespread press coverage. He worked with Gilberto on a UK-wide tour where Gilberto and members of his legal team discussed the case, his plight and the plight of the many other victims in the region. This work was also part of a wider campaign to change the UK law to make UK-based corporations accountable for human rights and environmental abuses abroad. Gareth has an LLM in International Environmental Law and has worked with various human rights and environmental organizations in the UK, India and

Colombia. He specializes in advising NGOs on law and policy and bringing cases against governments and multinational corporations. He now works as an independent consultant.

Tara Van Ho is a lecturer at the University of Essex School of Law and Human Rights Centre in the UK, and currently co-president of the Global Business and Human Rights Scholars Association. She was previously an assistant professor and a post-doctoral fellow at Aarhus University in Denmark, where she examined the impacts of businesses on land and water in Palestine, Myanmar and Colombia. It was in furtherance of her Colombia research, which was facilitated by the NGO Dejusticia, that she met with the Cajamarca and Ibagué environmental and human rights defenders featured in her chapter. After her visit, what had seemed like a clear legal victory was taken away from the defenders, undermining their right to participate in decisions that directly affect several human rights, including their health and livelihoods. The following year also proved to be one of the deadliest for human rights defenders, with a clear link in the targeting of those fighting business impacts on human rights. She therefore wrote this chapter with trepidation given the ever-changing and increasingly dangerous situation in Colombia for the defenders featured in her chapter, but with knowledge that they want their story out.

INDEX

www.ingramcontent.com/pod-product-compliance
Ingram Content Group UK Ltd.
Pitfield, Milton Keynes, MK11 3LW, UK
UKHW041830100926
8556IPUK00002B/109

9 781785 272264